IRISH ACADEMIC PRESS
DUBLIN • PORTLAND, OR

First published in 2009 by Irish Academic Press

2 Brookside,
Dundrum Road,
Dublin 14, Ireland

920 NE 58th Avenue, Suite 300
Portland, Oregon,
97213-3786, USA

www.iap.ie

British Library Cataloguing in Publication Data
An entry can be found on request

978 0 7165 2980 4 (cloth)
978 0 7165 2981 1 (paper)

Library of Congress Cataloging-in-Publication Data
An entry can be found on request

Printed in Great Britain by the MPG Books Group, Bodmin and King's Lynn

Dedicated to my parents, John and Betty Reidy
and to Kathleen

Contents

List of Tables

Acknowledgements

I offer my deep gratitude to Dr Bernadette Whelan, the supervisor of my doctoral thesis at the University of Limerick, who, through her professionalism and generosity, has been my greatest supporter from the very beginning of this work. It has been my privilege.

I acknowledge the assistance of the Irish Research Council for the Humanities and Social Sciences. I appreciate the faith that has been placed in this project by Lisa Hyde and Irish Academic Press: I thank them for this opportunity.

Gregory O'Connor, Senior Archivist, National Archives of Ireland, has been hugely instrumental in directing me towards the sources and answering my many questions with courtesy and much patience. I am also grateful to the staff of the National Archives Reading Room for their efforts on my behalf. I would like to acknowledge the National Archives of Ireland and the Director of the NAI for granting permission to use the cover image and the institution's 1909 plan.

I offer sincere thanks to Mary Guinan-Darmody and John O'Gorman, Tipperary Studies, Tipperary (NR) County Library, who facilitated my many research visits with professional courtesy and good humour. I thank those who agreed to be interviewed for this book, for sharing their memories and impressions of Clonmel borstal. I also acknowledge the assistance of the following archives and libraries: National Library of Ireland; Mary Immaculate College Library, Audio-Visual Section; Noelle Dowling, Dublin Diocesan Archive, Drumcondra; Garda Síochána Archive, Dublin Castle; Gluckman Library, University of Limerick; Hardiman Library, National University of Ireland, Galway; Tipperary County Museum, Clonmel; Local Studies Library, Ennis, and the Irish Architectural Archive. I am grateful to Archbishop Diarmuid Martin for allowing me to use material from the McQuaid Papers. I am deeply indebted to Ken Bergin, Jean Turner, Siobhan Morrissey and Anna Maria Hajba, of Special Collections, University of Limerick Library, not only for their outstanding help and expertise but for the memorable and sometimes unusual times we shared. Thank you. To those in Clonmel who contributed to this project I offer my heartfelt thanks; I wish to acknowledge the invaluable assistance provided by Margaret and John Rossiter for helping me to understand the existing geography of the borstal and its few remaining walls. Liam Ó'Duibhir made numerous enquiries on my behalf, which I greatly appreciate.

Much credit is due to Brendan Crawford, Declan, Patricia and Cathal Fitzpatrick and Kevin and Edel Copeland, all of whom provided refuge during the various phases of research.

Dr Ruan Ó'Donnell has provided much support as Head of the Department of History, University of Limerick over the past number of years and I thank him for his leadership. I also thank Dr John Logan, who was instrumental in starting me down this path and for serving as Internal Examiner for my doctoral thesis. Dr Alistair Malcolm has been of particular support and I thank him for his friendship and advice, particularly during the early years of my research. My thanks also to the wider Department of History at the University of Limerick for their support over the past number of years, particularly Susan Mulcahy and Anne Marie O'Donnell. I am also grateful to my colleagues in the Department of History, Mary Immaculate College, Limerick; Mr Liam Irwin, Head of Department, and Dr Liam Chambers, Dr Maura Cronin, Dr Deirdre McMahon and Dr Una Ní Bromeil for offering me such unwavering encouragement. I express my thanks to Dr John O'Callaghan for offering his valuable insights on specific aspects of this book. I am honoured that Professor Gearóid O'Tuathaigh, National University of Ireland, Galway, acted as External Examiner for my doctoral thesis and I thank him for his comments and advice. A long time ago, Dr Caitriona Clear, National University of Ireland, Galway, inadvertently planted the seed of my original interest in the history of crime and its punishment in Ireland and I am grateful for that early inspiration. Dr Oonagh Walsh, University College Cork, has shared her expertise on the subject of institutional history on several occasions and I thank her for those insights.

I am fortunate to have met my friend and colleague Dr Mary McCarthy at the outset of this journey. I thank her for her encouragement and enormous personal and professional support from the beginning. I am also grateful for the friendship, good humour and wise counsel of Ms Odette Clarke and Dr Catherine O'Connor. I extend my deepest gratitude to Ellen Murphy for the years of friendship, unquestioning loyalty and sound advice.

The following colleagues and friends, at the University of Limerick, past and present, have provided me with a context that has been positive, professional and hospitable. I thank them sincerely: Brendan Bolger, Julie Brazil, Dr Ciara Breathnach, Adrian Cormican, Aoife Geogheghan, Senan Healy, Deirdre Kelleher, Niamh Lenahan, Professor Anthony McElligott, Dr Angus Mitchell, Lorna Moloney, Patti Punch and Dr Nadine Rossol. A number of family and friends continue to provide much-needed strength and distraction: Nora Fahy, Maura Reidy, Michael Healy, Cáit and Ellen Healy, my aunt Margaret Kennedy and my uncle Matthew Reidy.

I thank my parents, John and Betty, my brothers Gerard and Seán and their respective partners, Heather and Joanne. Finally, I thank Kathleen for patiently supporting all my research endeavours and always remaining the better half.

Chronology

1775 English prison reformer John Howard makes his first visit to Ireland

1779 John Howard's second visit to Ireland

1782 Committee to Enquire into Prison Conditions in Ireland is established

1786 Sir Jeremiah Fitzpatrick is appointed the first inspector-general of prisons in Ireland

1812 Elizabeth Fry makes her first visit to Newgate prison in London

1819 Ireland's first penitentiary opens at Grangegorman Lane in Dublin

1847 Vagrancy Act is passed in Westminster

1847 Spike Island in Cork is occupied as a public works prison

1850 Mountjoy prison opens in Dublin

1853 Transportation from Ireland ends

1854 Irish Convict Prisons Board is established

1858 Reformatory Schools Bill is passed for Ireland

1869 Ireland's first industrial school opens in Dublin

1876 Elmira State Reformatory is opened in New York state

1878 General Prisons Board for Ireland is established, with Captain Walter Crofton as its first chairman

1894 House of Commons sets up a committee under the chairmanship of Herbert Gladstone to investigate the state of the penal system

1895 The report of the Departmental Committee on Prisons is published

1895 Prison Commission chairman Sir Edmund Du Cane resigns the following day

1895 Evelyn John Ruggles-Brise is appointed chairman of the English Prison Commissioners

1897 Ruggles-Brise tours the Elmira Reformatory

1900 Pre-experimental penal reformatory opens at Bedford

1901   English Prison Commissioners launch a penal reformatory for juvenile-adult male offenders at the convict prison at Borstal in Kent

1901   Juvenile Offenders Act is passed

1906   A wing of the county jail at Clonmel in County Tipperary is separated off for the treatment of juvenile-adult offenders

1906   Clonmel Discharged Prisoners' Aid Society is founded

1908   Prevention of Crime Act is passed

1910   Ireland's first and only borstal institution is established after all remaining adult convicts are removed from Clonmel prison

1910   Borstal Association of Ireland is founded

1914   Criminal Justice Administration Act is passed

1917   On 12 December, Boys' Town is opened by Father Edward Flanagan at a rented boarding house on Dodge Street, Omaha, Nebraska

1918   Since 1914, approximately 424 discharged inmates of Clonmel borstal have served with British armed forces in World War One

1918   Richard Bagwell dies in Clonmel

1919   General Prisons Board claims a success rate of 78 percent since 1908 in the reformation of inmates of Clonmel borstal

1922   Irish borstal institution is removed from Clonmel to temporary premises at Clogheen workhouse and later to Kilkenny

1924   Borstal returns to Clonmel

1928   General Prisons Board is dissolved

1938   7 September, motion picture *Boys Town* is released

1940   Borstal is removed to temporary premises at Cork prison

1946   Monsignor Edward Flanagan visits Ireland

1947   Borstal returns to Clonmel in January

1948   15 May, Monsignor Flanagan dies in Berlin

1948   Borstal is re-named St Patrick's Borstal Institution, Clonmel

1956   Five decades after its foundation in Clonmel, the Irish borstal institution is permanently removed to Dublin, where it is re-opened on the North Circular Road.

Abbreviations

BAI	Borstal Association of Ireland
CDPAS	Clonmel Discharged Prisoners' Aid Society
CR	Correspondence Register
CSORP	Chief Secretary's Office Registered Papers
GPB	General Prisons Board
NAI	National Archives of Ireland
NLI	National Library of Ireland
RIC	Royal Irish Constabulary
SVP	Society of St Vincent de Paul

Preface

My initial interest in the history of juvenile crime and its punishment in Ireland originated during my undergraduate studies ten years ago. While examining certain lines for potential investigation I quickly understood that there existed a number of gaps in the literature. Several areas of both male and female juvenile criminality in nineteenth and early twentieth-century Ireland remained under-researched. Questions of identity, socio-economic status, types of criminality and the experience of punishment were largely unanswered when compared with the exhaustive research that has been done on the history of criminal youth in Britain. As a research student I was presented with the opportunity to address some of these questions. Taking on board the advice of several more experienced colleagues I decided that the most effective route for such an initial study would be to examine some of these issues through the prism of an institution.

Clonmel borstal provided a significant opportunity for a deep exploration of juvenile criminality and would offer a unique window into a specific class of offender. An early examination of sources showed that the inmates originated from all parts of Ireland, although the majority represented two major urban centres. The nature of their criminal activity would also be fertile ground for examination. An analysis of the social and economic factors that shaped the lives of offenders would help to answer some important questions, although, as expected, this would fall short of providing definitive explanations for juvenile criminal acts. As a somewhat complex form of punishment for this specific young male criminal, borstal treatment itself promised to reveal important insights into the state response to his crime.

The principal archive of Irish borstal history is as complex as it is rich. Held by the National Archives of Ireland within the correspondence of the General Prisons Board, the material is part of a wider collection of documents relating to the administration of all of the institutions controlled by that agency. For the most part, these institutions comprised the country's decreasing number of local and convict prisons; two establishments, the borstal in Clonmel and the State Inebriate Reformatory in Ennis, could be described as more specialist in nature and targeted specific cohorts of offenders. The GPB correspondence relating to the borstal runs to thousands of documents, covering subject-matter that is at the same time mundane, intriguing and useful. They include items such as letters between institutional staff and the GPB, the Borstal Association of Ireland, the English borstals, local clergy, potential future employers for discharged inmates and numerous other agencies. Many documents generated in the institution have also survived in this collection. These include inspection reports, disciplinary proceedings, dietary and medical records, education and training documents, as well as accounts of noteworthy visitors to the borstal. Collectively, this material amounts to the most significant available account of life in Clonmel borstal prior to Independence. Practically, from the point of view of the historian, the collection presents a number of difficulties that make both research and referencing somewhat more laborious. The GPB correspondence tends to be unwieldy in its organisation; this is in no way the fault of the National Archives but rather a reflection of the manner in which documents were originally filed by those in Dublin Castle. This necessitates the adoption of a somewhat unique referencing system when citing documents from the GPB correspondence. The Four Courts fire of 1922 also ensures that there are inevitable gaps, although this remains the most complete and important repository for research on the Irish prison and borstal system.

Significantly, the fate of this book is dictated by a seventy-year rule governing the availability of most prison records at the National Archives. This means that a similarly detailed study of borstal administration beyond the mid-1930s is not possible at this time. This inevitably leads to a heavier reliance, for the post-1922 period, on miscellaneous sources such as Dáil debates, newspapers, official reports and a limited number of significant personal testimonies. A quantitative analysis of the inmates is not an option beyond 1928 because this is the cut-off point for the register of inmates. Such constraints ensure that there is very little room for manoeuvre for the researcher as these are problems that are not easily circumvented. Likewise, a comprehensive oral history of inmates has not been possible in the absence of a register of inmates for the period from which discharged boys may still be living today. It is hoped that this study will prove a worthy basis for a more complete analysis of the

1922–1956 period when those records are eventually released. Indeed, the most welcome addition to further research on this subject-matter would be the emergence of former inmates of Clonmel borstal to share their experience of daily life in the institution and the rehabilitation process to which they were subjected.

Despite the fact that the combination of all of these sources, particularly the material contained within the GPB correspondence and the register of inmates, provides detailed accounts of the backgrounds and crimes of those detained in Clonmel borstal, this book will not refer to any boy by his real name. Wherever an inmate is referred to by name, this name is completely fictional.

CHAPTER ONE

Introduction

For the greater part of the nineteenth century, the judicial and penal systems of Ireland and England struggled with the problem of how to treat juvenile offenders. The imprisonment of children in the same environment as adult convicts had long been deemed morally and practically undesirable. The introduction of the reformatory school system in 1858, and of industrial schools a decade later, alleviated but did not solve the problem. Such measures were taken partially because of a mid-Victorian panic amongst the middle class in England about the sharp rise in incidences of juvenile crime.[1] By 1880 there were still over one thousand children incarcerated in Irish prisons; approximately one hundred and fifty were under twelve years of age.[2] The introduction of the borstal system to Ireland in 1906 heralded a new era as penal policy-makers recognised the need for arrangements specifically designed to treat juvenile male offenders. Notwithstanding a renewed focus of attention during the second half of the nineteenth century, there remains the need for in-depth historical research on juvenile crime in Ireland. In those studies that do examine the issue, there is often little or no reference to Clonmel borstal institution, despite it being the first and, for fifty years, the only such establishment in what is now the Republic of Ireland. As with juvenile crime, in-depth studies of Clonmel borstal may not have been possible in the past due to a lack of awareness of primary sources.

From the late eighteenth century onwards, an increasing number of prison reformers and politicians were concerned about the imprisonment and welfare of Ireland's criminals and engaged in a recurring and vibrant debate on the development of the penal system. Indeed, it was clear that groups in Ireland demonstrated a far more enlightened attitude towards the prison system than was the case in Britain. Many initiatives put forward by the government in London from the mid-1800s onwards were in fact inspired by earlier innovations in Ireland. Among these was the borstal institution.[3] The borstal system was established in Britain at the beginning of the twentieth century in response to the growing crisis of juvenile male offenders. In 1895, the Gladstone Committee of the House of Commons, investigating the state of prisons, found that in the preceding year 16,000 prison sentences had been imposed on males under the age of twenty-one. After serving a short sentence, most offenders deteriorated in character and disposition.[4] Following extensive consultation and examination, the English Prison Commission chairman, Evelyn Ruggles-Brise, in 1900 devised an idea for a new type of penal reformatory dedicated exclusively to the treatment of males between the ages of sixteen and twenty-one. The system was extended to Ireland in 1906 with the opening of an institution in Clonmel in County Tipperary. While much scholarship has been devoted to the English borstal institution, little attention has been paid to the Irish system.

The foundation of the first borstal institution in Britain in 1901, and in Ireland in 1906, was the outcome of almost a century of political and societal debate that had extended across two continents. The opening chapter of Nial Osborough's *Borstal in Ireland: Custodial Provision for the Young Adult Offender 1906?1974* refers to Ireland's role in this process.[5] Osborough's study of the borstal system in Ireland stands alone as the only substantial work on the subject. It is commonly referred to by other scholars writing penal histories of the late nineteenth or early twentieth century. The book examines the borstal system in Ireland, both north and south, up to and including 1974.[6] Once he establishes the legislative structure of juvenile justice as it emerged from the late nineteenth-century debate, the background is outlined for the foundation of borstal. Though making reference to the results of the Gladstone Committee investigation in Britain, he does not outline in any detail the conditions that created the need for such an institution in Ireland.

Osborough employs a key source of information on the borstal system in Ireland: the annual reports of the General Prisons Board (GPB). These provide limited, but essential, detail on the arrangements at the Clonmel institution. Osborough uses the annual reports to underline some of the considerable problems Clonmel faced, including the ongoing issue of unsuitable training facilities for the inmates. He also allows his source to give voice to the Borstal Association of Ireland (BAI), the aftercare body whose annual reports were cited by the GPB. The work of the BAI was crucial to the early life of the system but the extent to which its comments were utilised in the GPB reports is limited. Some of the Association's own reports have survived but a far more comprehensive account of its work was regularly detailed in the pages of the Clonmel newspaper *The Nationalist* during the period.[7] Osborough makes some use of *The Nationalist* but this current work utilises this valuable local contemporary source to its fullest extent.

Though Osborough's study stands as the sole authority to date on the borstal system in Ireland, it is the work of Roger Hood that must form the basis of any primary or secondary study on the system as a whole.[8] His authoritative work *Borstal Re-assessed* is widely regarded by scholars of penal history as the pre-eminent source for the system that developed in England and Wales at the opening of the twentieth century. Hood uses source categories similar to those of Osborough, including parliamentary committee reports, House of Commons debates and police commission reports. He skilfully interrogates the bureaucratic terminology of each of his sources in an attempt to identify its hidden connotations. He employs similar skill in examining a book by the founder of the borstal system, Sir Evelyn Ruggles-Brise, and a memoir on him by the Anglo-Irish writer Shane Leslie.[9] Ruggles-Brise was the legendary reforming English Prison Commissioner whose expertise and ideas contributed much to the early success of the borstal in England.[10] In opting to explore these books, *Borstal Re-assessed* utilised what can often be a fundamental source, the personal account of one who was a driving force behind the idea in question. Discussion in the important newspapers of a given period can often establish a sense of wider attitudes to the creation of an institution such as the borstal. *The Times* newspaper provided Hood with an opportunity to complement his existing official sources with published letters and leading articles that conveyed something of the general disposition of élite society towards Ruggles-Brise and his new penal reformatory.

The relevance of Hood's work to this book is mixed. *Borstal Re-assessed* opens with an account of the legislative manoeuvres and penal demands that necessitated new thinking about a class of male offender known as the juvenile-adult. Like Osborough, Hood used legalistic descriptions of the different processes involved in the foundation of the system. What sets Hood's work apart, however, is that each aspect is explained in considerable detail and every decision is accounted for in generally non-legal terms. He devotes substantial discussion to specific matters, for example how the Prison Commissioners decided upon the age category of offenders, and goes on to consider the progress of the English borstal system, particularly after 1921. Hood's work becomes an essential secondary source for this book in the area of borstal aftercare. This aspect of the penal system was a product of the nineteenth century, when philanthropic groups were formed to provide support for discharged prisoners. Using its annual reports, Hood outlines the development of the Borstal Association in England from a minor body to an integral and legislated component of the borstal process.

Hood provides an essential basis for English, Irish and indeed international scholarship. The book does not, however, penetrate the daily workings of the borstal to any great extent, which is not its intention. Though persistent but unavoidable reference to various reports, committees and periods tends to compromise the clarity of an otherwise balanced and accessible work, *Borstal Re-assessed* is both detailed and analytical, highlighting many of the issues faced by those charged with implementing the system. For all its practicality, the book frames all of the major controversies surrounding juvenile offenders within the theoretical context that emerged throughout the nineteenth century. Indeed, any effective penal history must pay attention to contemporary intellectual opinion.

Few, if any, first-hand accounts of Clonmel borstal institution have survived, if they existed in the first place. Writing in *The Bell* in 1940, Edward Fahy provided some insight.[11] He opens with a profile of the young offender, pointing out that many adult criminal careers begin at a young age. He goes on to underline the importance of not breaking the offender's spirit but activating reformation from within, empowering the individual to stimulate change for himself.[12] This was the essence of borstal treatment. After devoting some discussion to the court process through which offenders passed, Fahy turns his attention to Clonmel, at which point the tone of the article becomes decidedly negative. Indeed, he provides a very bleak assessment of the country's only borstal, questioning how its building ever came to be selected for its purpose.[13] A detailed physical description of the complex is offered, particularly the exterior recreational and work areas. Fahy traces the link between the physical layout of the institution and the nature of the intended treatment programme. Physical drill, sports and work were central to borstal treatment, yet Clonmel provided little or no opportunity for such activities. While it had been frequently stressed by the founders of the borstal system that it should not be referred to or viewed as prison, the facility at Clonmel possessed all the distinctive features of its former role as the South Tipperary gaol. The presence of a 'gigantic wall' as well as their 'gloomy' cells ensured that the boys were constantly reminded of the distrust with which they were regarded, something that would surely have affected their attitude.[14]

Central to the borstal philosophy was the idea of the detainee as an individual. Borstal boys were known as inmates and were never referred to as prisoners. Following the appointment of Alexander Patterson as English Prison Commissioner in 1922, they were called 'lads'. This was just an expression of Patterson's less militaristic approach to borstal treatment as he sought to imbue his subjects with a sense of personal authority and responsibility. Later in the twentieth century the borstal 'lad' became known as a 'trainee'. McConville highlights an aspect of the system's foundation that is largely ignored by most writers, emphasising the tensions that existed within the 1894?5 Gladstone Committee on Prisons.[15] Not every committee member supported the idea of a new penal reformatory and neither did all of the witnesses who appeared before it. What becomes clear is that the borstal institution, in England at any rate, was very much a product of the Victorian notion of the prison and its supporters would spend much of their time in the early decades attempting to throw off that image.

One of the central aims of this book will be to identify and discuss the juvenile penal structure that emerged during the Victorian age. The nineteenth century penal environment in Britain and Ireland was a melting-pot of ideas, committees and reform movements. Identifying a system of juvenile justice among this continuous upheaval necessitates a much deeper understanding of wider penal affairs during the nineteenth century. Tim Carey attempts to extricate the establishment of Mountjoy prison from this context. His book *Mountjoy: The Story of a Prison* is essentially a history of Ireland's original 'model prison'.[16] This book is a rich account of prison conditions, from the depravity of the eighteenth century to the reform movements that eventually led to a modern prison system. It opens with a useful outline of the administration, or absence of it, of the eighteenth-century prison system in Ireland. Carey paints a picture of a debauched cauldron of moral depravity that was characteristic of Ireland's forty locally run prisons. He goes on to outline some of Dublin's most notorious prisons with vivid descriptions of strange and disorderly places within which murder, rape and robbery were commonplace.[17] The cruel and harrowing eighteenth-century prison did not categorise its inmates on the basis of class, age or gender. Men were incarcerated with women, children with lunatics, there was no order in prisons, which were devoid of any form of social norm. Carey describes the development of a prison reform movement in the mid-nineteenth century that would place Ireland at least fifty years ahead of England in terms of penal innovation. While there is little or no reference to the plight of juvenile offenders, Carey's work is important as the system he describes affected all elements of the internal social structure of the prison community. One of the legacies of the dire prison conditions of the eighteenth century and the subsequent reform movement was that they would both inspire later prison reformers, including Sir Walter Crofton and particularly Ruggles-Brise, to the recognition that a different approach was necessary for young offenders.[18]

This book will also examine the young offender himself. Who was the juvenile-adult male offender? What was his role in society? What was the nature of his existence before he offended? What was the progress of his criminal career? At what point, and how, was it cut short by his borstal detention? Radzinowicz and Hood contend that the 'young offender' was a Victorian creation. Prior to the nineteenth century, no age differentiation existed in the trial process, punishments or the methods by which they were imposed.[19] As well as addressing many of these questions, this book will turn its attention to the life of the offender inside borstal.

While Margaret O'Callaghan, Elizabeth Dooley and others devote considerable attention to the influential mid-nineteenth century developments in the Irish prison system, most studies do not take account, to any substantial extent, of the place of younger people in prison.[20] Although Osborough's *Borstal in Ireland* is a major study of penal provision for young offenders in Ireland, it is based largely on legislative, rather than institutional or official, sources. Many studies also fail to take account of the crucial distinction within the term 'juvenile offender'. It is important to separate the 'juvenile-adult offender' from other elements of the broad cohort of delinquent and law-breaking young people. This study, therefore, scrutinises the borstal itself and presents an account of the work of an institution that had a unique, albeit low, profile in the Irish penal system for half a century.

Emsley points out that the historiography of criminality, as well as the statistics themselves, suggests that crime was a male sphere in the eighteenth and nineteenth centuries. The various aspects of criminal behaviour, such as aggression, competitiveness and initiative, were all adopted as central to 'normal' masculine conduct.[21] Wiener supports this suggestion with his contention that at this time problems of violence, ideas of gender and the operation of the law all took a more prominent position in culture and consciousness. In parallel to this, they converged on one issue in particular, that of controlling male violence, especially that directed towards women.[22] History has tended to portray the male criminal as brazen and astute. The young male criminal from the eighteenth and nineteenth centuries has in particular become identified, in historiography and popular culture alike, with Charles Dickens' 'Artful Dodger'. The Irish juvenile-adult male offender class can be roughly divided in two. One was this Dickensian 'street-wise' youth who possessed all the cunning and wit of a man twice his age. He was the 'Artful Dodger' and he and his companions were often 'run' by a Fagin-like, older, criminal mentor. The other was the boy who fell into criminality somewhat accidentally – he may have committed his first offence and was unlucky enough to be caught, or too inexperienced to escape detection. He was the more innocent offender and did not possess the wiles of the 'Artful Dodger'. This book also examines the interactions between these young male inmates in the controlled environment of a borstal. It will reveal the underlying tensions brought about by the incarceration of a large group of awkward, post-adolescent young men, not yet psychologically mature. Such friction often gave rise to violence and to a phenomenon that sociologists have labelled 'subcultures of solidarity'.[23] An example of this behaviour occurred at Clonmel borstal when inmates from one specific geographical region grouped together in support of a boy from the same area, who had been accused by warders of a transgression. While studies such as *Gender and Sexuality in Modern Ireland* have taken account of the concepts of manliness at the outset of the twentieth century, a more in-depth study of so-called 'ordinary' and deviant young men is needed.[24] Gender historians have largely neglected the juvenile male offender in Irish penal institutions.

The development of the penal system in Ireland is, in many ways, drawn together by two distinctive strands during the nineteenth century, both forming the background to the birth and early progress of Clonmel borstal. Firstly, the composition of the British administration in Ireland had a direct and obvious bearing on the development of the prison

system. Following the Act of Union of 1801, the most senior British official in Ireland was the lord lieutenant, who functioned as the head of
government. His policies were devised at cabinet level in London but he
did have the benefit of a high degree of individual discretion. After the
legislative union in 1801, the role of the lord lieutenant was somewhat
diluted by the office of the chief secretary. As the chief secretary became
more powerful during the nineteenth century, due to the fact that his
presence was required in London to speak on Irish affairs when parliament was in session, the role of the lord lieutenant diminished.
Although the lord lieutenant was his superior, his presence in London
on a regular basis ensured that the chief secretary came into frequent
contact with cabinet members and policy-makers, inevitably enhancing
his authority.[25] The office of the lord lieutenant faced possible abolition
on a number of occasions during the nineteenth century but survived
until 1922 mainly due to political apathy.[26] One of the most significant
acts in the birth of the modern Irish penal system was the appointment
by the lord lieutenant of two inspectors-general of prisons in the late
eighteenth century. This important government intervention in the
development of prisons will be considered in greater detail in Chapter
2. By the late nineteenth century, meanwhile, the office of chief
secretary had attained a much higher status, and became accountable to
parliament for twenty-nine government departments.[27] One of these
departments was the GPB, founded in 1877 as the central authority for
the administration of the Irish penal system. The Board outlasted the
British administration in Ireland.

The Irish exchequer came under the full control of the British
treasury by 1817. British officials had already decided that the Irish
treasury department was inefficient and under-performing. In
contrast, the London government had developed a fiscal system that
gave the treasury considerable control over the efficiency of all departments and it became 'a persistent agent of administrative reform'.[28] The
treasury was a key department for all of the agencies of state and this
book emphasises its importance to the prison and borstal systems.
One indication of its extensive control over the expenditure of government agencies was that treasury officials vetted many elements of
Clonmel borstal for viability and cost-effectiveness.

The second strand forming the backdrop to the prison and borstal
systems was the series of turbulent political and social events that dominated Irish life and the public discourse during the nineteenth and
early twentieth centuries. The Great Famine of the mid-nineteenth

century had a devastating effect on the Irish population. The role of public institutions of care and punishment, such as workhouses and prisons, came into sharp focus during this time. The development of the prison system in particular was heavily influenced by events that took place during the Famine years, most notably the passing of the Vagrancy Act of 1847. In the second half of the nineteenth century, the historiography of crime in Ireland tends to be dominated by events arising from the land wars that began in the late 1870s. Yet, as this book will clearly demonstrate, most of the offences for which borstal offenders were convicted were not related to agrarian or political events. Nor is there any evidence that the operation of Clonmel borstal was greatly affected by the home rule issue, which had been a preoccupation of constitutional nationalists since the 1870s. Similarly, the institution's population seem to have been unaffected by the growth of radical nationalism that had been progressing throughout the nineteenth century. There is only limited evidence to suggest that internal agitation was caused by anti-British sentiment. Despite the fact that a major component of this book examines a period of considerable political strife, none of the borstal offences appear to have been of a political or agrarian nature. Through the censorship of letters and newspapers, the inmates of Clonmel were somewhat isolated from the unrest in Irish life between 1906 and 1921.

After the passing of the Prevention of Crime Act in 1908, the principal sentencing authority for borstal offenders was the court of assize. This was a judicial system that had its roots in the thirteenth century, and provided the principal local venue for criminal trials in Ireland. The role of this court evolved over the centuries and by the late nineteenth century judges of the assize travelled the country holding seasonal court sessions, where they presided over civil and criminal matters.[29] The juries of these courts were typically filled by individuals who were appointed through property or other qualifications. Although Catholics formed a large part of the jury panels, there was some disquiet that the individual members were chosen by local sheriffs who often discriminated on religious grounds.[30] Vaughan points out that, by the 1870s, these courts had begun to impact on the lives of ordinary men in much the same way as the confessional or the national school.[31] The press reporting of court of assize sessions offers a revealing insight into these same lives.

The central primary source for much of this book is the register of inmates for Clonmel prison and borstal institution, 1903?23.[32] It provides a comprehensive report on each individual inmate based on information collected at the time of admission and discharge. Name, age on arrival, physical description including height, weight, complexion, hair and eye colour, and details of any unusual markings on his body are provided. Such information serves to humanise and individualise the boys so that they become more than just numbered inmates. Information is also provided on the background of each boy, with his most recent place of residence as well as his place of birth both recorded. The register also gives the name and address of the next-of-kin of the inmate, allowing the researcher to determine with some accuracy whether or not he was living with parents or guardians at the time he offended. Information on the previous occupation of each inmate provides an opportunity to identify and analyse employment trends among the borstal population. Further, a comprehensive account can be created of the offences of borstal inmates, and subsequent sentences administered to them. Finally, the method of discharge can be reconstructed. In many cases a boy did not serve his full sentence but was discharged on licence, to be returned to the borstal should he re-offend within the period of his parole. Such detail is useful in determining the medium-term success, or otherwise, of the borstal system.

The GPB was the Irish equivalent of the English Prison Commissioners, the Home Office agency that controlled the English penal system. The Board consisted of three members and often took the lead from the English Prison Commissioners, indicating that the penal systems of both countries were largely operated along the same lines. Part of the control involved regular inspections by visiting justices and other officials from the Board. The borstal was included in the GPB annual reports, which offer an appraisal of the state of prisons in Ireland.[33] For these reasons, the institutional authorities at Clonmel maintained the register of inmates, which was subject to regular inspection. This accounts for the professional manner in which that register was maintained and preserved.

The work of the BAI is central to the period between 1906 and 1921. It was an organisation whose annual reports would prove vital to the understanding of the system in existence for the aftercare of the boys once they left the institution.[34] The reports were compiled by its committee and were based on the activities of its members, who not only assisted discharged inmates but also supported the work of the institution itself. Each report provides much practical detail on the daily functioning of the borstal and the challenges faced by discharged boys, though Chapter 8 will raise a number of questions regarding the veracity of some aspects of their content.

One of the most important sources for the study of the Irish penal system between 1877 and 1921 is the voluminous GPB correspondence. Held at the National Archives of Ireland (NAI), it contains all of the surviving correspondence between the headquarters of the Board and the institutions under its administration. For Clonmel borstal, the copies of correspondence include communications between the GPB, the institution and the BAI, on every conceivable issue from the number of apples that should be given to inmates, to the application of discipline. It contains complete sets of correspondence on disciplinary measures that were taken against particular inmates who were alleged to have misbehaved and became the subject of proceedings. These allow for the compilation of a number of case studies that provide insight into borstal discipline. The survival of a number of the Board's own inspection reports reveals something of the official opinion of the work that was being undertaken at Clonmel. These reports are noteworthy because they were often critical of the institution when necessary but the criticisms were never made public. The intense activity of the BAI is laid bare by an examination of this vast resource. The honorary secretary of the Association, William Casey, is revealed as its driving force, whether it was lobbying for more land for training or for a change in sentencing policy. The GPB correspondence also contains a number of important images. An architectural plan of the Clonmel gaol complex was commissioned by the GPB in 1909 in anticipation of the changeover to a full borstal institution. It offers an important visual image of the extent of the space available and the limitations that resulted from placing the institution in an unsuitable urban setting. An analysis of these documents reveals a penal authority that was intent on moving away from the traditional approach to juvenile offenders, towards a new, more personalised method. The actors in this modernisation process were earnest about the task at hand and determined to leave nothing to chance in establishing a system that had proven successful in England.

Access to comprehensive primary sources for much of the post-1921 borstal institution is hampered by a seventy-year rule, which means that Chapters 9 and 10 do not benefit from the type of detailed analysis possible for the earlier period. Nonetheless, the GPB and later the Irish

Department of Justice continued to publish annual reports that serve to provide the official record of the progress of the institution up to 1956. The borstal was often the subject of debate in Dáil Éireann at crucial moments in its later history. This was particularly true during the 1940s, when Fine Gael deputy James Dillon persistently highlighted what he felt were the poor conditions. Public comments by the Irish-American Roman Catholic founder of Boys Town, Monsignor Edward Flanagan, also came under some animated scrutiny in the Dáil. These debates will be used along with some of the extensive newspaper reporting on the controversy and its subsequent impact on Clonmel borstal. A number of residents familiar with the borstal between the late 1930s and its closure in 1956 were interviewed and provide some useful insights into the role of the institution and its final governor. One interviewee had a number of associations with the institution, firstly having made her confirmation alongside six inmates and later because of her assistance in the production of a play staged in the borstal by a local drama group.

This book opens with an examination of the place of the juvenile offender in the Irish penal system in the century prior to the introduction of the borstal system. It identifies the needs of children and young people within the penal system, making reference to the key developments in prison reform. The influence of a number of significant reformers, such as John Howard and Elizabeth Fry, ensured that a steady pace of change was maintained between the 1770s and the early 1900s. The development of a penal theory by Walter Crofton and its subsequent imitation throughout the world, including by the prison authorities in New York state, provided the permanent link between the nineteenth and twentieth-century penal systems. After being successfully tried and tested at penal reformatories, first in Bedford and later in Kent, the Crofton principles came full circle when they returned to Ireland with the opening of Clonmel borstal institution in a portion of the county gaol in May 1906. The state of juvenile offending and criminality in general were factors that potentially contributed to the decision to locate an institution in Ireland, ultimately leading the penal authorities in Dublin to end the experiment in 1910 and convert the gaol into a fully functioning borstal institution. This book then focuses on the juvenile-adult offender class at Clonmel, identifying those districts most commonly represented among the inmates and assessing the possible reasons. A profile of the borstal offender, including previous occupations, social class, education, religion and family circumstances, is fundamental to a deeper understanding of juvenile criminality. This will help further to locate the juvenile-adult male offender in early twentieth-century Irish society. The measures used to exert control and maintain order, while at the same time encouraging a sense of self-discipline, were a key element of the system inherited from Kent. All borstal disciplinary measures emanated from the grading system within which all inmates existed. An examination of the daily routine, similar to that in the adult prison, reveals the structure of the 'borstal day'. Separately and together, education, training and religion were each essential to the physical, intellectual and moral development of the juvenile-adult offender. The physical facilities for the provision of these services in Clonmel will be evaluated and the long and protracted debate that surrounded the institution's inability to provide adequate training in manual trades to inmates will be assessed. All of the boys were released into the care of the BAI: Chapter 8 will give a detailed analysis of the work of that body, questioning the effectiveness of its role within the overall system. Using anecdotal evidence, the often difficult readjustment to society of ex-borstal offenders, sometimes in the light of local hostility and exploitation, will be considered. The practice of discharging inmates to fight with the British army in the First World War was commonplace in borstal institutions and Clonmel was no different. The post-Independence section begins with an account of a Civil War incident that almost brought the Irish borstal system to a premature end. This period also witnessed a number of key developments in government administration as the institution came under the control of the new Irish Free State. One of the striking aspects of this era is the apparently diminished public role of the BAI. The final chapters will focus on what was the inevitable decline of Clonmel borstal. The institution had suffered under both British and Irish administration from the dual problems of severe under-funding and a lack of imagination. Having attracted the clearly unwanted attention of Monsignor Edward Flanagan in 1946 the borstal enjoyed something of a rebirth in the immediate post-World War Two period but largely because of judicial reluctance to avail of this particular sentencing option it had entered its closing years.

This book is intended as an institutional history of Clonmel borstal. It does not pretend to offer a comprehensive analysis of juvenile crime and its punishment in Ireland but rather seeks to throw some light on a hitherto neglected sub-category of offender. The juvenile-adult male offender class may not have been large in size compared with the numbers detained in industrial and reformatory schools but is no less worthy of its place in the historiography of crime and punishment in Ireland. Neither does this book offer line-by-line comparisons with the other institutions of detention and care for criminal and neglected young people. Rather, it will place the borstal in the context of the existing juvenile penal system. While institutions such as the Magdalen asylums, and the industrial and reformatory schools, rightly continue to exercise the minds of researchers, the recording of their histories is farther advanced than that of the borstal. Exhaustive comparisons between the borstal and those institutions would be futile at this stage as this would distract from the creation of this initial singular institutional history. This is not to say that such comparisons are not appropriate: they are necessary if a more complete understanding of the juvenile and indeed the adult penal system is to be achieved. Instead, this book intends to put forward a very specific analysis of the practical application of a treatment process, devised at the dawn of the twentieth century by British prison managers of the late Victorian era and delivered over the course of five decades, with little adjustment, to inmates of the Irish borstal in Clonmel.

NOTES

1. John Black, 'The Victorian origins of a "Group 4" prison service', *History Today*, 43, 10 (October, 1993), p. 10.
2. S.J. Connolly, *The Oxford Companion to Irish History* (Oxford: Oxford University Press, 1998), p. 477.
3. Later chapters of this book will detail the relationships between various initiatives.
4. R.R. Cherry, 'Juvenile crime and its prevention', *Journal of the Social and Statistical Inquiry Society of Ireland*, 1907–12, xxii, p. 436.
5. Nial Osborough, *Borstal in Ireland: Custodial Provision for the Young Adult Offender 1906–1974* (Dublin: Institute of Public Administration, 1975).
6. The borstal institution survived in Clonmel until 1956, when it was transferred to Dublin and renamed St Patrick's Borstal Institution.
7. Some of the annual reports of the Borstal Association of Ireland have survived for the period of this book and will be used as a primary source on their own, outside the context of Osborough's book.
8. Roger Hood, *Borstal Re-assessed* (London: Heinemann, 1965).
9. Sir Evelyn Ruggles-Brise, *The English Prison System* (London: Macmillan, 1921).
10. Shane Leslie, *Sir Evelyn Ruggles-Brise: A Memoir of the Founder of Borstal* (London: John Murray, 1938).
11. Edward Fahy, 'The boy criminal', *The Bell*, 1940, 1, 2, pp. 41–51.
12. Fahy, 'The boy criminal', p. 42.
13. Fahy, 'The boy criminal', p. 46.
14. Fahy, 'The boy criminal', p. 47.
15. S. McConville, 'The Victorian prison: England 1865–1965', in N. Morris, D. Rothman (eds), *The Oxford History of the Prison: The Practice of Punishment in Western Society* (Oxford: Oxford University Press, 1995), pp. 117–50.

16. Tim Carey, *Mountjoy: The Story of a Prison* (Dublin: The Collins Press, 2000). The 'model prison' was the term given to Pentonville prison in London, upon which Mountjoy was styled.
17. Carey, *Mountjoy: The Story of a Prison*, p. 6.
18. Carey, *Mountjoy: The Story of a Prison*, p. 8.
19. Leon Radzinowicz, Roger Hood, *A History of English Criminal Law and its Administration from 1750* (London: Clarendon, 1986).
20. Margaret O'Callaghan, *British High Politics and a Nationalist Ireland: Criminality, Land and the Law under Forster and Balfour* (Cork: Cork University Press, 1994). E.E. Dooley, 'Sir Walter Crofton and the Irish or intermediate system of prison discipline', in Ian O'Donnell and Finbarr McAuley (eds), *Criminal Justice History* (Dublin: Four Courts Press, 2003), pp. 197–220.
21. Clive Emsley, *Crime and Society in England* (Oxford: Oxford University Press, 2005), p. 92.
22. Martin Joel Wiener, *Men of Blood: Violence, Manliness and Criminal Justice in Victorian England* (London: Cambridge University Press, 2004), p. 9.
23. R. Emerson Dobash, Russell P. Dobash and Lesley Noaks, 'Thinking about gender and crime', in R. Emerson Dobash, Russell P. Dobash and Lesley Noaks (eds) *Gender and Crime* (Cardiff: University of Wales Press, 1995), p. 2.
24. Anthony Bradley and Maryann Gialanella Valiulis (eds), *Gender and Sexuality in Modern Ireland* (Massachusetts: University of Massachusetts Press, 1997).
25. S.J. Connolly, 'Aftermath and adjustment', in W.E. Vaughan (ed.), *A New History of Ireland: Ireland under the Union, 1801–70* (10 vols, Oxford: Oxford University Press, 1989), v, pp. 4–5.
26. Connolly, *Oxford Companion to Irish History*, p. 329.
27. Connolly, *Oxford Companion to Irish History*, p. 86.
28. R.B. McDowell, 'Administration and the public services, 1800–70', in Vaughan (ed.), *A New History of Ireland*, p. 542.
29. Connolly, *Oxford Companion to Irish History*, p. 30.
30. R.V. Comerford, 'Ireland 1850–70: post-famine and mid-Victorian', in Vaughan (ed.), *A New History of Ireland*, p. 388.
31. W.E.Vaughan, A.J. Fitzpatrick (eds), *Irish Historical Statistics: Population 1821–1971* (Dublin: Royal Irish Academy, 1978).
32. Between 1906 and 1910, the names and profiles of young men sentenced to borstal detention at Clonmel were not recorded separately from adult prisoners, making identification difficult. It is not until the register reaches August 1910, when adult prisoners were removed from Clonmel prison, that an accurate analysis of borstal inmates can take place. It is for this reason that this book will begin its detailed examination of the inmates in 1910 rather than in 1906, the year the borstal experiment began.
33. NLI, GPB, annual reports, 1878–1921.
34. Clonmel Borstal Memoranda, GPB/XB5

CHAPTER TWO

Emergence of juvenile penal policy in Ireland, 1779–1901

The perception and treatment of the juvenile offender class in late eighteenth-century Ireland were different to the situation that had emerged by 1900. The late eighteenth-century penal authorities made little attempt to subject offenders to any form of separation or classification and there was no significant attempt at reformation. Prison constituted a range of unregulated institutions devoid of any form of standardisation and lacking a central bureaucracy. There was an awareness among social and political élites of the presence of children and young adults in prisons with older, more seasoned convicts but this did not result in action. The seeds of change were not sown until 1775, with the first visit to Ireland of the English penal reformer John Howard. This chapter will examine the development of the Irish prison system from the late eighteenth century onwards, specifically tracing the evolution of public and political attitudes to juvenile offenders from the second half of the nineteenth century. It will go on to examine the many problems that afflicted the prison system, particularly with the decline of transportation, as well as the growing awareness of the difficulties associated with punishing and reforming juvenile offenders. Further to this, the chapter will investigate the importance of Captain Walter Crofton's pioneering Progressive Stage System (or Intermediate System) as an inspiration for the penal reformatories at Elmira in New York, Borstal in Kent and, eventually, Clonmel.

THE RISE OF THE PRISON IN IRELAND

The penal system that evolved during the nineteenth century differed considerably from that existing just one hundred years earlier. Carey provides an engaging account of an eighteenth-century system that was disorganised and corrupt, physically and morally contaminated by the excesses of human nature. By the later years of the century, the

Irish system consisted of over forty county and borough prisons and 112 bridewells, the latter being used for the punishment of debtors and petty offenders.[1] Each institution was administered at a local level, their construction and maintenance paid for by a grand jury.[2] This was the extent of its influence, however, because each prison was privately operated. Such unregulated private control provided widespread opportunities for corruption. Irish prisons, according to Carey, were 'characterised by a strange type of disorder'.[3]

The earliest stirrings of modernisation in Ireland's penal institutions began in 1775 with the arrival of the English prison reformer John Howard. This visit, and his second in 1779, did little to precipitate immediate change but both are significant in that they mark the beginning of a series of prison reform movements that would see Ireland become an innovator in the science of incarceration. Born in Hackney in 1726, Howard was an inconsequential figure until his appointment as sheriff for Bedfordshire in 1773. Part of his remit was to supervise the gaols that fell within his jurisdiction and he took the unusual step of actually visiting one; this affected him so much that it became the issue to which he dedicated the remainder of his life. Disturbed by what he saw and appalled by the indifference of the local magistrates, he embarked on a 50,000-mile tour of every English prison to investigate the condition of prisoners.[4] In 1777 he published *The State of Prisons in England and Wales*. During his 1779 visit to Ireland, he was disturbed to find boys under the age of twelve detained for up to two years because they had nobody to pay the necessary release fee to the sheriff or gaoler.[5] Taylor argues that, though he shocked his audience, Howard's work should not be explained away merely as a humanitarian response to the problems he encountered. Howard was a pragmatist and his findings were unacceptable on several different levels.[6]

The Irish political establishment was ready to embrace Howard's ideas only in 1782, when the Irish House of Commons established a Committee to Enquire into Prison Conditions. Several members of parliament, annoyed at having limited autonomy, seized on the prison system as the one area where they could wield some power ahead of London. Howard's testimony before this committee, along with repeated investigations, persistently concluded that Ireland's prisons were among the worst in Europe. The various prison acts of the 1780s brought the first practical reforms, with a much more proactive role for the grand jury as well as the introduction of regulations designed to improve the general physical and moral condition of each prisoner. In May 1786 the first inspector general of prisons, Sir Jeremiah Fitzpatrick, was appointed in Ireland, half a century before a similar office was established in England.[7] What followed is described by Carey as an 'unprecedented and since unparalleled period of prison construction'. By 1788, thirty-three prisons were either planned or in progress. It was an impressive first wave of prison reform and, though it did not, to any great degree, address the crucial issue of the separation of prisoners, it did establish a foundation that would sustain the system developed by future reformers.

Another penal initiative had its roots in the 'confinement crisis': when the newly independent American colonies refused to accept any further transported prisoners. Penal authorities in London proposed a penitentiary that would solve the problem. Heaney describes this penitentiary as an attempted alternative to transportation, reforming prisoners in a national institution through solitary confinement, hard labour and religious instruction.[8] This marked one of the earliest acknowledgements of the need to reform, as well as punish, prisoners. The opening of convict colonies in Australia in 1791 eliminated the immediate need for a penitentiary but the idea remained active. In 1792, the concept reached the statute books in Ireland. Its strongest supporter there was Jeremiah Fitzpatrick, who questioned the overall effectiveness of transportation. The penitentiary was tested on a trial basis but lay dormant until it was eventually opened on a full scale at Grangegorman Lane in Dublin in 1819.[9] The penitentiary in Dublin was initially deemed a success but eventually came to be frustrated by persistent political and religious quarrels; it closed in 1831. While it is agreed that much of the theory behind the project was ill-conceived, it did at the very least represent an attempt at innovation. Many of the core principles of the penitentiary faded from view when it closed its doors, but certain familiar threads from this period would be found in later initiatives.

A new crisis in Ireland's prison system emerged in parallel with the development of the penitentiary. The reform movement initiated by Howard had long since finished and the end of the Napoleonic wars presented a prison overcrowding crisis as victorious soldiers returned to find little in the way of material prosperity and often turned to crime. Between 1815 and 1818 the prison population in Ireland rose by over eight thousand.[10] In England, meanwhile, against conventional wisdom and in the face of well-intentioned opposition, English

Quaker philanthropist Elizabeth Fry in 1812 made an unprecedented visit to the women and children in London's Newgate prison. Deeply religious and humanitarian by nature, Fry was horrified by the conditions with which she was confronted and initially set up a school for the children of Newgate. Four years after her first inspection, she returned to form a ladies' visiting committee and began preaching to the female prisoners. Her presence proved influential and seemed to bear out the argument that religion could not only reform, but also bring about a change in character.[11] Inspired by the work of Elizabeth Fry, similar committees began to appear as affluent ladies with good intentions visited prisons across the country. A new reform movement was now in train, seeking to individualise the prisoner with a central focus on education. By the 1820s, a new round of county prisons was under construction, in Down, Kildare, Meath, Kerry, Galway and elsewhere.[12] The condition of the individual prisoner had generally been improved from its late eighteenth-century state, but the coming decades would bring a new set of challenges that would call for an entirely original and more scientific approach. This period would also see an increased awareness, by the authorities and the prison reformers, of the juvenile offender.

OLD CHALLENGES AND NEW INNOVATIONS

Perhaps the strongest challenge to mid-nineteenth century prison administrators was the decline of transportation. Between 1791 and 1853 more than 200 ships transported 39,000 Irish convicts to Australia.[13] Transportation of juveniles was commonplace, driven by the theory that banishing them to another country would have the effect of permanently disengaging them from their criminal connections at home.[14] When transportation from Ireland ended in 1853 it presented a considerable difficulty to a system that was already in trouble. A select committee of parliament was set up in 1856 and demanded that the length of penal servitude sentences be equal to that of transportation sentences.[15] Such a recommendation would serve to ensure that those prisoners already putting pressure on the system, by not being transported, would now be incarcerated for longer. Transportation had already been in decline but the penal authorities could scarcely have been prepared for the onset of the calamitous Famine in the late 1840s, which ultimately forced a complete rethink of the convict system.

Dooley cites the Great Famine as one of two conflicting influences over the Irish penal system in the mid-nineteenth century. The Famine produced high emigration and mortality, leading to population reduction. This, in turn, led to increased employment opportunities and better wages. However, a second influence would serve to counteract much of this. The Vagrancy Act of 1847 introduced short sentences for a larger number of offences, thus trebling the convict population between 1847 and 1850.[16] The introduction of this legislation at that particular moment was a disastrous miscalculation by the British government. As the Famine took hold it was obvious that normally law-abiding people would be forced into petty crime in order to survive. The full horror of the situation is represented by the fact that by 1849 over 100,000 people were incarcerated in Ireland's prisons. In 1849 alone, 1,300 of those died in prison.[17] Among the responses to this overcrowding crisis was the opening of a number of new prisons, among them, following consultation between Irish and British administrators, the Irish version of London's Model Prison at Pentonville.

The establishment of Mountjoy prison in Dublin was the result of a fact-finding tour of the English system in 1846 by Major Cottingham, the superintendent of prisons. He returned with the recommendation that Ireland needed its own version of Pentonville.[18] In the same year, Captain Joshua Jebb, the surveyor general of prisons in England and the driving force behind Pentonville, arrived in Ireland to advance plans for such an institution. A site on the North Circular Road in Dublin was found and plans were presented to the lord lieutenant in 1847.[19] Mountjoy eventually opened in 1850, the largest of three such institutions established during this period: Spike Island in Cork Harbour in 1847 and Philipstown in 1850. While these developments were undoubtedly welcome, absorbing some of the pressure from an overburdened penal structure, the most daring innovations were still ahead.

In direct response to the abolition of transportation, a new Convict Prisons Board was established for Ireland in 1854 under the chairmanship of Captain Walter Crofton. He and his fellow directors had no legal authority to manage Irish prisons until August 1854, when the Penal Servitude Act gave them the power to address overcrowding and to separate adults and juveniles. The condition of prisoners continued to be physically and morally reprehensible: they were housed in badly designed buildings, staffed by officers who were not fit to hold such positions. Most of the prisoners were uneducated and, therefore, lacking in confidence and self-respect. The greatest problem, however, was the large number of prisoners sentenced to penal servitude.[20] As a means of addressing these difficulties, Crofton adopted some ideas originally set forward by Captain Alexander Maconochie.[21] Given that the Crofton scheme developed in Ireland was actually a refinement of one that was partially developed in England in 1853, some credit should be given to Sir Joshua Jebb. Crofton is largely credited as the pioneer of the system because he actually brought it from theory to reality.[22] The scheme became known internationally as the Irish, or Intermediate, System (or the Progressive Stage System).

Many of the guiding principles of the borstal idea first emerged in the Intermediate System. Under this arrangement a prisoner passed through three stages in the course of their sentence. The initial stage consisted of nine months of severely enforced solitary confinement. The convict was forced to remain idle during this time as Crofton argued that it presented him with an opportunity for reflection and the realisation that work is a privilege.[23] The second stage in the process was known as the public works or associated stage. It was on this stage that Crofton's successors in England would later base the borstal system. Following their period of solitary confinement, convicts were sent to public works prisons – in England it was Dartmoor or Portland, while in Ireland it was Philipstown or Spike Island. They were given the opportunity to earn marks through their efforts in the areas of discipline, education and labour. The incentive was eligibility to move through five classes: probation, third class, second class, first class and exemplary class, each bringing increased privileges. As an effort at penal reform, this system was a genuine breakthrough. No longer were policy-makers wholly obsessed with punitive sentences but with the reformation and individualisation of the prisoner. Dooley cites statistics claiming that up to 75 per cent of prisoners entered this second stage.[24] The final part of the sentence was known as the intermediate stage, after which the system took one of its names. This stage could be described as a halfway house, under which the prisoners worked as regular labourers with little surveillance. During this time they lived in huts with no special measures imposed to prevent their escape.[25] Dooley describes the intermediate establishment at Smithfield in Dublin in terms of a lodging house, where convicts were unsupervised at mealtimes and often performed messenger duties around the city.[26] Crofton's friend and supporter, Baron Franz

Von Holtzendorff of the University of Berlin, underlined the importance of some level of supervision during this stage. The practice of discharging prisoners on a ticket-of-leave would only be valuable if their conduct could be observed at all times.[27] Crofton's scheme did not outlive its founder, but it was sufficient to make a considerable international impact, with aspects of the system adopted around the world; it received particular acclaim in the United States.

The Economist and the *Freeman's Journal* praised the system. Penal reformers, such as Count Cavour from France and E.C. Wines from the United States, hailed it as a much needed breakthrough. From 1857, many groups, including the National Reformatory Union, the Social Science Association and the reformatory movement, joined together in calling for the adoption of the Crofton system in England. During the following decade the English prison system did indeed move closer to that of Ireland, though never adopting all of its features.[28] The Third International Prison Congress in Frankfurt in 1857 called for its broad acceptance. The effects in Ireland were striking. Between 1853 and 1862, committals to Mountjoy declined by over 50 per cent and by 1870 the average daily number of inmates fell to one third of the 1854 level. In 1873 two empty wings of the prison were sealed off to save on gas and coal.[29] The system was discontinued in 1865 but Crofton had succeeded where many penal innovators had previously failed. His legacy in this respect was varied. His theories undeniably had an impact on penal philosophy but his influence manifested itself at a practical level. Indeed, several American states partially implemented many aspects of his system. In fact, it was not for eleven years after its collapse that the influence of the Intermediate System really came to the fore in that country, when the prison authorities focused on the specific problem of the juvenile offender. Crofton did not live to see the evolution of his Intermediate System into a penal reformatory for young male offenders. He utilised his interactions with society, the press and politicians to cultivate the policy-makers in a way that enabled them to better project their ideas and formulate their social policies. He died at his home in Oxford in 1897.[30] Parallel to the growth of his system in the 1850s and 1860s, the prison authorities in both Ireland and England set about addressing the crime and punishment of young people.

THE YOUTHFUL OFFENDER – PUNISHMENT AND REFORM

The terms juvenile offender, young offender, juvenile delinquent or youthful offender were among several applied to those generally under the age of sixteen. These terms are important to this book as they tended to change with the progression of penal science in the nineteenth century and eventually led to the development of a new term and the identification of an updated category of offender. Schlossman describes the change in attitude towards the so-called juvenile delinquent during the early nineteenth century. Popular disquiet over indiscipline among young people in general eventually turned into a widespread unease about working-class children: the middle and upper classes generally believed that they constituted some type of urban underworld.[31] One of the consequences of the economic growth of the nineteenth century was that it made it more affordable for more people to 'drink themselves into belligerent intoxication'.[32] Nonetheless it should be noted that, as the nineteenth century progressed, it was accepted that the young people who tended to occupy the various penal, reform or care institutions had not always demonstrated criminal tendencies. Many were incarcerated for petty criminality but, for others, detention was seen as necessary for reasons beyond their own control or responsibility. Sometimes a child was seen as being at risk of abuse and was removed from those circumstances until that risk could be eliminated or until the individual became adult or perhaps moved elsewhere. Parents were often unable to care for all of their offspring for health, economic or other reasons and so the child was at risk of vagrancy or delinquency and eventually found him or herself at the mercy of the penal authorities. The grounds were many and varied but by the 1850s it was clear that the authorities felt morally obliged to devise a more concerted approach to the care of such young people, criminal or not.

In 1854 the first report of the director of convict prisons for Ireland was placed before the lord lieutenant. It underlined the fact that a large and unacceptable number of juveniles under fifteen years old were held in Irish prisons. They also reported that the most urgent problem facing the system was the ongoing practice of placing young people in gaols with older, hardened criminals.[33] The report recommended that some government-owned land with access to a rail link to Dublin should be made available for the purpose of constructing a juvenile reformatory.[34] Institutions exclusively dedicated to the imprisonment or care of juveniles were not unheard of at this time. In 1837 a juvenile prison was set up at Parkhurst on the Isle of Wight but conditions were far from ideal, with boys regularly constrained by chains during school hours. The masters of the institution were typically criminals themselves and Parkhurst was generally controlled by a sense of menace.[35] At a time when religious organisations were increasing their participation in the care of delinquent children, it was a natural progression that the churches, particularly the Catholic Church, would become involved in the development and administration of the Irish version of the system that had been operating in England since the first Reformatory Schools Act of 1854. It was not until 1858 that a Reformatory Bill acceptable to the Catholic Church was agreed for Ireland.[36]

One of the key sticking points in extending the reformatory school to Ireland had been the issue of clerical involvement. The Catholic Church would support the Act only after it was enshrined in law that a young offender would be sent to a school managed by those of his own faith. The authorities in Dublin Castle placated the Catholic Church by meeting these demands. The Irish reformatory school, started in 1858, provided 'reformative treatment' for offenders convicted of minor as well as serious offences.[37] The 1858 bill stipulated that juvenile offenders between the ages of twelve and sixteen years convicted before a judge should be sent to a juvenile reformatory school for not less than one year and not more than five, with a preliminary prison term of fourteen days preceding the reformatory sentence. The impact of the reformatory on juvenile offending was not immediate but, by 1863, the directors of convict prisons were reporting a marked decrease in the numbers of juveniles imprisoned in Mountjoy.[38] The reformatory initiative begun in 1858 was only the beginning of the movement to take control of criminal or wayward young people. The authorities gradually succeeded in removing juveniles from convict prisons but the problem of disadvantaged, endangered and abandoned juveniles had not been resolved and a further institution, the industrial school, was conceived for this purpose.

If the reformatory showed signs of succeeding in its task of removing criminal children from prisons, then the purpose of the industrial school was to identify and target those that had the potential to become criminals. As with the reformatory system, England had moved ahead of Ireland by implementing the Industrial Schools Act in 1857. When the Irish version of the Act initially came before the

House of Commons in 1867 it was met with fierce opposition, particularly from Ulster Protestant members, who regarded it as a threat to poverty-stricken and disadvantaged children of their own faith.[39] The Act was ultimately accepted, however, and the first industrial school in Ireland was established in Lakelands in Dublin in 1869, under the management of the Irish Sisters of Charity. The system provided for certain classes of children up to the age of twelve found begging, receiving alms or wandering in the street without appearing to have a home, proper guardianship or support. It also catered for those found destitute, orphaned or in the care of a parent who was serving a term of imprisonment or spending time in the company of the criminal classes.[40] By the end of 1869, twenty-one industrial schools had been established. Two of the most important initiatives in the nineteenth-century crusade to eradicate juvenile crime were well underway by the early 1870s. But, as time moved on, so too did the nature of the problem. The last decades of the century brought a new class of juvenile offender and a realisation that the penal system could not remain static.

THE ELMIRA REFORMATORY

Just as Irish and English penal administrators had puzzled over the punishment and treatment of juvenile offenders, so too had their counterparts in the United States. The US prison system had been just as unsuccessful as the European one in this respect. The reformatory idea first entered US political and penal discourse in 1865 with the publication of a report by the secretary of the Board of State Charities of Massachusetts, Franklin Benjamin Sanborn, on the Crofton system tested in Ireland a number of years earlier.[41] The report played a key role in the decision of the authorities to create an institution of reformation for young adults. Such an establishment would provide some type of aftercare for its young subjects and US prison specialists envisaged something along the lines of the third, or intermediate, stage of the Crofton system. Other elements of that system would also inspire the Americans, however. In 1867, the secretary of the New York Prison Association, Dr E.C. Wines, began consultations with Crofton. He eventually presented a report on the Irish system to the Association, declaring it to be the best possible model for any new reformatory.[42] After considerable debate, the institution that came to be regarded as the most important development of the US penal system in the nineteenth century was launched in July 1876. Over the following decades, the Elmira State Reformatory in New York State attracted controversy and admiration in equal measure. As Radzinowicz and Hood pointed out, Elmira 'sometimes fascinated and sometimes repelled the progressive and the traditional forces of the Old World'. One way or the other, it could not be ignored.[43]

The Elmira Reformatory was described as ambitious in scale, not so much like a prison but more a college or a hospital, with an exterior that gave the impression of over-indulgence.[44] On the other hand, according to Dressler, it did maintain some of the physical characteristics of a high security prison with its barred cells, locked corridors and basic safe custody provisions.[45] Costing over one and a half million dollars to build, it could cater for 1,400 inmates. The cost and scale of the complex alone were enough to set it apart from any previous efforts in the field of juvenile detention. Elmira was intended for first-time juvenile offenders between the ages of sixteen and thirty or those who were in the early stages of their criminal careers and were therefore seen as ideal candidates for reformatory treatment. Among those admitted were the illiterate and the homeless.[46] The managers implemented a type of grade or mark system inspired by Crofton's Progressive Stage System, whereby inmates were categorised as superior, average or inferior. This was based on their educational achievement, their performance at work and, of course, their conduct. Placement in the higher categories ensured more favourable conditions of detention for an inmate and brought him closer to release on parole, while life for those in the inferior grade meant quite the opposite. According to Rotman, the educational programme was the basis for the entire system at Elmira and was designed in consultation with college professors, public school principals and lawyers. Included on the curriculum were sports, religion and military drill, as well as the school subjects of the time. The programme also provided vocational training, such as tailor cutting, plumbing, telegraphy and printing.[47] As the system grew and evolved, greater focus was placed on academic subjects, trades, and physical and military training. Elmira's superintendent, Zebulon Reed Brockway, was forced to place particular emphasis on physical and military training after industrial production by inmates was restricted by the state legislature. However, the trades training programmes were actually expanded over the years.[48] The entire premise of the Elmira project was driven by the vision and ideology of Brockway. As a German penologist, Dr

Hintrager, pointed out at the International Prisons Congress in Brussels in 1900, 'Brockway is the system.'[49]

Three basic principles were enshrined in the Elmira system: young offenders should be considered as potentially decent citizens; reformatory methods would be more effective than a basic custodial sentence; and, finally, this would therefore necessitate the employment of a distinctive type of treatment.[50] Despite the progressive nature of this approach, Elmira failed to fulfil its objectives in the way Brockway had hoped. Firstly, there was controversy surrounding the imposition of discipline at the reformatory and it is alleged that Brockway from time to time sanctioned physical punishments. A state investigation in 1894 declared that discipline in the institution was not in line with its stated ethos of humanity. Discipline was achieved through an atmosphere of fear of harsh punishment and not through encouragement to good behaviour, theoretically one of its central principles. Another reason the institution did not live up to the challenge was outside Brockway's control. Within two decades it had twice as many inmates as it could cater for and this impeded programmes that were obviously designed for lower numbers. Further to this was the fact that, despite the stated objective that the institution should receive only first offenders, the reality was that up to one third of the inmates were habitual or seasoned criminals.[51] Elmira did have its success, however, and was widely copied across the United States. Dooley underlines the connection between both systems by describing Crofton's influence on the Elmira principles as serving 'as an intellectual bridge between the hemispheres at a trying moment'.[52] Like Crofton's Intermediate System, Elmira became an inspirational force whereby many influential figures in penology recognised the wisdom behind the idea, even if the application was somewhat deficient.

THE STATE OF PRISONS IN IRELAND, 1880–96

The late nineteenth century witnessed the onset of a sense of malaise in the prisons of Ireland and Britain.[53] The most important development in Ireland during this time was the establishment in 1878 of the GPB, with Crofton as its first chairman. The Board acted as the central authority for the country's local and convict prisons. From the outset it published annual reports, which served as a vital tool not only in the battle to halt the moral decline of Irish prisoners but also in the fight against bureaucracy. Each report brought together much needed raw statistical data on the prison population, with an account of every individual institution under the Board's control. Though hardly a solution to all of the problems, for the first time a profile of the Irish prison system as a single entity became clear and perhaps led to a realisation of the true nature of the challenges that lay ahead. The very existence of the GPB ensured a structured and systematic framework within which political and social thinkers alike could finally get to grips with a sprawling and incoherent network.

While the general condition of prisoners had improved over the course of the previous century, many significant problems continued to undermine the work of administrators and prison governors alike. Overcrowding had been largely addressed by earlier prison-building programmes but the absence of proper classification posed insurmountable difficulties as offenders of all ages, both genders and all levels of criminality were housed together. Highlighting this situation in 1899, Hercules MacDonnell, a medical doctor associated with the system, pointed out that the organisation of prisoners must have been extraordinarily difficult in practice, given that theorists could not even seem to agree on a suitable response.[54] Recidivism was also a considerable burden on the system, with many prisoners frequently returning to gaol within weeks. Writing fourteen years earlier, MacDonnell had pointed to the absence in Ireland of discharged prisoners' aid societies.[55] He argued at the time that the difficulty that discharged prisoners encountered in getting work, coupled with the speed with which they fell back into criminality, was a direct result of no-one taking an interest in them upon their release.[56] MacDonnell's grievance in this respect was echoed repeatedly by the GPB annual reports during the 1880s and 1890s.

The problem of dealing with young offenders was comprehensively addressed in 1881 by former GPB member John Lentaigne, who concluded that most children commenced a career in crime after being initially jailed for begging. Highlighting the need for stronger parental and domestic discipline, he outlined a number of fundamental arguments against the imprisonment of those under a certain age. Prisons, he claimed, were constructed to increase the isolation and solitude of their inhabitants and this dulled the mental powers of a child, making him 'morbidly sensitive to real or imaginary wrongs'. The most positive features of his nature are blocked out and replaced with 'a spirit of resistance to all laws, human and divine'.[57] MacDonnell later pointed to inequality in the administration of justice with the example of a man who may receive a one-month sentence for 'kicking his wife into fragments', while a child may get two months in prison for stealing a loaf of bread in order to fend off starvation. 'Our law', he wrote, 'is no respector of persons, neither is it of the nature of the criminal.'[58] Public and political understanding of the juvenile offender was about to undergo a revolutionary overhaul, however, as the British government sought to respond to this and numerous other problems. In 1894 a committee was established to investigate the prison system and make recommendations. One of the most far-reaching outcomes of the work of this committee was the creation of a specific sub-category of the juvenile offender class.

THE GLADSTONE COMMITTEE

Appointed by Home Secretary Herbert Asquith, the Departmental Committee on Prisons, most commonly referred to as the Gladstone Committee, was set up as a response to these problems and the general poor moral condition of convicts leaving English prisons.[59] The committee had a bold and far-reaching agenda as it sought to come to grips with a system that was in need of a thorough overhaul and effective leadership. Under the chairmanship of Herbert John Gladstone, son of the prime minister, the committee was directed to examine six different but inter-related aspects of the system. Firstly, it would consider the nature of the accommodation provided for inmates, particularly those in local prisons. Secondly, the long-standing and unresolved question of how to deal comprehensively with juvenile and first offenders would come under scrutiny. Prison labour and recreation would constitute the third area of enquiry as the authorities sought to improve the moral and physical condition of discharged inmates. Fourthly, it would examine the system of prison visits and communications. Fifthly, the committee was ordered to look into the regulations governing prison offences. The final issue was the appointment of deputy governors and warders.[60] The committee was given *carte blanche* to enter all prisons, investigate some of the most persistent problems in the English system and compile an appropriate set of recommendations. Among the most dramatic findings in the Gladstone Committee report was its set of recommendations on juvenile offenders.

In the first of three conclusions on juveniles, the committee reported that 16,000 prison sentences had been imposed on those below the age of twenty-one during the preceding twelve months. Secondly, the average boy was worse in character and disposition after serving such a sentence. The third conclusion was that criminal instincts were generally formed between the ages of sixteen and twenty-one. In effect, it was found that the career of the habitual criminal had its origin between these ages.[61] While these conclusions refer for the most part to the state of the English system, the same central authority, the Home Office at Whitehall, also administered the Irish local and convict prisons.

In 1882 there were in Ireland twenty-seven large local prisons and eleven minor prisons under the control of the GPB. In addition there were four convict prisons, including Spike Island, Lusk and the male and female prisons at Mountjoy. The proportion of male offenders in the juvenile category remained higher than that of females during this period. There were 5,906 males between the ages of sixteen and twenty-one incarcerated in Ireland's local prisons during the year ending 31 March 1882. This represented 15 per cent of the inmates of local prisons that year. The figure for females of the same age group was 5.6 per cent. The proportion of juvenile males incarcerated peaked during the following year at over 16 per cent and declined gradually thereafter, usually by no more than a single percentage point per year. The figure for juvenile females declined equally slowly and stood at just over 2 per cent by 1896, while males of this age still represented close to 9 per cent of the prison population. In 1895, this one category of sixteen to twenty-one year old males made up almost 11 per cent of the population of local gaols in Ireland.[62] The figures for England were consistent with the situation in Ireland but it did not automatically follow that future recommendations would be applied in both jurisdictions simultaneously.

How to respond to these findings was not easy. Prison could not be part of the solution because it had been found to be part of the problem. Boys of this age could not be sent to a reformatory because the maximum age for that institution was sixteen. The Gladstone Committee recommended extending this to eighteen but the English Prison Commissioners and the Liberal government were both reluctant to accept the notion of reformatory treatment for adults. The alternative suggested by the committee was a penal reformatory but debate arose as to the extent it should be penal as opposed to a reformatory. A distinction had always existed between the two principles.[63] To overcome the problem of the age range of the offenders, the Prison

Commissioners decided upon a new category of habitual criminal. The juvenile-adult offender was seen as too old for exclusively reformatory methods and too young for the harsh punitive regime of a prison. This went some way towards solving the problem but the issue remained as to the nature of the penal reformatory that would house this new class of offender. The day after the publication of the report, Edmund Du Cane, the chairman of the English Prison Commissioners, retired. The formidable challenge of devising such a penal reformatory fell to his successor as chairman, Evelyn Ruggles-Brise.

The Gladstone Committee members were commended for their even-handed assessment but their report was nonetheless critical of outdated and 'discredited' methods.[64] In much the same way as Crofton in Ireland, and Brockway at Elmira, Du Cane was the embodiment of the English penal system during a reign that lasted from 1869 until 1895. He was a strict authoritarian who believed in punishment rather than reform: in prisoners enduring the darkness of the prison and the harshness of the regime. His opponents were strengthened by the reality that the existing system had been deemed a failure and, in fact, contributed more to a rise in crime and criminal behaviour than to a decline.[65] Indeed, Du Cane's prison 'regime of a silent world shrouded in almost complete darkness' lasted well into the twentieth century, despite the best efforts of those who followed him.[66] His successor was diametrically opposed, if not outright hostile, to Du Cane's ideas. Du Cane was widely unpopular among penal reformers. The *Daily Chronicle* described him as the man who managed the English prison system with a 'barbaric philosophy'. The newspaper greeted his demise as Prison Commission chairman as 'the inevitable end of a discredited system'.[67]

A Prison Commissioner under Du Cane, and a former civil servant, Evelyn John Ruggles-Brise was born in Finchingfied in Essex in 1857, the son of a Conservative MP, Sir Samuel Ruggles-Brise. It appears that Ruggles-Brise Jr was very much shaped by his experiences at private school prior to his time at Eton, notably the persistent hunger: 'I was always hungry, day and night, and nobody cared.' Along with a number of other boys, he regularly visited the fields around the school, where he milked the cows into a tin that had once held barley sugar. The boys also ate peas from a neighbouring garden and on one occasion, when confronted by the schoolmaster, Ruggles-Brise managed successfully to invent an alibi and denied his involvement.

The guilt of this lie, and the hunger he suffered at the school, both haunted him for the remainder of his life.[68] Ruggles-Brise was a sensitive young man and it was apparently this characteristic that shaped many of his values during his tenure as chief of the English prison system. His education continued at Eton and Balliol College, Oxford, and in 1881 he entered the Home Office, where he served as principal private secretary to four home secretaries.[69] During this part of his civil service career, Ruggles-Brise participated in some of the most controversial and high-profile events of the era. In his capacity as a senior officer of the Home Office, he was heavily involved, at official level, in the investigation into the infamous Whitechapel murders of 1888. In the subsequent years, Ruggles-Brise climbed the ranks of the civil service to become a Prison Commissioner in 1892. In the context of his professional life, he was noted as a humanitarian, compassionate and progressive. These characteristics were never more evident than in his attitude to Oscar Wilde, imprisoned at Reading Gaol in 1895. Ruggles-Brise ordered that Wilde should be given suitable work within the prison such as gardening, bookbinding or a position in the library. He also instructed that Wilde be furnished with a pen, ink and foolscap paper in his cell to facilitate his writing. He is credited by Wilde's biographer, H. Montgomery Hyde, as 'perhaps the most enlightened and humane prison administrator so to be in charge of the service'.[70] A wide range of improvements marked his tenure as chairman as he sought to modernise the prison system, both structurally and bureaucratically. This earned him a reputation as a leading prison reformer.

His appointment as chairman of the Prison Commissioners was something of a baptism of fire for Ruggles-Brise as he was forced to confront the findings of the Gladstone Committee.[71] Resolving the age category question continued to occupy the minds of both the Commissioners and the political classes. The nature of the treatment to be administered to such offenders also posed a dilemma. Ruggles-Brise turned his attention to the Elmira Reformatory as a possible model for the English solution. He took up an earlier invitation to visit the New York state institution and inspect the reformatory methodology applied to its juvenile offenders. He was impressed with the principles of the Elmira method, which were very much in line with the recommendations of the Gladstone Committee. The Elmira system advanced the hypothesis that all juvenile offenders had the capacity to be good citizens. Reformation, they believed, would render more favourable results than imprisonment. By accepting those two principles, it must be recognised, therefore, that an exceptional course of action was necessary to strike an appropriate balance between reformatory and punitive measures.[72] This was the set of criteria under which Elmira functioned. Ruggles-Brise generally supported these ideas but he was critical of the reformatory methods carried out there.

He believed that Elmira's existing age category (sixteen to thirty years) was quite unrealistic as it treated men as boys and would never be accepted by the English public. Further to this, he sensed he had witnessed a system that was excessively relaxed and extravagant.[73] On the other hand, he pointed out that it would be unwise to believe that this contributed in any way to lower standards of discipline.[74] However, the positives outweighed the negatives in Ruggles-Brise's reaction to Elmira and he returned to England with a more coherent set of ideas that needed to be refined and applied to his own country. The following three years saw an animated debate between the political and administrative systems regarding the age category for inmates of the proposed English reformatory. The Prison Commissioners were generally happy with a minimum age of sixteen but discussion continued on the cut-off point. Ruggles-Brise supported the Gladstone Committee recommendation that twenty-one would be a suitable upper age limit. Eventually, he decided that sixteen to twenty-one was the most suitable age category on the basis that recalcitrant offenders could not be seen as children but neither could they be accepted as adults. Ruggles-Brise based this conclusion on psychological evidence that this was the period when a boy was most likely to follow the route into permanent criminality. The age category had thus been agreed but it could not be accepted until put to the test. The Prison Commissioners later summed up the exact nature of the boys with which they were dealing.

> This is a delicate plant to cultivate when the soil is hard and barren and unreceptive, as it must be in the case of many of these young persons whom we style 'juvenile-adults', and whose criminal character has already become ingrained in many cases by the succession of short-sentences of imprisonment which public opinion is now condemning, not only as an ineffective, but as a harmful method of dealing with crime.

The initial experiment got underway in the early months of 1900, when eight young prisoners from the London area were singled out for special treatment and transferred to Bedford prison, 'one of England's smallest local gaols'.[76] This was a very modest and cautious trial. In implementing a new treatment process with a new class of inmate, Ruggles-Brise was bent on success but not at the cost of losing public support. Within three months the governor at Bedford reported that the progress of his young subjects had far exceeded his expectations. 'The scheme,' he argued to the prison commissioners, 'is a commendable one and worthy of any trouble and expense the State may incur.'[77] This allowed Ruggles-Brise to enshrine the 'juvenile-adult offender' as a formal element of the criminal classes and provided him with sufficient political and moral authority to place his experiment on a permanent footing.

Four basic tenets governed the new penal reformatory. First, inmates were subjected to strict classification. Second, the institution was regulated by a rigid code of discipline. Third, the inmates were engaged in hard work. The final and arguably the most significant principle dictated that inmates were to be subjected to a strict period of regulated supervision upon their discharge.[78] For the first time, the state now had some control over the lives of inmates beyond the period of their detention. This was a type of containment procedure whereby the authorities could monitor their subjects and rein in repeat offenders or those who renewed previous criminal acquaintances. Before being sent to the reformatory, an offender would be observed in the local prison. His parents or guardians, employers and the police would be consulted and a report prepared for the authorities.[79] The penal reformatory advanced from the experimental phase twelve months after it had been initiated at Bedford. In early 1901, a group of youths, again selected from London area gaols, arrived in chains at a convict prison near a small village in Kent. Some adult prisoners remained incarcerated there but the juvenile-adults were held in a completely separate area. The name of that village was Borstal. One of the most enduring, enlightened and sometimes controversial penal initiatives of the twentieth century was born.

The late nineteenth century saw the start of a movement towards a modern prison system in Ireland. What emerged over the following century came about because of the initiatives of individuals or small groups of reformers rather than any widespread political or public revulsion at the conditions endured by convicts, young and old. John Howard's representation to the Irish parliament inspired many. One such was Elizabeth Fry, whose many personal attributes led to some of the most radical changes in prison conditions during the nineteenth century. The dual challenges of the 1845–51 Famine and the mid-century's phasing out of transportation forced a re-think for prison administrators as goals became overcrowded and desperate. The establishment of the Irish Convict Prisons Board in 1854 marked an important step forward as its first chairman, Captain Walter Crofton, implemented the first major social scientific programme. The Progressive Stage System or Intermediate System won widespread international respect and, it must be argued, served as an inspiration long after its demise. The development of the industrial and reformatory school systems ensured that large numbers of children, previously detained in prisons, but not always as convicted criminals, were now housed in progressive facilities more appropriate to their age and development. The US penal authorities, however, were already ahead of their Irish and English colleagues with the opening of the Elmira Reformatory in New York State in 1876, though the Elmira reformation programme received some criticism for the elaborate conditions in which its inmates were housed. As the nineteenth century came to a close, the English government, recognising that major problems still existed in the way it administered punishment, set up the Gladstone Committee to examine the most challenging aspects of the system. A new class of male offender aged between sixteen and twenty-one was identified as being of the age at which the career of the habitual criminal was formed. Under the guidance of new chairman Evelyn Ruggles-Brise, the English Prison Commissioners set about devising a new penal reformatory in line with the recommendations of the committee. The resulting reformatory at Borstal in Kent lent its name to a system that would dominate its field for the greater part of the twentieth century. Borstal became synonymous with the individual reformatory treatment and militaristic discipline of generations of young adult males.

NOTES

1. Connolly, *The Oxford Companion to Irish History*, p. 463.
2. A grand jury comprised a group of between twelve and twenty-three men, drawn from the landlord class, who held local judicial and administrative powers. It levied taxes at local level to pay for the maintenance of roads, bridges, gaols and courthouses.
3. Carey, *Mountjoy: The Story of a Prison*, p. 6.

4. Randall McGowen, 'The well-ordered prison: England, 1780–1865', in Norval Morris, David J. Rothman (eds), *The Oxford History of the Prison: The Practice of Punishment in Western Society* (Oxford: Oxford University Press, 1998), p. 87.

5. Joseph Robins, *The Lost Children: A Study of Charity Children in Ireland, 1700–1900* (Dublin: Institute of Public Administration, 1980), p. 108.

6. David Taylor, *Crime, Policing and Punishment in England, 1750–1914* (London: Macmillan, 1998), pp. 145–6.

7. Carey, *Mountjoy: The Story of a Prison*, p. 12.

8. Henry Heaney, 'Ireland's penitentiary 1820–31: an experiment that failed', in Ian O'Donnell, Finbarr McAuley (eds), *Criminal Justice History* (Dublin: Four Courts Press, 2003), p. 175.

9. Heaney, 'Ireland's penitentiary', p. 176.

10. Carey, *Mountjoy: The Story of a Prison*, p. 23.

11. McGowen, 'The well-ordered prison', p. 95.

12. Carey, *Mountjoy: The Story of a Prison*, pp. 24–31.

13. Carey, *Mountjoy: The Story of a Prison*, p. 35.

14. Radzinowicz, Hood, *A History of English Criminal Law*, p. 139.

15. Dooley, 'Sir Walter Crofton', p. 197.

16. Dooley, 'Sir Walter Crofton', p. 198.

17. Carey, *Mountjoy: The Story of a Prison*, p. 40.

18. Designed by John Haviland and implemented by Joshua Jebb, Pentonville was established in 1846 in preparation for the oncoming decline of transportation.

19. Carey, *Mountjoy: The Story of a Prison*, pp. 38-9.

20. Dooley, 'Sir Walter Crofton', p. 199.

21. Alexander Maconochie was the superintendent of Norfolk Island penal colony in the 1840s.

22. Gladys J. Putney, Snell Putney, 'Origins of the reformatory', *Journal of Criminal Law, Criminology, and Police Science*, (December, 1962) 53, 4, p. 438.

23. Dooley, 'Sir Walter Crofton', p. 201.

24. Dooley, 'Sir Walter Crofton', p. 202.

25. Radzinowicz, Hood, *A History of English Criminal Law*, p. 516.

26. Dooley, 'Sir Walter Crofton', p. 202.

27. Franz von Holtzendorff, *The Irish Convict System: Most Especially Intermediate Prisons* (Dublin: W.B. Kelly, 1860).

28. Lawrence Goldman, 'Crofton, Sir Walter Frederick', *Oxford Dictionary of National Biography* (http://oxforddnb.com/view/printable/65325) (28 November 2006).

29. Carey, *Mountjoy:The Story of a Prison*, p. 113.

30. Lawrence Goldman, 'Crofton, Sir Walter Frederick', *Oxford Dictionary of National Biography* (http://oxforddnb.com/view/printable/65325) (28 November 2006).

31. Stephen Schlossman, 'Delinquent children: the juvenile reform school', in N. Morris and D. Rothman (eds), *The Oxford History of the Prison: The Practice of Punishment in Western Society* (Oxford: Oxford University Press, 1995), p. 365.

32. Wiener, *Men of Blood*, p. 9.

33. Cited by P. Carroll-Burke, *Colonial Discipline: The Making of the Irish Convict System* (Dublin: Four Courts Press, 2000), p. 112.

34. Carroll-Burke, *Colonial Discipline*, p. 98.

35. Robins, *The Lost Children*, p. 295.

36. Jane Barnes, *Irish Industrial Schools: 1868–1908* (Dublin: Irish Academic Press, 1989), p. 42.

37. Barnes, *Irish Industrial Schools*, p. 42.

38. Robins, *The Lost Children*, p. 298.

39. Robins, *The Lost Children*, p. 301.

40. Barnes, *Irish Industrial Schools*, p. 42.

41. David Dressler, *Practice and Theory of Probation and Parole* (New York: Columbia University Press, 1959), p. 121.

42. Putney, Putney, 'Origins of the reformatory', p. 441.
43. Radzinowicz, Hood, *A History of English Criminal Law*, p. 378.
44. Radzinowicz, Hood, *A History of English Criminal Law*, p. 378.
45. Dressler, *Practice and Theory of Probation and Parole*, p. 123
46. Radzinowicz, Hood, *A History of English Criminal Law*, p. 378.
47. Edgardo Rotman, 'The failure of reform', in Norval Morris, David J. Rothman (eds.), *The Oxford History of the Prison: The Practice of Punishment in Western Society* (Oxford, 1998), p.155.
48. Putney, Putney, 'Origins of the reformatory', p. 443.
49. Sir Evelyn Ruggles-Brise, *Prison Reform at Home and Abroad: A Short History of the International Movement since the London Congress, 1872* (London: Macmillan, 1925), p. 96.
50. Hood, *Borstal Re-assessed*, p. 7.
51. Rotman, 'The failure of reform,' p. 156.
52. Dooley, 'Sir Walter Crofton', p. 213.
53. The General Prisons Board (GPB) annual reports provided a statistical account of the numbers of prisoners incarcerated in institutions under its control in a given year, with each one categorising inmates by age and gender. It is a helpful coincidence that all of the early reports up to and including 1896 provided details on the numbers of inmates between the ages of sixteen and twenty-one years. Taking a fifteen-year period from 1882 until 1896, it is, therefore, possible to assess the progress of this category of offender in Ireland.
54. Hercules MacDonnell, 'Prisons and prisoners: suggestions as to treatment and classification of criminals', *Journal of the Social and Statistical Inquiry Society of Ireland*, 1899, 10, p. 442.
55. Chapter 8 will provide a fuller account on the state of prison aftercare in Ireland in the late 1800s.
56. Hercules MacDonnell, 'Review of some of the subjects in the Report of the Royal Commission on Prisons in Ireland', *Journal of the Social and Statistical Inquiry Society of Ireland*, 1885, 13, p. 620.
57. John Lentaigne, 'The treatment and punishment of young offenders', *Journal of the Social and Statistical Inquiry Society of Ireland*, 1881, 13, p. xxxii.
58. MacDonnell, 'Prisons and prisoners', p. 444.
59. Carey, *Mountjoy: The Story of a Prison*, p. 122.
60. NLI, *Report from the Departmental Committee on Prisons*, vi, 1 [C 7702-1], H.L. 1895, 3.
61. Hood, *Borstal Re-assessed*, p. 4.
62. NLI, *Seventeenth Report of the General Prisons Board for Ireland*, x [C-7560], H.L. 1894, 5, xvii, 69.
63. Hood, *Borstal Re-assessed*, p. 5.
64. Radzinowicz, Hood, *A History of English Criminal Law*, p. 579.
65. Christopher Harding, 'The inevitable end of a discredited system? The origins of the Gladstone committee report on prisons, 1895', *Historical Journal*, (September, 1988) 31, 3, p. 593.
66. John Black, 'The Victorian origins of a Group 4 prison service', p. 4.
67. Harding, 'The inevitable end of a discredited system?', p. 591.
68. Leslie, *Sir Evelyn-Ruggles-Brise: A Memoir of the Founder of Borstal*, p. 8.
69. Philip Priestley, 'Brise, Sir Evelyn John Ruggles', *Oxford Dictionary of National Biography* (http//www.oxforddnb.com/view/printable/35864) (28 November 2006).
70. H. Montgomery Hyde, *Oscar Wilde: A Biography* (London: Farrar, Straus and Giroux, 1976), p. 306.
71. For a detailed account of the negotiation process leading up to the founding of such an institution, see Hood, *Borstal Re-assessed*, pp. 5–13.
72. Hood, *Borstal Reassessed*, p. 7.
73. Radzinowicz, Hood, *A History of English Criminal Law*, p. 380.
74. Ruggles-Brise, *The English Prison System*, p. 91.

75. NLI, *Report of the Commissioners of Prisons and the Directors of Convict Prisons in England*, iv, [Cd-1278], H.L. 1900-1, xx, 11–12.
76. Radzinowicz, Hood, *A History of English Criminal Law*, p. 384.
77. Hood, *Borstal Re-assessed*, p. 14.
78. Hood, *Borstal Re-assessed*, p. 15.
79. Norman S. Hayner, 'English schools for young offenders', in *Journal of Criminal Law and Criminology*, (January–February 1937) 27, 5, p. 702.

CHAPTER THREE

Extension of the borstal system to Ireland, 1906–10

The successful launch of a penal reformatory in England in 1901 raised the possibility that the underlying principles could be applied elsewhere. By 1903 the regime had been extended to Bedford and Dartmoor prisons. The idea attracted the attention of penal policy-makers in Ireland, where social thinkers and commentators had long been calling for improvements in the treatment of children and young people within the criminal justice system. The task of devising a similar method of dealing with young offenders in Ireland fell to the GPB.

This chapter will examine the process that led to the opening, in 1906, of the first borstal institution in Ireland, at Clonmel in County Tipperary. An examination of the condition of young offenders in Ireland during the early years of the new century is necessary in order to locate the juvenile-adult offender within the criminal classes. The chapter will examine the composition of Ireland's prison population in the year prior to the introduction of the borstal, placing particular emphasis on the country's soon-to-be-established juvenile-adult offender class. It will continue with an analysis of the penal history of Clonmel, focusing specifically on the building that would become the place of detention for many troubled post-adolescent men. In discussing the origins of the borstal in Ireland it is essential that the local context of the institution also be examined. To this end the chapter will attempt to explain why Clonmel was chosen as the site for the first borstal. The analysis will then address the first tentative steps of the borstal system in Clonmel with an examination of its beginnings, somewhat unorthodox in the context of the wider Irish penal system.

THE PHYSICAL, LEGAL AND SOCIAL CONDITION OF JUVENILE OFFENDERS

By 1900 Ireland was in a state of economic stagnation. Mulhall claims that 'visitors to Ireland at the turn of the century were shocked by what they saw.'[1] Western Europe and the United States enjoyed a convincing economic performance, while parts of Ireland seemed 'a world apart'.[2] There was no better reflection of this situation than in the near death of a number of once great industries. The mighty forces of distilling, brewing and milling had all deteriorated substantially by the early 1900s. Even the thriving linen industry in the northern part of the island had stagnated. Emigration and high mortality rates became the norm after the mid-nineteenth century Famine. Much of the remaining population, particularly in urban areas, existed in conditions where low wages and poor housing vanquished any hope of circumventing the cycle of poverty.

One of the most striking causes of crime, particularly juvenile offending, in early twentieth-century Ireland was the widespread poverty that permeated the lower classes and remained a serious obstruction to societal development. The absence of any real educational or economic advancement inevitably ensured persistently high levels of offending. The workhouse was crucial in supporting the poor but beyond this provision there was little assistance available. In fact, the only form of support available beyond the workhouse was outdoor relief. Under this scheme, a person was paid, by the local poor law union, approximately one shilling and four pence per week, a negligible amount even by nineteenth-century standards.[3] At the turn of the century, 159 poor law unions provided assistance to 43,043 people and 58,365 people received outdoor relief.[4] With such high levels of poverty, it was inevitable that the country would experience considerable societal degradation, particularly in major urban centres.

Many of the Clonmel inmates came from Dublin. Much of the city's population lived in accommodation that was grossly unsuitable for human habitation. In 1911 approximately 60 per cent of Dublin's 128,000 working-class inhabitants were deemed to be living in unsatisfactory housing conditions, with 118,000 people occupying just 5,000 tenement houses, 1,500 of which were classed as wholly unacceptable.[5] The inhabitants of Dublin endured the worst slums of the British Isles, or indeed north-western Europe, during the first two decades of the twentieth century.[6] These conditions meant that diseases such as typhoid and tuberculosis were prevalent. Low wages or unemployment ensured that slum dwellers endured the added burden of malnutrition. The majority of those employed in Dublin in 1901 worked in unskilled and low-paid labouring jobs: out of a total male labour force of 40,000 just one quarter worked in skilled professions like printing, engineering, leatherworking or clothing. More than 7,000 were messengers of some kind and approximately 23,000 were labourers.[7] Ó Gráda cites statistics set out by the French writer Paul Dubois in 1901. It was claimed that 36 per cent of families in Dublin lived in one-room tenements. By comparison in London 15 per cent lived in similar conditions, with 11 per cent in Cork. In Belfast this figure was just 1 per cent.[8]

Belfast was the other major contributor of inmates to Clonmel borstal. The environment was not very different from that in the poor parts of Dublin. Belfast had its own share of urban decay and poor living conditions at this time, though perhaps not on the same scale as Cork or Limerick. Lyons showed that industrialisation brought a 'precarious prosperity' to Belfast, which exhibited the common patterns of intensive labour, poor housing conditions, malnutrition and disease. Such perceptions must, however, be measured against the reality that Belfast experienced a resurgence during the late nineteenth century that was unequalled anywhere else in Ireland during that period. Rapid population growth often meant that the majority of housing was new and purpose built, yet the city suffered a high mortality rate and larger families tended to experience the same effects of overcrowding as the wider working-class populations of southern Irish cities.[9]

The conditions endured by those living in rural Ireland were different from those of urban areas. Undoubtedly, in the second half of the nineteenth century, farm productivity was enhanced by a decline in the number of holdings of less than one acre from 570,338 in 1851 to 485,455 in 1911. The percentage of holdings of less than 15 acres fell from 49 to 40.[10] Ferriter indicates that this increase in larger agricultural units and an expansion in the banking and railway sectors constituted reasons for optimism at the outset of the twentieth century.[11] The declining population brought about a move away from using human labour towards reliance on horsepower. Machinery was more widely used and in creameries and co-operatives replaced traditional production methods.[12] The extension of the creamery system had the effect of boosting productivity in dairying, particularly in isolated locations.[13] In general, the economy at the beginning of the twentieth century remained dominated by the agricultural sector: in 1901, as many as 59 per cent of all working males were employed in farm work, while this figure was as high as 85 per cent in Mayo and

Leitrim.[14] Ireland's agriculture, however, was generally shifting away from traditional methods of production and embracing a more commercially driven approach. This resulted in an improvement in living standards but it did leave the Irish economy in a weak position in the face of changes in the wider global market, where Ireland was not a significant player.[15] This apparent urban-rural divide was very much reflected amongst the borstal population in later years. It was also particularly telling that the institutional aftercare body, the BAI, worked tirelessly to place discharged inmates in employment in the countryside rather than in any town or city.

This book will consider the condition of the lives of juvenile-adult offenders when they entered the borstal institution in Clonmel. At this point, however, it is worth noting the occupations of the wider prison population in the year prior to the introduction of the borstal system. The labouring classes accounted for the vast majority of occupations, with 14,535 committals to the country's local and convict prisons. The second largest occupation represented was that of prostitution, with 3,863 registered in that profession. Mechanics and skilled workers made up the third cohort, with 3,368 individuals. Shopkeepers and dealers were in fourth position, with 2,826 committals. The remaining categories included domestic service, factory work and those enlisted in the various military forces. Just ten prisoners were listed as holding professional employment.[16] These figures confirm that the overwhelming majority of Ireland's prisoners were unskilled labourers. This was despite an improvement in access to education. The 1851 census indicates that 46.8 per cent of the population were deemed illiterate. This figure decreased steadily after this time and by 1911 had dropped to 11.9 per cent.[17] The growth in educational opportunities ensured that a greater number of people could now either read, write or do both. As Guinnane argues, a rise in literacy rates had an economic impact.[18] Yet, with their limited opportunities for advancement and the associated poor wages, it was among the lower classes that the very heart of the country's criminal underworld resided.

On the eve of the introduction of the borstal system in Clonmel in 1906, the judicial statistics for Ireland reveal habitual offending as the most problematic feature of the Irish prison system. Out of 29,259 prisoners admitted to local prisons, bridewells and convict prisons during 1905, 22,205 had at least one previous conviction. This meant that over three quarters, or 76 per cent, of those imprisoned in that year were habitual offenders.[19] At any age, habitual offenders became immune to the regime of the prison because their repeated short sentences removed any sense of foreboding from the threat of imprisonment. The scale of the problem becomes evident when that figure of 29,259 committals during 1905 is broken down even further. Over 9 per cent, or 2,719, had been convicted just once, 1,907 (6.5 per cent) on two occasions. At the upper end of the scale, 5,410 of these inmates had been convicted on at least twenty prior occasions, accounting for 18.5 per cent of all those sent to prison in 1905. A further 3,605 (12 per cent) had attracted between eleven and twenty prior convictions.[20] The report showed that habitual offending was certainly a problem in Ireland during this time and perhaps accounts for the GPB's action the following year in seeking a remedy that would stem the growth of these figures in at least one age category. The attorney-general for Ireland, Lord Justice Cherry, later described the habitual offender as 'that hideous pest'. He concurred with the popular view that his criminal career was the result of the 'degrading effect on his character' of prison discipline and his inability, through ignorance or lack of opportunity, to gain employment upon discharge.[21]

The judicial statistics included a category that corresponded exactly with the age range of the juvenile-adult offender. The total number of males and females between the ages of 16 and 21 years convicted during 1905 was 2,607. Of this number, 1,948 (almost 75 per cent) were male. Female prisoners of juvenile-adult age accounted for the remaining 659 or 25 per cent.[22] These data would have underlined to the penal authorities the emergence of a serious problem in the same age category that had been identified by the English prison administrators ten years earlier. It presented the Irish penal authorities with a strong argument for following the lead of their counterparts in England. Political or agrarian challenges to law and order had the potential to be widespread during this time but even these were limited and sporadic. For example, during 1906 and 1907, agrarian unrest arose in parts of Connacht and Leinster, when small farmers attempted to take possession of lands held by large-scale graziers.[23] Among the most commonly mentioned offences in *Hue and Cry: The Police Gazette* in May 1906 were burglary, larceny, forgery, unlawful carnal knowledge, assault and animal theft.[24]

Despite the political tensions that existed in Ireland at this time the relationship between the police and ordinary people was surprisingly good. In his profile of policing in Ireland from 1822 to 1922, O'Sullivan claims that the period 1890–1916 was an important one for the Royal Irish Constabulary (RIC). The lack of serious political violence coupled with a low crime rate by the turn of the century allowed the RIC to become a fully integrated civil police force like any other.[25] Samuel Waters, a retired RIC officer, reported in 1906 that relations with the general public were on the whole friendly during his career, which spanned eleven stations across nine counties.[26] The civilised nature of this relationship was undoubtedly instrumental in maintaining law and order because the RIC were particularly skilled at procuring information from the public without necessarily resorting to any form of interrogation or even formal questioning. Officers often entered the houses of inhabitants of their district on the pretext that they were passing and needed a light for their pipe or some such ruse. Such tactics usually worked because the constables themselves were typically the sons of small farmers and were quite capable of communicating with ordinary people.[27]

Numerous labels were applied to deviant young people. In the larger towns and cities the problem of 'juvenile street traders' exercised official minds. Reformatories, industrial schools and the workhouse continued to provide sanctuary, shelter or punishment for 'young offenders' and 'delinquents' of different ages. The juvenile-adult offender category was still in the post-experimental stage in England and the notion of such a class of criminal had not yet reached Ireland. Wayward children and young people were often the product of the slum conditions that were so prevalent in much of urban Ireland. Many of the most serious social problems, including crime, were concentrated in certain small geographical areas where poverty and low morality fed off each other and the poor were caught in a vicious circle stimulated by destitution and lack of opportunity. Younger children were particularly vulnerable to these conditions.[28] These children were born into a socio-economic environment ensuring that a certain percentage of them were destined for a criminal career, fuelled initially by the requirement to fulfil their basic need to survive.

The development of the reformatory and industrial school systems in the second half of the nineteenth century were important benchmarks in the creation of a modern juvenile justice system in Ireland. As outlined in Chapter 2, the industrial school was an institution for convicted and abandoned children under the age of twelve. By 1900 there were seventy industrial schools in Ireland, accommodating 7,591 children.[29] While many were discharged to the care of family or friends, to employment or emigration, a certain percentage progressed each year to the reformatory school. Dublin barrister E.D. Daly, writing in 1901, identified an immediate problem inherent in the industrial and reformatory school systems. After the taxpayer had contributed for many years to the care and reformation of a child, the state had no legal role in his or her life beyond the period of detention. Daly believed that children and older juveniles were most likely to be carried back to the source of their original negative influences.[30] One of the primary aims of both of these systems was to remove children from adult prisons but, as Osborough points out, the legal framework in which the reformatory school operated often only served to exacerbate their problems.[31] A reformatory term was preceded by a mandatory two-week prison sentence, thus ensuring that this category of offender was guaranteed exposure to the very environment from which the school was established to protect them.

In the early years of the twentieth century a number of legislative manoeuvres sought to take control of the various problems surrounding juvenile and child offenders. The method and nature of incarceration was not the only challenge posed to the penal authorities and social thinkers. Issues also arose surrounding the practice of bringing children accused of criminal acts before courts at the same time as adults. Juveniles were forced to appear alongside drunkards, prostitutes and those accused of serious offences. In this respect the authorities had not developed a full appreciation of the need for the complete separation of adults and juveniles at all stages of the criminal justice process. The first decade of the new century also saw a change in attitude towards the level of criminal responsibility that was attached to wayward children.

The first significant act of legislative reform in this area was the Juvenile Offenders Act 1901, which made substantial inroads in addressing some of the difficulties surrounding juveniles and children in the criminal justice system, both in Ireland and in Britain. The writer Oscar Wilde had made a considerable impact on British society with his accounts of the condition of children in Reading Gaol. The chairman of the English Prison Commission, Evelyn Ruggles-Brise, pledged to do his utmost to eliminate the problems.[32] One of the first ways the Juvenile Offenders Act sought to address this issue was to ensure that children who were held on remand or sent forward for trial were not held in a gaol while the action against them took its course. The Act allowed them to be sent to the custody of a suitable guardian 'other than a gaoler who looks after thieves and debased women'.[33] Children could be sent to an orphanage, a boy's or girl's home, police court missionaries or perhaps a police sergeant and his wife.[34] A further provision of the Act declared that children should not be in contact with adult prisoners while going to and from court.

As well as finding further ways to remove children from prisons, the Juvenile Offenders Act also confronted the issue of responsibility. In line with the ongoing evolution of social thought in this field, it was recognised that children had diminished responsibility and that parents should be forced to provide for their physical and moral care. Daly pointed out in 1901 that the Act would prove to be a 'source of discomfort' for wayward or drunken parents who did have earning ability and potential but yet chose to relinquish the care of their children to an industrial school at the expense of the state.[35] The Act allowed magistrates to deal severely with such parents by ordering them to take responsibility for their children and their actions or face prison themselves. The 1901 Act was an early manifestation of a new and enlightened approach not only to crime and punishment but also to children and juveniles. It did not resolve all the problems, however, and in many ways it marked only the beginning of a new era redefining the legal position of the young person.

In the field of child welfare, one of the key legislative initiatives of the twentieth century was passed in 1908. The Children's Act established, among other provisions, a juvenile or children's court. The Act directed that cases involving minors should be heard completely separately from those involving adults. If a case could not be heard in a separate building then a different room should be used. Court sittings for adults and children were not to take place at the same time. Further to this, the Act decided that members of the public with no direct involvement in a child's case should be refused entry to their trial.[36] The removal of children from the company of adults at this first stage of the criminal justice process had not been fully addressed by the Juvenile Offenders Act in 1901.

The 1908 Act also afforded greater protection to children in danger through cruelty or neglect. It strengthened existing laws to further safeguard the young against the abuse of strangers or their own parents.[37] Ferriter argues that the Act was of considerable significance as it was the instrument upon which Ireland went on to base many subsequent child protection measures.[38] The Act was also described as marking a 'revolutionary change of attitude' in the area of criminal responsibility.[39] In line with an evolution in thought alluded to earlier, juvenile offenders were no longer viewed as small adults fully responsible for their own crimes. The 1908 Act emphasised a greater degree of parental responsibility in an apparent attempt to guide society towards a new understanding, and indeed redefinition, of childhood. The third strand in the juvenile penal system was the treatment process applied to the borstal offender. The introduction of the Prevention of Crime Act 1908 meant that there was now a fully functioning juvenile penal system for the vast majority of young offenders up to and including the age of twenty-one years. The borstal system had been operated in England for seven years and in Ireland for two on a non-statutory footing (it was not until 1908 that it became permanent).

It should be pointed out that the Prevention of Crime Act 1908 was not solely concerned with underpinning the borstal system. There were other aspects of the wider criminal justice system that always needed the attention of policy-makers but for the purposes of this book it is only necessary to examine those areas directly involving juvenile-adult offenders. Ironically it was the chairman of the Gladstone Committee whose final report led to the foundation of the borstal system, who had the ultimate responsibility for formulating the Prevention of Crime Act 1908 and guiding it through the House of Commons. Herbert Gladstone had, by 1908, become home secretary in the Asquith-led Liberal government and was now positioned to finally implement many of the recommendations of the 1895 committee he chaired.[40]

One of the first areas of borstal law to receive attention in the Prevention of Crime Act 1908 was sentencing policy. Under the Act, an individual between the ages of sixteen and twenty-one, convicted on indictment of an offence for which they were likely to receive a sentence of penal servitude or imprisonment, could be detained in the borstal institution for a minimum of one and a maximum of three years.[41] Early discharge was possible if, after six months, he showed satisfactory progress. This discharge was conditional on his behaviour, which would be monitored to a large extent by whatever after-care body was attached to a given institution. If he re-offended he was automatically returned to serve out the remainder of his sentence. Likewise, if it became apparent that he was associating with people of negative influence or was in danger of falling back into lawless ways, he would be sent back.[42] The Act also allowed for mobility between the various penal institutions. If an inmate of the borstal was deemed incorrigible, he could be transferred to an adult prison. On the other hand, the courts also had the power to administer a borstal sentence to any suitably aged boy who was deemed to have broken the rules of a reformatory school.[43] The Prevention of Crime Act 1908 did not mark the beginning of the borstal system in Ireland but merely established it in law. The system had in fact existed in Ireland, in Clonmel, since 23 May 1906.

FROM LOUGH STREET TO RICHMOND STREET –
THE BIRTH OF CLONMEL PRISON

Prior to the arrival of the borstal in Clonmel, the town was home to an array of different penal institutions. In the early nineteenth century there was a house of correction, a sheriff's gaol, a marshalsea for debtors, a house of industry (or workhouse) and a county gaol.[44] The original county gaol, located in Lough Street, was built in the late seventeenth century and by the eighteenth century it was called 'the strongest prison in Ireland' at the time.[45] Due in no small part to poor management, the prison subsequently encountered a number of problems, including overcrowding, rampant disease and repeated escapes.[46] Conditions in the gaol met the seventeenth and eighteenth-century vision of an Irish prison – severely cramped accommodation, sickness, mixed gender incarceration and dark, unhealthy dungeons.[47] The Lough Street gaol was closed in the 1780s to be replaced by a new facility in Richmond Street. This was part of the Irish prison building project inspired in part by the efforts of John Howard. The structure encompassed 42 large single cells, 198 smaller cells, 12 solitary cells, 13 day rooms, 16 work rooms and 24 yards. It was capable of housing around 340 prisoners at one time.[48] An 1828 report from the inspectors-general of prisons in Ireland criticised the inadequacy of this county gaol and a process of change started in 1830, leading to the reconstruction of the complex by 1835. This development, coupled with the introduction of the district asylum in 1834, saw the elimination of certain prisoner categories, including criminals and lunatics, from the gaol, leaving mostly the poor, infirm and orphans.[49] Clonmel gaol suffered the same problems as most similar institutions in Ireland during the mid-nineteenth century. Serious overcrowding came about, firstly, because of an increased crime rate during the period 1845–51. The 1847 Vagrancy Act placed considerable strain on the gaol.[50] The decline of transportation pushed an already pressurised system to breaking point.

None of the available evidence for this period provides a good reason for Clonmel gaol being selected as the site for Ireland's borstal experiment. The GPB annual reports provide an important insight into the overall state of the system and the first mention of the introduction of the borstal method to Ireland comes in the 1906 report. Without fanfare the report announced that 'a reformatory class of Male Juvenile Adults, i.e., prisoners between sixteen and twenty-one years of age has been started in Clonmel prison'.[51] The report went on briefly to acknowledge the English system upon which this experiment would be based and made reference to some of the physical changes that would be made. There was no mention of the basis for Clonmel's selection. The first annual report of the newly formed Clonmel Discharged Prisoners' Aid Society (CDPAS) offered a reason of sorts. It stated that the gaol had been chosen for the experiment because 'he [William Casey, honorary secretary] supposed they considered the prison there had suitable buildings'.[52] Another explanation centred on the local landlord and barrister Richard Bagwell, also mainly credited with attracting the borstal system to the town. Bagwell was not only an important figure locally but was also a commissioner for education, a renowned historian and later became the founder of the BAI. However, there is no concrete evidence to support either interpretation.

Clonmel never seemed like a natural location for such an institution. The town was located in one of the most fertile and affluent agricultural regions in the country. The nineteenth-century economic profile of the town was wholly dominated by the agricultural sector. In the years prior to the 1845–51 Famine almost one third of the population of Clonmel was employed in agriculture. Specific trends within this sector had a knock-on effect on industry in Clonmel as the nineteenth century progressed. A downturn in tillage farming, for example, played an important role in the decline of the once vibrant corn milling industry in the town: by 1891, just twelve people in the town of Clonmel were employed in milling. This was a trend that was also mirrored on a national scale, when South Tipperary farming, in the second half of the century, moved away from corn and towards livestock production. This in turn gave rise to brisk business in dairy-related industries such as butter and bacon production, as well as tanning. While the tanning industry in the town went into a steep decline in the later decades of the century, butter and other dairy production flourished with the opening of a major creamery and a number of rural sub-stations. Despite this, employment in agriculture generally declined in the surrounding areas during the late nineteenth century. By the dawn of the new century, the largest employers in Clonmel tended to be in service industries such as transport, the army and local government.[53]

Little is known about the local reaction to the arrival of the borstal system. The likelihood is that it had little or no impact on the daily lives or consciousness of most local people. There had been a gaol of one type or another in the town since the eighteenth century; the new regime would be behind the prison walls and, therefore, out of sight of the town's inhabitants. Reaction in the local press was muted. On 11 April 1906, *The Nationalist* did extend a warm welcome to the new initiative. As well as praising the system that was already operating in England, the paper outlined some of the changes that had been made in Clonmel gaol in anticipation of the arrival of the first juvenile-adult offenders. Two new officers had been appointed and the female or number two prison, which had been unoccupied for most of the past twenty years, was 'fully prepared and equipped after the style of the Borstal foundation'.[54] Apart from providing employment and an outlet for local food and other miscellaneous supplies, a key way in which the gaol would have contributed to the local economy was through the need for building maintenance.

Each GPB report outlined any works of reconstruction or maintenance that had taken place at any given prison during the previous twelve months. Works of reconstruction and repair took place by one of two different means: by contract/external labour, or by prisoner labour. All Irish prisons were subjected to various levels of repair and renovation and Clonmel was no exception. Some tasks assigned to outside contractors were moderately easy and could include something as simple as replacing a lock or repairing a roof.[55] Other projects were fairly significant, a good example being the construction during 1893 and 1894 of six warders' cottages.[56] Overall, Clonmel gaol underwent extensive reconstruction during the period from 1879 to 1906. While prisoner labour was utilised where possible, it always fell to more skilled and experienced outside contractors to take responsibility for larger-scale, more specialised work. The reno-

vation of the disused female prison in 1906 marked the beginning of
the end of more than two centuries of conventional penal discipline
in Clonmel.

BORSTAL BEGINS IN IRELAND:
THE EXPERIMENT AT CLONMEL, 1906–10

It is important to bear in mind that the borstal institution in Ireland
began life in a disused section of an existing local prison and was not
specifically constructed to fulfil the purpose of a penal reformatory
for juvenile-adult offenders. In keeping with the philosophy of the
borstal method, the number two prison in Clonmel was renovated,
with the aim of keeping the juveniles completely separated from the
adult prisoners. In 1907, in his annual report to the GPB, Governor
John Connor of Clonmel Prison and Borstal Institution noted some of
the modifications that were made to the number two prison to facilitate the treatment of the juvenile-adults. The new unit included a
schoolroom, a recreation room 'and a large and commodious carpenter's shop'.[57] Immediate physical comparisons with the first experimental English institutions at Bedford and Borstal are not possible as
the key authorities on the subject do not provide such descriptions
until later. However, the penal authorities in Ireland, both in GPB
headquarters in Dublin Castle and in Clonmel prison, maintained
close contact with their counterparts in England, so the likelihood is
that Ireland's experiment was closely modelled on the original. The
GPB and the Clonmel prison authorities designed a facility that could
house up to fifty-four boys but anticipated no more than twenty.[58] As
Osborough points out, this was a rather cautious estimate.[59] It turned
out that the authorities completely underestimated the number of
juvenile-adult offenders in Ireland, a fact that would eventually lead
to a considerable expansion of Clonmel.

In the early years of the borstal system there, the GPB was charged
with the task of selecting suitable inmates. Due to the fact that the system remained experimental and was, therefore, not grounded in law,
boys could not be sentenced directly to a term of detention in the
borstal. The GPB instead decided to select boys between the ages of
sixteen and twenty-one who had been sentenced to not less than nine
months in prison. This was considered the shortest period in which
reformatory treatment could possibly succeed.[60] Throughout the final
two decades of the nineteenth century, sentencing practices remained

an area of contention between the GPB and the courts. The Board repeatedly expressed concern at the high number of short sentences imposed: it was felt that reformation of any prisoner was not possible in the short terms passed by the judiciary. Once the borstal system became operational in Clonmel the various interested parties again began to express their disquiet with sentencing. In 1908 the GPB reported that one of the principal challenges to the borstal system was the high level of minimum sentences. In the previous year, thirteen out of the thirty-three juvenile adults sent to Clonmel had been sentenced to the minimum nine-month term necessary to secure them a place.[61] As the founders of the borstal system in England had learned, one of the keys to the success of the treatment was that those implementing it would have sufficient time to work with the offender. Two years into the English borstal experiment it was decided to raise the minimum sentence to twelve months, as the six-month period initially set by the Prison Commissioners was deemed too short to make any significant impact. This was a time in England when lengthy sentences were rare for juveniles.[62]

'I beg to report the arrival of the first Juvenile Adult from Waterford Prison.'[63] In this brief but highly significant one-line letter, Governor John Connor announced the commencement of fifty years of borstal in Clonmel prison. In the initial three to four-year period all of the boys sent there came from other prisons in Ireland rather than directly from the courts. In the ten-month period from May 1906 to March 1907 a total of eighteen boys were received at the institution. Four came from Londonderry, three each from Mountjoy and Belfast, and two from Cork, with Waterford, Galway, Kilkenny, Clonmel, Castlebar and Tullamore providing one each.[64] Upon the release of the thirtieth report of the GPB in mid-1908 the number rose to thirty-five.[65] In its report for the year 1909–10, the Board announced that, since the foundation of the system, 137 young men had been subjected to borstal treatment in Clonmel prison, forty-six of whom were still in custody.[66] The Board provided a breakdown of the origins of the boys at Clonmel during the twelve-month period leading to the publication of the 1910 report. Fifteen came from Belfast, fourteen from Dublin, six from Cork, three from Londonderry, three from Tullamore, and two each from Sligo and Waterford, with one each from Dundalk, Armagh, Tralee, Limerick and Kilkenny.[67] These early trends were indicative of a strong pattern that continued to emerge: the overwhelming majority of borstal inmates originated from the country's largest urban centres. In keeping with the original concept of borstal treatment, the conditions afforded to boys in Clonmel were somewhat different from those of the ordinary adult prisoners. The facilities and the routine were devised with the purpose of inducing better behaviour through a combination of a tough and unwavering routine along with education and training. The juvenile-adults were subjected to a strict routine, into which was built a comprehensive programme of education, training, physical drill and religious guidance. Many features of the overall treatment process applied to the boys at the borstal evolved and improved over time. Though the facilities were somewhat humble, those involved in the institution on a daily basis were encouraged by the positive responses not only of the boys, but also of those charged with their reformation and care.

The initial reactions of the various interested parties to the borstal system can be best measured by their public statements. It should be remembered that, between May 1906 and August 1910, John Connor was not only governor of the borstal institution but of all of Clonmel prison. During those years, the juvenile-adult class was very much in the minority in the overall prison population there. In his first report on the borstal institution, published by the GPB in 1907, Governor Connor demonstrated a clear understanding of, and enthusiastic approach towards, the task that lay ahead. These qualities were undoubtedly key to the early success of the experiment. Two chaplains worked at Clonmel prison during these years and their early reaction to the work of the institution left little room for doubt. In 1907, the Roman Catholic chaplain, and local parish priest, Canon Flavin was brief but direct in stating that 'the extension of the Borstal system to this country I think is a great blessing'.[68] At the annual meeting of the CDPAS in May 1908, Flavin again expressed his strong approval of the institution's progress by pointing out that its work was not only of tremendous benefit to the boys but also to the community into which they were returned.[69] For his part, the Rev. Mr Smith, the Church of Ireland chaplain, was lavish in his praise of the system. He declared in 1907 that it was 'eminently qualified to help forward the reformation of these youths' lives'.[70]

The ability of the Clonmel borstal to effect such change was to take an important step forward in 1908 with the passing of the Prevention of Crime Act. The term was purely theoretical, an idea based on a treatment process devised between 1895 and 1900 and named after the place in which it was first applied. The fact that the term borstal passed so quickly into the penal lexicon is more a tribute to the success of the idea rather than to any legal instrument. Before 1908, therefore, the penal reformatory that was operational at the number two prison in Clonmel may have been referred to as a borstal institution, or indeed a borstal school, but such terms were purely unofficial as the approach continued indefinitely on an experimental basis. The Prevention of Crime Act 1908 gave official status to the establishments at Clonmel and elsewhere as designated borstal institutions. The GPB made a point of underlining this change of status in its 1910 report. The institution was now a borstal and it should not be referred to as a prison. Sentences were no longer to be referred to as such, but as periods of detention. Most significantly, the boys incarcerated in the borstal were no longer to be known as 'prisoners' but as 'inmates'.[71] This particular re-adjustment was applied rigidly and the term prisoner rarely appeared on any official borstal-related document after this time.

There was a change too to the sentencing process for juvenile-adults. Power was given to the courts to send suitable boys to the institution. Judges could pass a borstal sentence of not less than one year or not more than three years, with a provision for release on licence after six months if appropriate.[72] The new legislation had immediate consequences for Clonmel and the idea of expansion became a necessary consideration. When the measures set out in 1908 came into effect in November 1909 there were twenty-two boys in Clonmel. Six months later this number had increased to fifty-four. With the alteration in the law and the consequent rapid expansion of the juvenile-adult offender class, the GPB for the first time put forward the possibility that the entire Clonmel prison complex might need to be designated for exclusive use as a borstal institution.[73]

By mid-1910 it had become clear that the borstal system in Ireland needed an overhaul. The GPB was faced with the decision as to whether or not to expand the system. The developments that had taken place at Clonmel prison since 23 May 1906 ensured that the authorities in Dublin Castle were faced with an easy and very obvious choice that would meet with little public or political resistance. The annual reports of the GPB and the CDPAS had been largely positive: the words of several influential individuals associated with the institution had particular resonance and undoubtedly fed into the decision-making process. Central to the judgement to move forward in 1910 would be the success of the institution in reforming its subjects and the statistics weighted in favour of expansion. The GPB reported in 1910 that, since its foundation, 137 boys had been committed to the institution. Of that number, forty-six were still in detention, four had been removed to adult prisons for various transgressions and eighty-seven were discharged. Of these, forty were confirmed as 'doing well', and nine could not be traced but had not come to the attention of the authorities. Others had entered various careers including the merchant service; five had married and had become 'respectable members of society'. The GPB claimed that, by May 1910, the institution had a success rate of 63 per cent.[74] To begin with, the authorities established a facility capable of accommodating just fifty-four inmates and, therefore, considerably underestimated the size of the juvenile-adult offender class in Ireland. Coupled with the success rates, this gave the GPB sufficient reason to recommend expansion. In August 1910, after the remaining adult offenders had been removed to other locations, Clonmel prison entered another era and became the first and only borstal institution in what would become the Republic of Ireland.

The early twentieth century saw a new dawn in Irish penal history. While many of the physical structures that housed the country's criminals remained part of the legacy of the early nineteenth century, a new momentum for change had gathered pace along an unstoppable course. One of the outcomes of this change was the completion of the process that saw the removal of children and the majority of young offenders from adult prisons. The identification, using scientific and psychological evidence, of a specific category of young criminal that became known as the juvenile-adult offender class is the most obvious example of the modernising influence of individuals such as Evelyn Ruggles-Brise and Herbert Gladstone. The early success of the new English penal reformatory at Borstal in Kent inspired the GPB in Ireland to establish a similar institution, with the purpose of effecting change in young Irish male offenders. A declining economy and a growth in unemployment, along with high levels of urban deprivation, ensured that Ireland's larger cities were a breeding ground for disaffected and criminal youth. The country's penal institutions suffered the same large-scale problems of habitual offending revealed in the English prison system a decade earlier. Taken collectively, the effects of the Juvenile Offenders Act 1901, the Children Act 1908 and the Prevention of Crime Act 1908 led to a change in political, social and public opinion. The introduction of the borstal to Ireland brought the key influential principles of the acclaimed Crofton system of the mid-nineteenth century back to the country in which they were first pioneered. The early success of the experiment was hastened by the enthusiasm of a number of different elements of the penal system and civilian society. This in turn led to an expansion of the system when the entire county gaol at Clonmel was taken over for the sole purpose of housing a borstal institution.

NOTES

1. Daniel Mulhall, *A New Day Dawning: Ireland at the Turn of the Century* (Cork: Collins Press, 1999), p. 85.
2. Mulhall, *A New Day Dawning*, p. 85.
3. Mulhall, *A New Day Dawning*, p. 69.
4. Diarmaid Ferriter, *The Transformation of Ireland, 1900–2000* (Dublin: Profile Books, 2004), p. 52.
5. Ferriter, *The Transformation of Ireland*, p. 61.
6. Cormac Ó Gráda, *Ireland: A New Economic History: 1780–1939* (Oxford: Oxford University Press, 1994), p. 241.
7. F.S.L. Lyons, *Ireland since the Famine* (London: Fontana Press, 1985), p. 278.
8. Ó Gráda, *Ireland: A New Economic History*, p. 241.
9. Lyons, *Ireland since the Famine*, p. 27.
10. Ó Gráda, *Ireland: A New Economic History*, p. 259.
11. Ferriter, *The Transformation of Ireland*, p. 32.
12. Connolly, *The Oxford Companion to Irish History*, p. 9
13. Ó Gráda, *Ireland: A New Economic History*, p. 259.
14. Timothy W. Guinnane, 'Age at leaving home in rural Ireland, 1901–1911', *Journal of Economic History*, (September, 1992) 52, 3, p. 656.
15. Seán Duffy, *Atlas of Irish history* (Dublin: Gill and Macmillan, 1997), p. 104.
16. NLI, *Judicial Statistics for Ireland*, I [Cd. 3112], H.L. 1904–5, xix, 29.
17. Ruth Dudley Edwards, *An Atlas of Irish History* (London: Routledge, 2005), pp. 223–5.
18. Guinnane, T., *The Vanishing Irish: Households, Migration and the Rural Economy in Ireland, 1850–1914* (Princeton: Princeton University Press , 1997), p. 65.
19. NLI, *Judicial Statistics for Ireland*, I [Cd. 3112], H.L. 1904–5, xix, 41.
20. NLI, *Judicial Statistics for Ireland*, I [Cd. 3112], H.L. 1904–5, xix, 63.
21. Cherry, 'Juvenile crime and its prevention', p. 436.
22. NLI, *Judicial Statistics for Ireland*, I [Cd. 3112], H.L. 1904-5, xix, 63.
23. Virginia Crossman, *Politics, Law and Order in Nineteenth Century Ireland* (Dublin: Gill and Macmillan, 1996), p. 186.
24. *Hue and Cry: The Police Gazette*, 1 May 1905. *Hue and Cry* was a Royal Irish Constabulary (RIC) publication, which was circulated to every police barracks in the country on Tuesday and Friday of each week. It provided details of those wanted for crimes by the RIC, the Dublin Metropolitan Police and, where relevant, the English police.
25. Donal J. O'Sullivan, *The Irish Constabularies, 1822–1922: A Century of Policing in Ireland* (Dingle: Brandon, 1999), p. 227.
26. Ferriter, *The Transformation of Ireland*, p. 65.
27. O'Sullivan, *The Irish Constabularies*, p. 222.
28. Ferriter, *The Transformation of Ireland*, p. 49.

29. Barnes, *Irish Industrial Schools*, p. 75.
30. E.D. Daly, 'The Juvenile Offenders Act 1901', in *New Ireland Review*, (November, 1901) 16, p. 150.
31. Osborough, *Borstal in Ireland*, p. 5.
32. Radzinowicz, Hood, *A History of English Criminal Law*, p. 627.
33. Daly, 'The Juvenile Offenders Act 1901', p. 149.
34. Radzinowicz and Hood, *A History of English Criminal Law*, p. 628.
35. Daly, *'The Juvenile Offenders Act 1901'*, p. 148.
36. Radzinowicz, Hood, *A History of English Criminal Law*, p. 628.
37. Ivy Pinchbeck, Margaret Hewitt, *Children in English Society*, Vol. 2: *From the Eighteenth Century to the Children Act 1948* (London: Routledge, 1973), p. 621.
38. Ferriter, *The Transformation of Ireland*, p. 49.
39. Pinchbeck, Hewitt, *Children in English Society*, p. 492.
40. Hood, *Borstal Re-assessed*, p. 20.
41. Radzinowicz, Hood, *A History of English Criminal Law*, p. 386.
42. Hood, *Borstal Re-assessed*, p. 21.
43. Radzinowicz, Hood, *A History of English Criminal Law*, p. 386.
44. Donal A. Murphy, *The Two Tipperarys* (Nenagh: Relay Books 1994), p. 137.
45. William P. Burke, *The History of Clonmel* (Waterford: Clonmel Library Committee, 1983), p. 171.
46. Burke, *The History of Clonmel*, p. 171.
47. Seán O'Donnell, *Clonmel: 1840–1900 – Anatomy of an Irish Town* (Dublin: Geography Publications, 2000), p. 31.
48. Burke, *The History of Clonmel*, p. 171.
49. Murphy, *The Two Tipperarys*, p. 137.
50. O'Donnell, *Clonmel: 1840–1900*, p. 32.
51. NLI, *Twenty-ninth Report of the General Prisons Board*, x [Cd-3698], H.L. 1905–6, xi, 55.
52. *The Nationalist*, 29 May 1907.
53. O'Donnell, *Clonmel – 1840–1900*, pp. 20, 23, 24, 25.
54. *The Nationalist*, 11 April 1906.
55. NLI, *Sixth Report of the General Prisons Board*, v [C-4158], H.L. 1883–4, iii, 96.
56. NLI, *Fifteenth Report of the General Prison Board*, xx [C-7174], H.L. 1892–3, v, 70.
57. John Connor, Governor, Clonmel Prison, quoted in NLI, *Twenty-ninth Report of the General Prisons Board*, x [Cd-3698], H.L. 1906–7, ix, 86.
58. *The Nationalist*, 11 April 1906.
59. Osborough, *Borstal in Ireland*, p. 10.
60. NLI, *Twenty-ninth Report of the General Prisons Board*, x [Cd-3698], H.L. 1906–7, x, 10.
61. NLI, *Thirtieth Report of the General Prisons Board*, iii [Cd-4253], H.L. , 1907–08, xi, 31.
62. Hood, *Borstal Re-assessed*, pp. 15–16.
63. NAI, GPB, Correspondence register (CR), Governor Connor to GPB, 22 May 1906, GPB/6505/1906
64. NLI, *Twenty-ninth Report of the General Prisons Board*, x [Cd-3969], H.L. 1906–7, v, 86.
65. NLI, *Thirtieth Report of the General Prisons Board*, v [Cd-4253], H.L. 1907–8, viii, 19.
66. NLI, *Thirty-second Report of the General Prisons Board*, xxi [Cd-5286], H.L. 1909–10, xv, 29.
67. NLI, *Thirty-second Report of the General Prisons Board*, xxi [Cd-5286], H.L. 1909–10, xvi, 42.
68. NLI, *Twenty-ninth Report of the General Prisons Board*, x [Cd-3969], H.L. 1906–7, v, 88.
69. *The Nationalist*, 27 May 1908.
70. NLI, *Twenty-ninth Report of the General Prisons Board*, x [Cd-3969], H.L. 1906–7, v, 88.
71. NLI, *Thirty-second Report of the General Prisons Board*, xxi [Cd-5286], H.L. 1909–10, xvi, 41.
72. NLI, *Thirty-second Report of the General Prisons Board*, xxi [Cd-5286], H.L. 1909–10, xi, 44.
73. NLI, *Thirty-second Report of the General Prisons Board*, xxi [Cd-5286], H.L. 1909–10, xvi, 42.
74. NLI, *Thirty-second Report of the General Prisons Board*, xxi [Cd-5286], H.L. 1909–10, xvi, 22.

CHAPTER FOUR

Background of the Clonmel
borstal inmates, 1906–21

When the former county gaol at Clonmel in South Tipperary became a borstal institution in August 1910, it marked a new dawn in Irish penal history. Young men from troubled backgrounds who had fallen into lawless ways were taken to a place that was designed to change their lives. Irish prison administrators advanced their borstal institution beyond the experimental stage with the distinct advantage of knowing that the system had been tested and implemented successfully in Britain. The foundation of the original borstal institution was the result of over five years of consultation between prison administrators, politicians and contemporary medical and psychological experts.

This chapter will examine the condition of the lives of Ireland's borstal boys at the moment they entered the institution at Clonmel.[1] It will analyse the geographical origins of the inmates and explore their backgrounds by looking at their occupations, religious affiliations and education. It will identify those sections of society from which juvenile-adult offenders, and youthful criminals in general, were most likely to emerge. Secondly, it will look at the low level of provision for female juvenile-adults. Two important pieces of legislation, the Prevention of Crime Act 1908 and the Criminal Justice Administration Act 1914 both had serious consequences for the selection of borstal inmates and these will be discussed in detail. The underlying question is whether the criminal instincts of these boys were as likely to be a consequence of their circumstances and environment as of any psychological influence.

IDENTIFYING AND SELECTING BORSTAL INMATES

One of the most pressing tasks facing the members of the Gladstone Committee was to put forward a definition of the type of convicts that would occupy the proposed penal reformatory. The committee declared that males between the ages of sixteen and twenty-one years were at the greatest risk of descending into a life of professional and habitual criminality, according to evidence given by the chaplain of Holloway and Newgate prisons. After studying the profiles of about 2,000 prisoners he declared that 'it will be observed that there are more burglars at the age of eighteen than at any other age'.[2] At this early stage a clearer definition of the social class of criminal concerned was not forthcoming. The committee members were fixed on agreeing upon a suitable age category to define a juvenile offender, one that would not only address the problem but also satisfy public opinion. The task of further defining the most suitable type of criminal for the new treatment process fell, in the main, to the about-to-be-appointed chairman of the English Prison Commissioners, Evelyn Ruggles-Brise. In the interim, the Prison Commissioners were required to implement the recommendations of the Gladstone Committee report.

Indeed, this report amounted to a devastating indictment of the English, and by extension the Irish, penal system and the leadership of Prison Commission chairman Edmund Du Cane. An insight into the challenge faced by his successor can be gained from a retrospective account written in 1910.[3] Armed with the Gladstone Committee report and his own subsequent investigations, Ruggles-Brise and his fellow Commissioners developed a definite sense of who would benefit most from new reform methods. The practice of imposing repeated short prison sentences upon males aged between sixteen and twenty-one had been proven to have a detrimental effect. In such circumstances, the boys became all too familiar with the harsh regime of the adult prison. According to Ruggles-Brise, the sad effect was that the boys developed a 'cynical contempt for such deterring influences as the system affords these lads at the most dangerous, reckless, passionate, and, at the same time, most impressionable period of their life'.[4] He went on to cite evidence that the careers of many hardened criminals began in earnest between these ages. The records 'would show', he stated, 'that a considerable percentage had graduated to a high degree in the school of crime, through a succession of short sentences served in early youth between sixteen and twenty-one'.[5] The English authorities had identified their future borstal inmates. Ruggles-Brise and his colleagues had also designed the model upon which Ireland would base its borstal system. At this early stage the criteria qualifying a boy for admission to Clonmel borstal were the same as those in the English system, but some divergence emerged over time.

Clonmel borstal was modelled on the English system and there was little or no debate in Ireland on the identification of an appropriate type of criminal for selection. Irish discourse instead tended to focus on two areas. Firstly, the penal authorities sought to ensure that the reformatory methods to be applied at Clonmel would serve to arrest the descent of these offenders into a life of habitual criminality.[6] This was a long established condition of qualification. Secondly, particular emphasis was placed by the GPB on the role that the borstal would play in the rescue of its subjects from adult prisons. In an editorial published in April 1906, the local Clonmel newspaper, *The Nationalist*, endorsed the establishment of the borstal in the country. It pointed out that the initiative 'is a vast improvement on the old system, for everyone knows that association with adult criminals is ruinous for lads of such an age'.[7] In an address to the International Penitentiary Congress in 1910, the chairman of the GPB, J.S. Gibbons, argued that the borstal method saw the subject as being 'not reclaimable' but it gave him a far greater chance of reform than the ordinary prison system.[8] Like the English, the Irish prison authorities had a clear vision of the type of convict they would target with this treatment. He would already be an established criminal, someone who had experienced life in an adult prison and would do so again if the state did not intervene.

Gibbons also claimed that the borstal system was not intended for first-time offenders.[9] The borstal method was for boys at a more advanced stage of a criminal career. This thinking was in line with the intentions of both the Gladstone Committee and Ruggles-Brise, endorsed by the GPB. Yet the annual reports of the GPB show that the Irish system was significantly out of line with that of England in this regard. In the three and a half year period to 31 December 1909, forty-one inmates with no previous convictions were committed to Clonmel borstal.[10] A survey of GPB data between 1912 and 1921 shows that 245 inmates had no prior convictions.[11]

The GPB decided that there was no need for any sweeping provision for female juvenile-adults. The early GPB reports made only passing references to the female juvenile-adult offender class. In its first account of Clonmel borstal in 1907, the Board declared that the numbers of this class of offender were so modest that the establishment of a separate institution was unnecessary.[12] Further direct reference to the place of females in the borstal system came in 1911. In the previous year, in a move that can be seen as a vote of confidence in the work underway at Clonmel, the GPB established a Modified Borstal System in Belfast, Cork and Mountjoy prisons. Under this regime, juvenile-adults detained in these prisons were subjected, insofar as it was possible, to the same treatment process as the inmates of the borstal. But the female juvenile-adult population was still deemed too small in number even for this scaled-down version. Prison governors were instead directed to treat juvenile-adult females 'in accordance with the spirit of the Modified Borstal System'.[13] As in the late nineteenth century, the number of females of this age category committed to prisons in Ireland remained considerably lower than males.

It was not possible to detain every juvenile-adult male given a custodial sentence at Clonmel borstal. This was part of the reasoning behind expanding the system without actually opening a second institution in Ireland. The Modified Borstal System was designed to correct this situation by further isolating juveniles within adult prisons. In the five-year period from 1910 to 1914, 7,455 qualifying juvenile-adult offenders were committed to Irish prisons. Of this number, 5,361 were male, while 2,094 were female.[14] The GPB case against creating a separate category of female juvenile-adult offenders was reinforced by these figures and also by the lack of long sentences imposed on females. In 1911, for example, just four out of 344 female juvenile-adults were given sentences of four months or over.[15] The GPB argued that this phenomenon undermined the Modified Borstal System, as one of the key elements of successful treatment was time.

One of the most important consequences of the lack of legal status was that juvenile-adults could not be given a borstal sentence by the courts. Consequently, between 1906 and 1910 the responsibility for selecting offenders for borstal treatment fell to the GPB. The same qualifying criteria outlined earlier were employed by the GPB to select suitable inmates from prisons around Ireland for entry to the borstal. Only those sentenced to nine-months' incarceration and upwards were selected, as this was deemed the minimum time-frame for the treatment process to be successful.[16] The system was not enshrined in law until the introduction of the Prevention of Crime Act 1908, the effects of which came into force in 1909. The Act may have altered the legal status of the borstal but the objective remained the same.[17]

In the field of borstal law the principal change brought about by the Act was to transfer the power of sentencing to the judiciary. The existing courts of assize and quarter sessions were given the authority to impose upon suitable candidates sentences of not less than one year and not more than three.[18] A borstal sentence could now be imposed in place of a prison sentence or a period of penal servitude. The process

of selecting a candidate for borstal treatment began once a male of juvenile-adult age was committed to prison to await trial. The prison
governor was obliged to enquire from the police about the boy's character and family background. He also had to discuss with the medical
officer the boy's state of mental and physical health. The result of this
investigation, complete with the governor's recommendation as to the
suitability of the boy for borstal treatment, was then sent to the GPB.
The Board would review and, if necessary, amend these documents
before forwarding copies to the crown solicitor and the sentencing
judge.[19] This process provided the courts with the necessary information
for the preparation, or not, of a borstal sentence. The 1908 Act also provided for the release of inmates on licence from the borstal after six
months, under certain conditions.[20] The portion of Clonmel prison that
was already used for juvenile-adults was formally designated as a borstal
under the Act, coming into effect in late 1909. For the first time, serious
consideration was given to widening the scheme within the prison.

The changes introduced by the Prevention of Crime Act 1908 had a
number of important effects on Clonmel borstal. When the number two
prison was formally redesignated as a borstal on 27 November 1909,
there were twenty-two juvenile-adults in custody there. Within six
months this number rose to the maximum capacity of fifty-four.[21] This
expansion was a consequence of sentencing powers being transferred to
the courts, though it can also be viewed as a vote of confidence in the
system by the judiciary. But it also raised the question of how to accom-
modate the growing number of inmates. The legal changes brought
about between 1908 and 1910 had the effect of heightening public
awareness of the borstal. While there is no evidence of widespread press
reporting on the Clonmel institution, there certainly was greater public
reference to its work. In court sessions, judges made frequent reference
to Clonmel borstal, spelling out its benefits for the young man about to
be sentenced. This was subsequently reported in local, and some national, newspapers, and represented a key difference because, prior to the
1908 Act coming into effect, there was no public account of an offender being sent to the Clonmel borstal.[22]

Additional changes to the borstal system came about with the passing in 1914 of the Criminal Justice Administration Act. While magistrates' courts were prohibited from directly sentencing an offender to
borstal, they were given the power to forward him to the quarter sessions with a recommendation for such a sentence.[23] The other most
notable change to borstal law under the 1914 legislation was the

increase of the minimum borstal sentence to two years. As this chapter will later show, this had an implication for sentencing practice and countered the criticism of the judiciary by the GPB and BAI. The arrival of the borstal, with its need for lengthy periods of detention in order to bring about reform, fully exposed the power of the judiciary to undermine and indeed inflict serious damage upon the system.

The public relationship between the GPB and the judiciary can be characterised as one of polite disharmony. Prior to the passing of the Prevention of Crime Act 1908, the Board complained about the high number of minimum sentences. Thirteen out of thirty-three boys sent to Clonmel during 1907 received the minimum term of nine months. The Board described this phenomenon as 'the greatest drawback of the system'.[24] In 1910, the borstal aftercare body (still known at that stage as the Clonmel Discharged Prisoners' Aid Society – CDPAS) reacted positively to the longer sentences brought about by the Act. The CDPAS argued that the longer sentences would ultimately be more effective in bringing about desired changes in inmates. The crucial drawback of short sentencing was that an inmate could not acquire the skills of a trade and was, therefore, unqualified for employment upon his release. The benefit of the longer sentence was that a boy 'usually left the prison with sufficient knowledge of a trade to enable him to earn a livelihood'.[25]

There is sufficient evidence, however, to suggest that relations between the GPB and the judiciary were, for the most part, co-operative. The GPB correspondence register contains a number of enthusiastic enquiries from judges in various parts of Ireland expressing an interest in the work of Clonmel borstal. Such requests often came in advance of one of the seasonal assizes, when a judge was preparing his sentencing options. In 1911, for example, the GPB drafted a comprehensive response to Judge Kenny, who had requested some information on the operation of the system and his own obligations. The Board acquainted the judge with the procedure by which he could select a boy for borstal treatment and outlined the reasons why certain offenders were not suitable.[26] This reply also reveals the strong reliance of the GPB upon the lead given by the English Prison Commissioners, as it quoted extensively from that body's instructions to prison governors. With a heightened awareness in Ireland of borstal as a sentencing option, judges became curious about its working and local newspaper reporting shows that many were anxious to be seen to embrace this enlightened new endeavour.

GEOGRAPHICAL ORIGINS

The borstal at Clonmel was to be the only one of its kind in what would become the Republic of Ireland. Industrial schools and reformatories were spread over a much wider geographical area, while the borstal system served the entire population from one modest former convict prison in South Tipperary. Transport of inmates from court or prison in Belfast or Dublin would have been an arduous and expensive process. Visits from relatives or friends, when permitted, would have been almost inconceivable. Yet, it is the latter point that may have been on the minds of the decision-makers of the GPB as they sought to rid the inmates of previous unsavoury influences. A clear and comprehensive account of the last residence of each boy is set out in the prison register, which provides a detailed account of the background and physical state of each inmate held at Clonmel local prison and borstal from 1903 until 1928.

TABLE 4.1
GEOGRAPHICAL ORIGINS OF INMATES, 1910–21

County of origin	Number of inmates
Antrim/Belfast	160
Dublin	150
Cork	26
Londonderry	18
Tipperary	18
Louth	15
Down	10
Tyrone	9
Waterford	8
Kerry	7
Clare	6
Galway	6
Kilkenny	6
Carlow	5
Kildare	5
Limerick	5
Donegal	4
Wicklow	4
Cavan	3
Longford	3
Meath	3
Queen's County	3
Westmeath	3
Leitrim/Mayo/Offaly/Sligo	2 each
Armagh/Fermanagh/Monaghan/Roscommon	1 each
No fixed abode	25
Other	6
Total	516

Source: NAI, Prison register, Clonmel prison and borstal institution, 1903–23, GPB/1/7/14.

Between 1906 and 1921, approximately 660 juvenile-adult male offenders were committed to Clonmel borstal. The counties with the highest representation tended to be those that contained large urban centres.[27] The eleven-year period between August 1910 and October 1921 saw 160 juvenile male adults with Belfast as their last recorded address enter the borstal.[28] Table 4.1 indicates that Belfast had by far the highest number of inmates from a single county and that Dublin contributed the second highest, with 150 committals. The 1911 census reports a population of 480,000 in Belfast and 390,000 in Dublin.[29] It is clear that the borstal inmates came from all parts of the island.

Not surprisingly, inmates were more likely to emerge from cities because there were increased opportunities there for the type of criminal acts that carried sentences. While juvenile crime was not an exclusively urban phenomenon, Table 4.1 does give weight to the argument that discharged borstal inmates, particularly those from city areas, should be encouraged not to return to where they had originally acquired their criminal habits. The BAI particularly advocated the country life for those under their care, claiming that proper agricultural training would transform a 'city cornerboy' into a decent farm labourer.[30]

As the table illustrates, there was a dramatic difference between the number of inmates from Dublin and those from Cork, the third most represented county in the borstal. A mere twenty-six inmates from Cork entered during these years.[31] It is worth noting that Cork city had a population of just 76,000 in 1911 and was the third largest urban centre in Ireland.[32] It is clear then that national trends were replicated in the borstal population. Londonderry and Tipperary each contributed eighteen inmates during these years. Counties Louth and Down followed with fifteen and ten inmates respectively.[33] None of the other counties had ten or more inmates in Clonmel borstal. The numerical gap between the most and least populated centres was immense. The population of the west of Ireland in particular had declined dramatically during the period after the 1845?51 Famine. It may be concluded, therefore, that there was an overwhelmingly urban composition to the population of Clonmel borstal institution and this in turn suggests a higher concentration of habitual juvenile offending in these areas.

There were two final groups of inmates that are not categorised by county for the purposes of this study. Twenty-five inmates had their address listed on the register as 'no fixed', indicating that these boys were most likely homeless at the time of their conviction.[34] Most of these did have the name and address of a next-of-kin registered, suggesting that a family or economic problem could account for their homelessness. A final category listed in Table 4.1 is labelled 'other'. It was not included in the prison register in this format but was created as such for this study. It is a combination of last residences that do not fit into the categories listed thus far. Three of the inmates in this category had their last residence listed as a reformatory, while one had been in the care of a poor law union. One inmate was in the army, while another was from outside Ireland.[35]

PREVIOUS OCCUPATIONS

The inhabitants of Clonmel borstal claimed to have been employed in a variety of careers at the time of their conviction (Table 4.2). While the various GPB reports often characterised the inmates as 'unemployed' and 'lazy', the majority were listed in the Board's own register of inmates as having held some sort of position. The most common job was that of labourer, held by 259 (39.2 per cent) of the 660 inmates between 1910 and 1921.[36] This position carried a very broad definition in early twentieth-century Ireland, including work in agriculture, construction and even the retail sector, among others. The outstanding feature of labouring was that, of all the borstal occupations, it required the least skill and paid the lowest wages.

The number of labourers was over four times higher than that of the second most popular job: sixty-four messengers or message boys, accounting for 9.5 per cent.[37] Inmates who had worked in this job tended to be concentrated in urban areas. Newsvendors or newsboys accounted for forty borstal inmates, just over 6 per cent of the total. These were positions that required little skill and most certainly offered low wages. The preceding statistics confirm a number of widely held assumptions. It seems more likely that there was a higher inclination for juvenile crime among those in low-paid and unskilled occupations. This argument is strengthened by the fact that these particular jobs would have provided ample opportunity for offending. It should be noted that the majority of those committed to borstal had offended previously. Working as labourers or messengers in large urban areas, these rebellious young men had little chance of avoiding further encounters with the law. Nineteen borstal inmates (just over 2.5 per cent) had their occupation registered as 'nil', a comparatively low figure given that seventeen of these were incarcerated between 1910 and 1921.[38]

Only three occupations that could be described as requiring some degree of skill are included among the most common jobs. There were eleven painters in the borstal (accounting for just 1.5 per cent of all inmates), eight carpenters and seven shoemakers. There are many single number entries in the borstal register; some were skilled, such as service industry occupations like grocer's assistant, pantry boy or draper's assistant.[39] In some instances, it is not easy to understand how certain individuals, working in steady and skilled positions such as plumber, barber or watchmaker, could have continued to fall into crime; such jobs would also have been better paid. It would, however, be reasonable to question the validity of an entry that records a seventeen-year-old boy as a watchmaker. It is more likely that many of these boys may have been apprentices or assistants, rather than fully qualified practitioners of their craft. For the entire eleven-year period, just one inmate is registered as having worked as a farmer. It is the only entry that bears a stated connection to agriculture but it can be assumed that many of those employed as labourers worked on farms. Two inmates worked as 'heater boy in shipyard', another as a 'catch boy in a shipyard'. All three were from Belfast, the heart of shipbuilding in Ireland

TABLE 4.2

OCCUPATION OF INMATES IMMEDIATELY PRIOR TO BORSTAL DETENTION, 1910?21

Occupation	Number of inmates	% of total
Labourer	259	39.2
Message boy	64	9.5
Newsboy	40	6
Nil	19	2.5
Painter	11	2.13
Dealer	10	1.9
Mill worker	10	1.9
Carpenter	8	1.5
Shoemaker	7	1.35
Soldier	7	1.35
Machine boy	6	1.16
Porter	5	1
Cattle drover	4	0.7
Van driver	4	0.7
Baker	3	0.5
Pantry boy	3	0.5
Railway porter	3	0.5
Shop assistant	3	0.5
Barber/Fowl plucker/Herd/Tailor/Tinsmith/heater-boy in shipyard	2 each	0.38 each

Source: NAI, Prison register, Clonmel prison and borstal institution, 1903?23, GPB/1/7/14.

at that time. With such a wide assortment of different trades it can be expected that at least one will be unusual. One inmate, Patrick Whyte from Carlow had previously worked as a 'showman'. Thomas Healy, born in Dublin but of no fixed abode, had worked as a 'cinema operator', which was a reflection of the ongoing modernisation of society, as it was a position that was not likely to have existed when the borstal opened fourteen years earlier.[40] For the most part, these boys were incarcerated not because of their actual preceding crime, but because it represented a step too far. The conviction marked their coming of age as a habitual criminal and the offence itself is often incidental to the wider picture.

OFFENCES

While location, status and family background may have been instrumental, it was the direct actions of the boys themselves that brought them into contact with the borstal system. The records of such an institution provide a glimpse of the type of criminal activities in which young men were involved. Table 4.3 reveals that the boys at Clonmel were incarcerated for a variety of misdeeds. While the prison register provides an opportunity for a general assessment of those crimes, it does not yield many clues as to the circumstances of each one. What is known with certainty is that the borstal system was not designed for the faint-hearted first-time offender who stumbled into trouble by chance. It was created in the main for established criminals who had already acquired the characteristics that promised a future in crime.[41] These were boys who came from what the GPB and the BAI repeatedly labelled 'evil surroundings'.[42]

Larceny was by far the most common reason for borstal detention, with 352 convictions in Clonmel.[43] This can best be described as a form of theft or stealing and a definition of sorts can be found in Sir Robert Peel's Larceny Act of 1827. Under this legislation, larceny included the theft of very minor property such as apples, dogs or fish.[44] However, it can be assumed that the offence more often than not involved the theft of items of a much higher value such as money, jewels or cattle. On the register of inmates, a conviction for larceny is often accompanied by one for breaking and entering, or for receiving. The number of inmates convicted for breaking and entering was 114, the second most frequent offence. This was followed by the similar crime of housebreaking, for which 58 were convicted.[45] A likely distinction between these crimes is that those convicted of breaking and

TABLE 4.3
MOST COMMON OFFENCES AMONG INMATES, 1910?21

Offence	Number of convictions
Larceny	352
Breaking and entering	114
Housebreaking	58
Receiving	36
Shopbreaking	33
Malicious damage	20
Sexual	13
Burglary	11
Cattle stealing	5
False pretences	5
Felony	5
Forgery	5
Robbery	5
Assault	4
Manslaughter	4
Wounding	3
Embezzlement	2
Robbery with violence	2
Attempted murder	1
Criminal assault	1
Demanding money with menace	1
Escaping	1
Feloniously killing cattle	1
Highway robbery	1
Murder	1
Riot/Unlawful assembly	1 each
Striking	1

Source: NAI, Prison register, Clonmel prison and borstal institution, 1903?23, GPB/1/7/14.

entering probably violated premises of a commercial rather than domestic nature. The high instance of these three offences underlines the scenario of opportunity outlined in the previous section of this chapter. The scope for committing all three crimes was much higher in towns and cities than in less populated rural areas.

The fourth most common borstal offence was that of receiving. Thirty-six inmates received convictions for this crime and, as pointed out above, it often appeared on the register in conjunction with other connected offences. Thirty-three inmates were convicted of shopbreaking. Offences of a sexual nature were perpetrated by thirteen of the boys.[46] This is not a high figure but is greater than more mainstream offences such as burglary or robbery. Sexual crimes ranged from attempted rape to 'indecent assault of a girl under thirteen years of age'.[47] A search of local newspaper coverage of borstal-related court proceedings where the offence was sexual found little or no reporting. Outside of the sexual category, there were nine different offences that could be described as crimes against the physical person. The total number convicted for such offences was relatively low, accounting for just seventeen inmates between 1910 and 1921. The first of these was assault, committed by four inmates. A further four inmates were convicted of manslaughter, and three of wounding. Two boys were convicted of robbery with violence and one each of attempted murder, criminal assault, and riot. One had been convicted of murder. This inmate was sentenced to 'be hanged by the neck until he died' but this was commuted to penal servitude for life.[48]

There were some offences that were not in line with the more common categories outlined thus far. Harold Peters, aged fourteen and from Belfast, received two years' penal detention for escaping from Malone Reformatory. Seventeen-year-old Henry Davis, born in London but living in Dublin at the time of his conviction, was charged and convicted with striking his superior officer and sentenced to three years penal servitude. A soldier, he was tried before a general court martial in Dublin. Jon Wilson aged sixteen was sentenced by Cavan quarter session to three years' detention in the borstal for the larceny of a heifer. Sixteen-year-old Samuel Wall from Cork received a similar sentence for killing a calf. Richard Sweeney, of no fixed abode, was sentenced to three years' detention at Castlebar assizes for the larceny of an ass. James O'Brien was sentenced to two years' penal discipline for stealing six pounds and a half pint of whiskey. Eighteen-year-old Francis Gleeson and sixteen-year-old Thomas Barker were convicted of 'severing lead with intent to steal same'. Both were sentenced to three years.[49] While some of these may seem like harsh sentences, it should be noted that they were mostly levied upon young men who had appeared before the courts on one or more previous occasions.

RELIGIOUS AFFILIATIONS

Spiritual and moral guidance were a key element of borstal treatment and the founders of the system envisaged an active role for the chaplains of the institution. Their function was different from that of clergy in industrial and reformatory schools. In the borstal, the chaplains had no authority in the overall management structure. Instead, their principal function was to provide spiritual and moral guidance using a firm but kind approach. Another feature that distinguished borstal chaplains from their counterparts was their role in the aftercare of inmates.

As members of the Board of the BAI, they were involved in aiding the progress of inmates after they were discharged. In their capacity of members of this Board they also contributed to vital Association policy, whether being critical of judicial sentencing practices or government investment in the institution. Clonmel borstal institution provided two chaplains, one each for Roman Catholic and Church of Ireland inmates. The GPB report for 1906?07 provides a breakdown for the initial intake of borstal inmates. Of the twenty-seven committed during that year, eighteen were Roman Catholic, eight were Episcopalian and one was Presbyterian.[50] Figures for the religious affiliation of the borstal population from 1907 to 1909 are not available. Between 1910 and 1921, the overwhelming majority of juvenile adult offenders, over 560, were registered as Roman Catholic.[51] A number of other religious groups were represented: forty-eight were Church of Ireland; forty-four were Presbyterian. The Episcopalian and Baptist faiths each had one inmate in the borstal.[52] These figures are not necessarily reflective of any class division between Catholics and the other faiths. Protestants often endured the same impoverished conditions as those of Catholics, particularly in the major urban areas. Instead, they point to the fact that Catholics in Ireland far outnumbered those from the other churches and so this was reflected in the borstal population. In 1881, for example, 89.5 per cent of the Irish population was Catholic and 10.5 per cent was comprised by Protestant, Jewish and other groups.[53] There were no Jews or other non-Christians at Clonmel borstal between 1910 and 1921.

EDUCATION AND LITERACY UPON COMMITTAL

Writing in 1911, Lord Justice Cherry commended the borstal institution in Ireland for its success in educating its inmates. He claimed that most of the boys had been committed with extremely poor literacy levels but that many left with at least the ability to write a letter.[54] Yet, a majority of inmates were listed on the prison register as, upon entry, being able to read and write. A very modest number of inmates were illiterate.[55] When considering this apparently high level of literacy, however, it must be noted that the register does not reveal the extent to which the inmates were able to read and write. The GPB confirmed this in its annual report for 1911?12, when it described the educational standards of newly committed juvenile-adults as 'deficient'.[56] From this report onwards, as Table 4.4 indicates, the GPB included detailed annual statistics on the educational achievements of borstal inmates. These data included a comprehensive statistical account of the progress of the entire inmate population in both literacy and numeracy over the course of each year. The compilation and publication of such information not only allowed the system to measure its own effectiveness in educating borstal inmates, but also gave the middle and upper classes, upon whom the BAI was somewhat dependent for financial support, the opportunity to judge the success of the system. As this chapter is concerned with the state of inmates only on their admission to the borstal, it will focus on educational attainment levels at that point.

Table 4.4 indicates that, between 1911 and 1921, a majority of inmates (65.9 per cent), had some degree of literacy problem upon their admission. Of the total number committed during this ten-year period, 86 boys (16.6 per cent of those in detention), were unable to either read or write. Just fewer than 50 per cent, or 255 boys, were judged to be able to read and write imperfectly. The remaining 34 per cent, or 176 juvenile-adults, were able to read and write well, according to the GPB.[57] Indeed, as Guinnane points out, statistics on literacy often conceal a wide array of educational capabilities.[58] In fact, it was a prerequisite of the institution that, before an inmate could begin training for a trade such as carpentry or shoemaking, he first had to attain the required national standard of basic education. This process of education and training was administered in the context of a strict code of conduct with in-built mechanisms designed to reprimand those who failed to adhere to it. The educational achievements of

TABLE 4.4
EDUCATION OF INMATES UPON COMMITTAL, 1912–21

Level	1912	1913	1914	1915	1916	1917	1918	1919	1920	1921
Those unable to either read or write	8	10	10	12	9	11	7	3	4	12
Able to read and write imperfectly	51	45	34	14	12	16	23	18	11	31
Able to read and write well	9	2	12	23	9	20	19	16	17	39
Total committed during year	68	57	56	49	30	47	49	37	32	82

Source: NLI, GPB, annual reports, 1912?21

these boys as they entered the institution were more often than not indicative of their family backgrounds up to that point.

AGE AND PHYSICAL CONDITION

One of the conditions of entry to the borstal institution was that an inmate could not possess any serious physical or mental deficiencies.[59] Daily physical drill and training in manual trades were both fundamental elements of borstal treatment, and so full bodily health was essential. In certain limited cases an inmate could be admitted to the borstal but was exempted from physical drill if, for example, he suffered from an ailment that would not otherwise obstruct his progress, such as a heart condition. Juvenile-adult offenders in the borstal were between sixteen and twenty-one years old and Table 4.5 indicates that, between 1911 and 1921, the majority of inmates, almost 58 per cent, entered at the lower end of that age span. During this decade, 24 per cent of all those committed were aged sixteen and 33.5 per cent seventeen.[60] Table 4.5 shows that the judiciary was more inclined to sentence younger juvenile-adults to Clonmel borstal. This suggests a belief on the part of judges that borstal treatment would be most effective for younger offenders. While there was a substantial number of eighteen and nineteen year-old inmates, younger offenders would have been seen as particularly vulnerable and susceptible to criminal habits. It is not clear why an offender would be sentenced to borstal at the age of twenty-one but this did happen in 1917. At the Ulster winter assizes held in Belfast in December 1917, James Dickson, whose age was entered on the register as twenty-one and eleven twelfths years, was sentenced to three years' penal discipline for two cases of larceny and receiving.[61] His detention in Clonmel seems completely futile given that he would have been transferred to an adult prison when he turned twenty-two without any realistic chance of benefitting from borstal treatment. In fact, his detention would have caused an administrative headache for all parties concerned: the governor, the GPB and the BAI. This case is most likely an example of a judge not being properly acquainted with borstal law and procedure, an issue that arose on more than one occasion.

A number of inmates were admitted despite the fact that they had not yet reached sixteen years of age. Again, there was no official explanation for this apparent anomaly and the records of the GPB make no reference to these boys. One was a printer from Dublin,

TABLE 4.5
AGES OF INMATES UPON COMMITTAL, 1911–12 TO 1920–21

	1911 –12	1912 –13	1913 –14	1914 –15	1915 –16	1916 –17	1917 –18	1918 –19	1919 –20	1920 –21	Total
16 years	13	13	14	17	10	12	1	16	7	13	126
17 years	22	33	16	14	6	21	22	9	6	27	176
18 years	13	8	8	3	5	7	10	8	6	20	88
19 years	13	9	11	10	5	7	7	2	9	13	86
20 years	7	3	7	5	4	-	8	1	3	9	47
21 years	-	-	-	-	-	-	1	-	-	-	1

Source: NLI, GPB, annual reports, 1912?21

Timothy Coleman, aged fifteen years and ten months. On 6 December 1912, he was sentenced to three years' detention under the Children's Act 1908 for a felonious killing. Given that this inmate was close to turning sixteen, it is likely that the judiciary consulted the GPB prior to sentencing to establish what level of judicial discretion was permitted. Both parties may have agreed that a minor infringement of the rules was acceptable when an inmate was likely to benefit from borstal treatment. On 3 December 1913, Richard Sheridan, a painter from Limerick, aged fifteen years and two months, was sentenced to twelve months for housebreaking.[62] As this offender was not as close to borstal age as the first boy, his detention in Clonmel is somewhat more difficult to understand. This could be indicative of two things: it may show that the system was not fully understood by those carrying out sentencing or it may demonstrate a degree of flexibility of which the authorities were fully conscious.

While the prison register does not provide a comprehensive medical report on each inmate, it is possible to build a detailed physical profile of an offender. One column in the register is entitled 'Marks on person', which was completed following an examination on admission (such record-keeping was part of the normal routine for Irish prisons). Burns, tattoos, vaccination marks, warts, moles and even baldness were all recorded. One inmate was unflatteringly described as having his 'nose slightly set to the left'.[63] Much of the detail included in this column was of an intimate and indeed sexual nature. Very few of the borstal inmates seemed to be devoid of severe physical scarring of some sort, evidence of hard physical labour or violence. Height, hair and eye colour were noted, as was weight.

If an inmate suffered from a mental deficiency, epilepsy or was unable 'to do a full day's work at some occupation whether sedentary or active', he was precluded from admission.[64] His medical fitness for the institution was determined by the judge, the GPB and the police, prior to his sentencing in court. It was also stipulated by the Home Office that an offender must not be suffering from any 'active tubercular disease or other conditions likely to incapacitate him during training'.[65] The 'marks on body' column in the register does provide some limited medical information on incoming inmates. Some were registered as suffering from ailments such as poor eyesight, gingivitis, dental problems or a deformity of some type. It is likely that the borstal management would have compiled individual files comprising full medical reports but this information has not survived. As in all Irish prisons during this time, there was a medical officer attached to Clonmel borstal.

BORSTAL SENTENCING

Offenders entering Clonmel borstal in the period up to 1914 were likely to have been given much shorter sentences than those sentenced in 1921. In fact, the GPB and BAI did not hesitate to stress that the success of the system depended to a large extent on sentencing practices. Prior to the enactment in 1909 of the Prevention of Crime Act 1908, both bodies repeatedly lamented the reluctance of judges to impose longer sentences upon males between sixteen and twenty-one. The GPB originally set nine months as the minimum time in which reformation might have a chance of succeeding and that became the shortest sentence required for admission to the borstal.[66]

The Prevention of Crime Act 1908 stipulated that borstal sentences should be not less than one year and no more than three years. The evidence suggests, however, that judges were still reluctant to embrace the benefits of longer sentencing. Between August 1910 and December 1914, 229 offenders were sent to Clonmel borstal. Of this number, 57 (25 per cent) were given minimum sentences of one year, 56 sentences of two years and 116 (50 per cent) the maximum three-year sentence.[67]

These figures show that, even after the 1908 Act had been imposed upon the judiciary, approximately half were well below the maximum allowable sentence. In 1911, the BAI complained that the sluggish response of judges to the potential of the Act continued to hamper the operation of the system. Its members re-stated their long-held view that real reform could be effected only through the use of longer sentences and called for a three-year term in all cases. The 1911 report pointed out that, because a system of discharge on licence was in place, only a small number of inmates would actually serve the full three-year sentence. The Association argued that anything less than a three-year term would be of no benefit to these offenders and it was, therefore, worth applying to all. It maintained that a sentence of twelve or eighteen months was 'too short to make them perfect in a trade or to get them to forget the vagabond life they had been leading'.[68] In 1912 both the GPB and the Association continued to hold the line that the judiciary was not fulfilling its duty. The Board underlined the fact that they had no desire to hold an inmate for three years and many of those who had received that maximum sentence were indeed released within seventeen or eighteen months, having shown the necessary signs of reform.[69] The BAI pointed out that the maximum sentence was advantageous to an offender as he came to realise that his own behaviour dictated whether he would be released on licence or serve a longer term.[70] An example of judicial leniency was the case of James Condren, aged seventeen years, convicted of larceny and assault in April 1913. Condren was found guilty by a grand jury of robbing, stripping and severely beating a twelve-year-old boy the previous month. The judge described the offence as demonstrating 'a certain amount of mental depravity' before going on to sentence Condren to eighteen months in the borstal institution. While applauding the merits of the borstal and its potential benefits for this offender, the judge decided to take a 'merciful' view of this case, rather than send the accused to an adult prison.[71]

It was this mentality that exasperated the GPB and the BAI but, in its 1913 report, the GPB finally had reason to praise the judiciary, as there had been a rise in the number of maximum sentences. Of the sixty-six inmates committed to the institution in the previous year, thirty-nine had received the maximum sentence. The Board argued that this was a positive development that was in the interest of an inmate's welfare.[72] 1914 saw a change in borstal sentencing policy, permitting a reduction in tension between the GPB and the BAI on the one side and the judiciary on the other.

The Criminal Justice Administration Act 1914 amended borstal sentencing guidelines bringing the minimum term up to two years and retaining the maximum at three. Between January 1915 and December 1921, 324 boys were committed to Clonmel borstal. Of this total, 131 (40.4 per cent) were given the minimum two-year sentence and 193 (59.6 per cent) the maximum three-year sentence. Although a higher proportion of were now receiving maximum sentences, the Board and the BAI continued to protest at the reluctance of judges to take advantage of the 1914 Act. Two years later, the GPB mused that there were probably many young men at large and drifting into permanent criminality who had received several convictions for trivial offences, and would have benefited from a borstal sentence. Yet again, the Board reassured the courts that no inmate would remain in borstal for a day longer than was deemed necessary for his reformation.[73] In 1918, barely restraining its language, the BAI expressed the view that relevant members of the judiciary would be well served to actually visit Clonmel and see for themselves 'the enormous advantages to be obtained from the Borstal System'.[74] In this way, judges would be able to investigate the system at first hand and use this information when dealing with young offenders. According to the BAI, the further benefit of maximum sentencing for a boy was that his period of supervision after discharge was also likely to be longer, allowing for greater monitored stability. It also carried with it the threat of a longer period during which he could potentially be returned to the institution.[75] This type of incentive was part of the original design of the borstal treatment programme and was created for the purpose of encouraging prolonged periods of good behaviour on the part of an offender, both during his detention and after his discharge.

A brief insight into the nature of the relationship between the GPB and the judiciary on the sentencing issue can be seen in a line of communications in 1920 between the Board's secretary, Max Green, and the recorder of Belfast. Mr Green spelled out the case for longer sentencing, pointing out that the two-year term, which was by then the minimum, was still inadequate for the reformation of a young criminal. He pointed out that during the first eighteen months a hardened offender can be 'recovered to normal – after which we have to accustom him to honest effort'.[76] He went on to make clear that, under the borstal system's release on licence provisions, an inmate serving a maximum sentence could often be released early because he 'gets the advantage of the shorter sentence by manifesting himself that he is worthy of it'.[77] A short sentence should be earned, rather than handed down by a judge. In a reply to Green, the recorder defended the actions of judges. He argued that short sentences were often the most appropriate because anything else could be disproportionate and unjustified. However, he concluded that it was, for the most part, in a boy's interest to be given a longer sentence.[78] This exchange reveals little about the reasoning behind the judiciary's reluctance to fully embrace the ideals of those managing the borstal system. Sentencing issues were not referred to beyond the 1918 report of the GPB, something that could indicate greater co-operation by the judiciary. There was also the possibility that civil and political unrest between 1914 and 1922 distracted the authorities from engaging in such debate.

FAMILY AND DOMESTIC BACKGROUNDS

The register also supplies further evidence of the backgrounds of juvenile offenders. One column on the register required the name and address of the next-of-kin of each inmate. In almost every case that person is a parent, in a far lower number of instances a grandparent, while a number of inmates declared a sibling, an aunt or an uncle as their closest relative. This would not necessarily indicate that the parents were deceased: it was possible that an offender was estranged from his parents or had somehow been abandoned by his family. A small number of entries indicated that the parents' location was unknown.

In several instances, a name is given but the address is listed as 'no fixed' abode. In this case the address applied to both parents and son. Sixteen-year-old Peter Cullen seems to have come from a particularly bleak family background. His most recent residence is recorded as Trim Industrial School, while his next-of-kin was his mother, listed as being under the care of Drogheda union.[79] A similar situation existed for seventeen-year-old John Redmond. His next-of-kin was his brother, also at Trim Industrial School.[80] Seventeen-year-old Owen Maguire was a labourer from Dublin, convicted of larceny and sentenced to three years' penal discipline. His next-of-kin was his father, listed as an inmate of Dundrum asylum.[81] A number of next-of-kin entries simply read 'parents dead'. This was the case for sixteen-year-old Martin Dunn, whose last residence was recorded as the Salvation Army in Belfast. His next-of-kin was an unnamed stepfather residing at an unknown location in Scotland. Another entry for a seventeen-year-old inmate, Thomas Bracken, is even more stark. The entry for next-of-kin simply reads 'has none'.[82] In 1912, the *Freeman's Journal* described juvenile-adult offenders as 'victims of the neglect of parents'. Many of these boys came from homes that were marred by drunkenness, idleness and 'other forms of vice'. A life of criminality was the only inevitable outcome for such unfortunate boys.[83] The GPB chairman, J.S. Gibbons, presented a number of examples of the background of borstal inmates to the International Penitentiary Congress in 1910. One boy was twenty years old, with three previous convictions for drunkenness and larceny. He resided with his parents, 'who keep a low lodging-house, and are themselves downgraded people'.[84] They had often complained of being assaulted by their son. The chairman also referred to a twenty-year-old youth who had been convicted five times for larceny and drunkenness. For a number of years, this young man of bad character had been associating with prostitutes.[85] With evidence such as this, the presence of these young men in the borstal is easily explained. For many of these inmates, a borstal sentence was possibly the most significant and positive development in their short lives as it represented their best hope for an ordinary life.

Many of the inmates displayed the characteristics and confidence of experienced adult criminals. Boys from major urban centres tended to possess particular skill and tenacity. Three such individuals received borstal sentences in January 1914 at Belfast city sessions. William Parks and Patrick Kerr were seventeen years old and their occupations were listed as '[shipyard] catch boy'. A third boy, Michael Mulligan, a labourer, was sixteen.[86] All three pleaded guilty to breaking and entering no less than three domestic and commercial premises. During the previous September, they stole seven clocks, twenty-two knives, four pens, six brooches and three rings from the property of William Navey. In January, just over a week before the court sitting, they broke into the shop of William Stanfield. On an unspecified date, they stole 'a quantity of liquors' from the shop of W.A. Gilbey. The presiding judge, Walker Craig, declared that the boys showed an 'amount of precocity which really startled one'. He argued that their criminal careers must be stopped before they advanced any further and therefore the best option for the boys, their parents and society was to sentence them to two years each in Clonmel borstal institution.[87]

On many occasions, the boy or boys who eventually found themselves in court were accompanied by an older more experienced man during their criminal exploits. In March 1913, David Wilson, a twenty-year old-labourer, and Michael Wright, eighteen years old and also a labourer, appeared before Belfast city assizes.[88] Along with an older man, John Stanley, they pleaded guilty to breaking and entering the houses of Sarah Jane McGrath, Samuel H. McVeigh and Hugh Arthurs, over a number of days the previous January, and stealing a number of unspecified items. Stanley also pleaded guilty to breaking and entering, and stealing, from another house later in the month. His lawyer argued for leniency: Stanley was a married man with a young child, had been in the army and was of previous good character. The judge acknowledged this and expressed a desire to show leniency but pointed out the need to respond strongly to anyone contributing to the 'plague' of housebreaking in the city. He sentenced Stanley to six months in prison without hard labour, thereby, apparently, saving his army pension. It transpired that Wilson and Wright had no previous convictions but they were identified as suitable candidates for borstal treatment. They were of an age, according to the judge, when it was possible to save them from a life of crime.[89] He sentenced each to three years in Clonmel borstal.

The inner city areas of Belfast were obviously a breeding ground for youthful offenders and their crimes often explain why so many of the borstal inmates came from cities. Urban areas offered the type of opportunities that were not so readily available in the country. David Eccleston was a nineteen-year-old painter from Belfast who appeared before the city assizes in March 1913.[90] Together with two older men, William O'Donnell and Peter Finchley, Eccleston was accused of breaking and entering the premises of J.C. Blow and stealing a pair of scissors, a set of keys, an overcoat, two pairs of boots, a cheque book and other items. They were also accused of entering the 'counting-house' of Joseph Malcomson and stealing postage and other stamps to the value of £5, socks, a notebook and lead pencils. They were further charged with breaking into the 'counting-house' of J.C. Crawford, the property of Hugh Benson and the property of William H. White. While O'Donnell and Finchley were sentenced to three years' hard labour in regular prison, Eccleston was given three years in Clonmel.[91] He seemed to be a much more suitable candidate for borstal treatment than many others sent there. He met most of the key criteria outlined by Ruggles-Brise and the Gladstone Committee in that he was guilty of multiple offences, had proven bad associations and demonstrated the potential for a descent into serious criminality. It is not clear, however, if he had prior convictions.

It is clear that during these years Belfast, like other large urban centres, was a den of criminality and low morals. The opportunities for offending were furnished by the tempting number of premises to break into, but also by the presence of unscrupulous, Fagin-like characters who would encourage and often reward such behaviour. In October 1910, three young men, James Kelly, Peter Phillips and Daniel McIvinchey, aged seventeen, sixteen and seventeen respectively, appeared at Belfast general sessions, accused of various charges of theft and damage to the property of Messrs John Robb and Company.[92] Evidence was produced to show that the defendants entered through the rear of the premises by using a rope thrown over a wall. A detective, concealed on the premises, confronted the burglars but they resisted arrest and one of them bit his finger. It transpired that the accused boys had entered the property in order to steal lead piping, which would be sold on to 'marine dealers'. The presiding judge was highly critical of 'marine-store-dealers', pointing out that, if a boy of the defendants' age group entered their store after dark, while his accomplice waited outside with a donkey and cart loaded with lead, it should alert the dealer to the likelihood that the cargo was stolen. He declared that, if there were fewer 'marine-store-dealers' to whom such boys could sell lead, there would be less theft in the city. After the boys were found guilty of several of the charges laid against them, the judge weighed up his sentencing options. The most useful course of action, in his opinion, was to send all three to the borstal institution, rather than to an adult prison, where they would 'consort with jail birds'. He cited a report from the prison authorities stating that the boys were suitable candidates as they were well known to be keeping bad company and were in danger of sinking deeper into criminality. All three were sentenced to two years detention in Clonmel borstal.[93]

The negative influences of older characters were strongly evident in the case of nineteen-year-old Patrick Coogan, who appeared before Dublin city commission in February 1912.[94] Along with an older man, Michael Feeney, he was accused of passing a counterfeit coin at Church Street the previous month. Coogan pleaded guilty, Feeney not guilty. Giving evidence, Police Sergeant Moloney alleged that the coin was actually passed by the boy but he was in the company of Feeney and a woman. The prosecution claimed that the two older suspects got Coogan to pass the coin. Michael Feeney made a lengthy statement to the court, during which he called Coogan 'a lovely liar' and encouraged the jury to do 'their duty by their God and King'. The judge, Mr Justice Dodd, praised Feeney as intelligent and skilful but regretted that his abilities were wasted on crime. Thirty-eight years old and with sixteen previous convictions, he received a six-month prison sentence. The judge turned to Coogan and passed a sentence of three years in Clonmel borstal: 'You'll like it there,' he said, smiling. 'It is better than Mountjoy.'[95]

The streets of Dublin were just as much a criminal breeding-ground as those of Belfast. Juvenile-adult offenders often roamed the city in small gangs and crimes were not always committed by a lone perpetrator. Christopher Ellis appeared to be part of a small criminal gang. He was seventeen years old when he appeared before Dublin city commission in June 1912.[96] He pleaded not guilty to breaking and entering the home of Mrs Bridget Fanning at Ellis Quay and stealing a quantity of clothing that included eighteen shirts and a number of hats. Following the evidence of Mrs Fanning that the property did indeed belong to her and an account of the items stolen, the court heard evidence from 'a little boy' named Christopher Rogers. He resided with his parents at Hendrick Street and testified that at 6.00 am on the morning of the theft he was walking on Ellis Quay, having been sent by his parents to Benburb Street to get water for the house. He claimed that he saw Ellis and a number of other boys. Ellis broke a shop window and stole a large number of shirts and collars before running away. In his testimony, Ellis tried to discredit the child by claiming that he heard a policeman offer to pay him money to tell these lies. In summing up the case to the jury, Mr Justice Gibson declared that, if the present state of affairs persisted, they would all have to take out very high insurance on their properties. This type of crime was increasing and was being committed by young people who could not be severely punished. He stated that he was opposed to punishing young offenders except in exceptional circumstances: this was one such case, a daring crime committed in broad daylight. He pointed out that the boys engaged in this type of activity were not stealing the shirts in order to give them to the poor or to beggars but because they had someone behind them waiting to purchase them. Ellis was convicted and sentenced to three years in Clonmel.[97]

Juvenile-adult offending was obviously not restricted to the streets of Dublin and Belfast. Peter O'Riordan, a labourer from Dublin, appeared before Carlow petty sessions at the age of eighteen, in January 1921.[98] He was accused of the larceny of twenty pounds from the house of John Fallon, his employer. On 18 December, Fallon had returned from a trip to Tullow and had given the defendant ten shillings, putting the remainder of his money, which amounted to twenty pounds, into his waistcoat pocket. He slept in the same room as the defendant that night and the following morning Fallon and his niece went to mass. O'Riordan remained at the house, claiming that he was not ready and did not want to make his employers late. Upon returning from mass, Fallon found that the defendant was gone and the twenty pounds was missing from his waistcoat. RIC Sergeant Kelly gave evidence of arresting O'Riordan in Cavan.[99] He pleaded guilty to the charge of larceny and it emerged that he held previous convictions for larceny and for indecently assaulting a girl. Sergeant Kelly testified that the accused had had a bad start in life. The judge stated his wish 'to take the taint of the jail off the prisoner' and expressed a determination to give him an opportunity to reform himself. He sent him to Clonmel for two years.[100]

To say that these tragic cases were typical of the profile of the borstal offender would be a misrepresentation. The vast majority of the boys were listed as having the same last residence as their parents. A search of local newspaper court reporting shows that judges often looked favourably on the efforts of parents to restrain and control their sons. As Michael Davitt pointed out a number of decades earlier, many of the young criminals he encountered in jail did indeed have honest parents and were the product of good backgrounds.[101] This is illustrated by a case at the Cork assizes in July 1912, when a juvenile-adult offender, John Mason, was sentenced to three years' penal discipline in Clonmel after pleading guilty to stealing a waistcoat from a local draper. In court it emerged that Mason was a member of a 'respected' local family, and that his father was a contractor, to whom the boy was apprenticed. The boy's mother pleaded for leniency, blaming the crime primarily on the fact that her son had fallen into bad company. In passing sentence, the judge rejected her pleas but went to great lengths to emphasise his admiration for the efforts he knew she had been making with her son; 'The object [of borstal treatment],' said the judge, 'is reformation – not punishment.' After the boy had been led from the court, the judge asked counsel to reassure the parents that the three-year sentence did not mean he would necessarily spend that long in detention.[102]

By 1910 the former convict prison in Clonmel, transformed into the sole borstal institution in Ireland, had become a key weapon in a new fight against juvenile crime. Many of those who found themselves in the institution had come from troubled environments with limited opportunities and no hope of economic or social advancement. The post-Gladstone report debate on the nature of the proposed penal reformatory focused largely on the age of inmates. A clear difference emerged between procedures in the Irish and English borstal systems. Officially, the Irish system was identical, following the same rules of admission, including the age category of sixteen to twenty-one years. A number of inmates were admitted below the age of sixteen, however, a practice not in keeping with the stated intention of the founders. Low numbers of female juvenile-adults meant that a similar institution for girls was not necessary but the burgeoning numbers of males, unable to be absorbed by Clonmel, convinced the authorities to establish modified borstal systems in certain selected convict prisons. The reluctance of judges to impose sufficiently long sentences on juveniles, in both Ireland and England, was the source of ongoing tension between the judiciary and the GPB. This was addressed by the Prevention of Crime Act 1908 and the Criminal Justice Administration Act 1914, both of which increased the minimum sentences for borstal treatment. Though the borstal system accommodated inmates from almost every part of Ireland, the majority were from the cities of Belfast and Dublin. Inmates had been engaged in a wide range of occupations before conviction but the overwhelming majority had been in low-paid jobs that required little skill. The physical condition of inmates suggested that many had emerged from backgrounds marked by poverty and violence. A large number were raised in troubled and often disordered family settings, where criminality and immorality were normal. This should not be taken as a sweeping generalisation for all borstal inmates, however, as this is not supported by the evidence. If a typical Irish borstal inmate existed, he could be described as urban, under-skilled and under-educated. He was most likely a Roman Catholic from the lower classes, someone whose very existence epitomised dire economic conditions in the early twentieth-century Irish city.

NOTES

1. Using the annual reports of the General Prisons Board (GPB), as well as the institution's own prison register, this chapter will, insofar as is possible, develop a profile of a typical borstal inmate. It is based solely on information recorded in the days leading up to each boy's arrival at Clonmel borstal, before the attempted reformation process begins.
2. NLI, *Report from the Departmental Committee on Prisons*, vi, 1 [C 7702-1], H.L. 1895, 3.
3. NLI, *Proceedings of the International Penitentiary Congress*, vi [Cd-5286], H.L., 1909–10, xxxix, 3.
4. NLI, *Proceedings of the International Penitentiary Congress*, vi [Cd-5286], H.L., 1909–10, xxxix, 4.

5. NLI, *Proceedings of the International Penitentiary Congress,* vi [Cd-5286], H.L., 1909–10, xxxix, 6.
6. NLI, *Twenty-ninth Report of the General Prisons Board,* x [Cd-3698], H.L. 1906–7, x, 12.
7. *The Nationalist,* 11 April 1906.
8. NLI, *Proceedings of the International Penitentiary Congress,* vi [Cd-5286], H.L., 1909–10, xxxix, 12.
9. NLI, *Proceedings of the International Penitentiary Congress,* vi [Cd-5286], H.L., 1909–10, xxxix, 13.
10. NLI, *Thirty-second Report of the General Prisons Board,* xxi [Cd-5286], H.L. 1909–10, xv, 40.
11. NAI, Prison register, Clonmel prison and borstal institution, 1903?23, GPB/1/7/14.
12. NLI, *Twenty-ninth Report of the General Prisons Board,* x [Cd-3698], H.L. 1906–7, ix, 33.
13. NLI, *Twenty-ninth Report of the General Prisons Board,* x [Cd-3969], H.L. 1906–7,v, 70.
14. NLI, *Thirty-sixth Report of the General Prisons Board,* v [Cd-7409], H.L. 1913–4, x. 28.
15. NLI, *Thirty-fourth Report of the General Prisons Board,* vii [Cd-6365], H.L. 1911–2, viii, 18.
16. NLI, *Twenty-ninth Report of the General Prisons Board,* x [Cd-3969], H.L. 1906–7,v, 89.
17. Osborough, *Borstal in Ireland,* p. 6.
18. Osborough, *Borstal in Ireland,* p. 8.
19. NAI, GPB, Correspondence register (CR), GPB to Judge Kenny, 3 July 1911, GPB/1911/1832.
20. NLI, *Thirty-second Report of the General Prisons Board,* v [Cd-5286], 1909–10, ii, 43.
21. NLI, *Thirty-second Report of the General Prisons Board,* v [Cd-5286], 1909–10, ii, 43.
22. As pointed out earlier, prior to the implementation of the Prevention of Crime Act 1908, borstal sentencing, as such, did not exist. The process of selecting a boy for borstal treatment took place privately within the confines of the GPB in Dublin Castle, in consultation with the relevant prison governor.
23. Osborough, *Borstal in Ireland,* p. 8.
24. NLI, *Thirtieth Report of the General Prisons Board,* v [Cd-4253], H.L. 1907–8, xx, 14.
25. *The Nationalist,* 28 May 1910.
26. NAI, GPB, CR, GPB to Judge Kenny, 3 July 1911, GPB/1911/1832.
27. An accurate statistical account of borstal inmates prior to August 1910 is not possible as juvenile-adults were listed on the register with the adult convicts.
28. NAI, Prison register, Clonmel prison and borstal institution, 1903–23, GPB/1/7/14.
29. *Census of Ireland,* 1911, part ii, *General Report,* pp. 109–10.
30. NAI, Prison register, Clonmel prison and borstal institution, 1903–23, GPB/1/7/14.
31. NAI, Prison register, Clonmel prison and borstal institution, 1903–23, GPB/1/7/14.
32. *Census of Ireland,* 1911.
33. NAI, Prison register, Clonmel prison and borstal institution, 1903–23, GPB/1/7/14.
34. NAI, Prison register, Clonmel prison and borstal institution, 1903–1923, GPB/1/7/14.
35. NAI, Prison register, Clonmel prison and borstal institution, 1903–1923, GPB/1/7/14.
36. NAI, Prison register, Clonmel prison and borstal institution, 1903–1923, GPB/1/7/14.
37. NAI, Prison register, Clonmel prison and borstal institution, 1903–1923, GPB/1/7/14.
38. NAI, Prison register, Clonmel prison and borstal institution, 1903–1923, GPB/1/7/14.
39. NAI, Prison register, Clonmel prison and borstal institution, 1903–1923, GPB/1/7/14.
40. NAI, Prison register, Clonmel prison and borstal institution, 1903–1923, GPB/1/7/14.
41. Edward Fahy, 'The prisons', *The Bell,* 1940, 1, 2, p. 72.
42. This term appeared on numerous occasions in GPB and BAI annual reports between 1906 and 1921. It was also repeated in *The Nationalist* during these years.
43. NAI, Prison register, Clonmel prison and borstal institution, 1903–23, GPB/1/7/14.
44. Radzinowicz, Hood, *A History of English Criminal Law,* p. 620
45. NAI, Prison register, Clonmel prison and borstal institution, 1903–1923, GPB/1/7/14.
46. NAI, Prison register, Clonmel prison and borstal institution, 1903–1923, GPB/1/7/14.
47. NAI, Prison register, Clonmel prison and borstal institution, 1903–1923, GPB/1/7/14.
48. NAI, Prison register, Clonmel prison and borstal institution, 1903–1923, GPB/1/7/14.
49. NAI, Prison register, Clonmel prison and borstal institution, 1903–1923, GPB/1/7/14.
50. NLI, *Twenty-ninth Report of the General Prisons Board,* x [Cd-3969], H.L. 1906–7, v, 149.
51. NAI, Prison register, Clonmel prison and borstal institution, 1903–1923, GPB/1/7/14.

52. NAI, Prison register, Clonmel prison and borstal institution, 1903–1923, GPB/1/7/14.
53. Dudley Edwards, *An Atlas of Irish History*, p. 132.
54. Cherry, 'Juvenile crime and its prevention', p. 444.
55. NAI, Prison register, Clonmel prison and borstal institution, 1903–1923, GPB/1/7/14.
56. NLI, *Thirty-fourth Report of the General Prisons Board*, vii [Cd-6365], 1911–2, v, p. 27.
57. NLI, *Forty-third Report of the General Prisons Board*, vi [Cd-4479], H.L. 1920–2, iv, 121.
58. Guinnane, *The Vanishing Irish*, p. 65.
59. Cherry, 'Juvenile crime and its prevention', p. 444.
60. NLI, *Forty-third report of the General Prisons Board*, vi [Cd-4479], H.L. 1920–2, iv, 121.
61. NAI, Prison register, Clonmel prison and borstal institution, 1903–1923, GPB/1/7/14.
62. NAI, Prison register, Clonmel prison and borstal institution, 1903–1923, GPB/1/7/14.
63. NAI, Prison register, Clonmel prison and borstal institution, 1903–1923, GPB/1/7/14.
64. NAI, GPB, Clonmel borstal memoranda, circular letter from Home Office, Whitehall, London, 25 November 1919, Youthful Offenders, GPB/XB5.
65. GPB, Clonmel borstal memoranda, circular letter from Home Office, Whitehall, London, 25 November 1919, Youthful Offenders, GPB/XB5.
66. NLI, *Twenty-ninth Report of the General Prisons Board*, x [Cd-3969], H.L. 1906–7, v, 87.
67. NAI, Prison register, Clonmel prison and borstal institution, 1903–1923, GPB/1/7/14.
68. Quoted in NLI, *Thirty-third Report of the General Prisons Board*, v [Cd-3440], H.L. 1910–1, xvii, 7.
69. NLI, *Thirty-fourth Report of the General Prisons Board*, vii [Cd-6365], 1911–2, v, p. 44.
70. NLI, *Thirty-fourth Report of the General Prisons Board*, vii [Cd-6365], H.L. 1911–2, v, p. 13.
71. *Clare Champion*, 19 April 1913.
72. NLI, *Thirty-fifth Report of the General Prisons Board*, i [Cd-6996], H.L. 1912–3, xxxii, 44.
73. NLI, *Thirty-eighth Report of the General Prisons Board*, iv [Cd-8450], H.L. 1915–6, xx, 37.
74. Quoted in NLI, *Fortieth Report of the General Prisons Board*, iii [Cm-42], H.L. 1917–8, ix, 33.
75. NLI, *Fortieth Report of the General Prisons Board*, iii [Cm-42], H.L. 1917–8, ix, 34.
76. NAI, GPB, CR, Green to the Recorder of Belfast, 30 September 1920, GPB/1824/1911.
77. NAI, GPB, CR, Green to the Recorder of Belfast, 30 September 1920, GPB/1824/1911.
78. NAI, GPB, CR, recorder of Belfast letter to Green, GPB, 4 October 1920, GPB/1824/1911.
79. NAI, Prison register, Clonmel prison and borstal institution, 1903–1923, GPB/1/7/14.
80. NAI, Prison register, Clonmel prison and borstal institution, 1903–1923, GPB/1/7/14.
81. NAI, Prison register, Clonmel prison and borstal institution, 1903–1923, GPB/1/7/14.
82. NAI, Prison register, Clonmel prison and borstal institution, 1903–1923, GPB/1/7/14.
83. *Freeman's Journal*, 30 May 1912.
84. NLI, *Proceedings of the International Penitentiary Congress*, vi [Cd-5286], H.L., 1909–10, xxxix, 13.
85. NLI, *Proceedings of the International Penitentiary Congress*, vi [Cd-5286], H.L., 1909–10, xxxix, 14.
86. NAI, Prison register, Clonmel prison and borstal institution, 1903–1923, GPB/1/7/14.
87. *Belfast Newsletter*, 14 January 1914.
88. NAI, Prison register, Clonmel prison and borstal institution, 1903–1923, GPB/1/7/14.
89. *Belfast Newsletter*, 14 March 1913.
90. NAI, Prison register, Clonmel prison and borstal institution, 1903–1923, GPB/1/7/14.
91. *Belfast Newsletter*, 15 March 1913.
92. NAI, Prison register, Clonmel prison and borstal institution, 1903–1923, GPB/1/7/14.
93. *Belfast Newsletter*, 31 October 1912.
94. NAI, Prison register, Clonmel prison and borstal institution, 1903–1923, GPB/1/7/14.
95. *Dublin Evening Mail*, 9 February 1912.
96. NAI, Prison register, Clonmel prison and borstal institution, 1903–1923, GPB/1/7/14.
97. *Dublin Evening Mail*, 13 June 1912.
98. NAI, Prison register, Clonmel prison and borstal institution, 1903–1923, GPB/1/7/14.
99. *Nationalist and Leinster Times*, 29 January 1921.
100. *Nationalist and Leinster Times*, 19 February 1921.
101. Michael Davitt, *Leaves from a Prison Diary* (Shannon: Irish University Press, 1972), p. 120.
102. *Cork Examiner*, 21 July 1911.

CHAPTER FIVE

Classification and discipline of inmates, 1906–21

The majority of juvenile-adult offenders at Clonmel borstal were regulated only by the laws of the street before their burgeoning criminal careers faltered in the early stages. Some were raised in broken homes, or came from the care of parents who were themselves on the fringes of a criminal underworld. Many came from the streets of Dublin and Belfast and were beyond the control of their parents or guardians. This class of inmate was described by Sydney A. Moseley in 1926 as 'physically and mentally degenerate'.[1] The challenge faced by the governor and staff of Clonmel borstal was to bring about an improvement in the behaviour and outlook of the boys under their care. This chapter will assess the first of those four key weapons in this fight: the use of penal discipline as a means of exacting change and inculcating a sense of self-control in these boys.

In some ways, the idea of borstal discipline was wholly unoriginal, a combination of elements drawn from the penal system over the previous half century. The feature that set the borstal apart from previous initiatives was that this concept had never previously been used on this class of offender. The chapter will describe the legislative basis for borstal discipline and its evolution from a small-scale experiment to its constitution as a fully legitimate entity in the penal system under a 1908 act of parliament. Central to the reformation process at Clonmel was the grade system of classification, which sought to instil a sense of self-discipline by offering to the boys an ongoing scheme of incentives. The condition of life in the ordinary, special and penal grades will be discussed through an examination of the rules and regulations governing the institution. The grade system provided a means of strict social and physical control over the inmates and was a type of corrective measure designed to bring about positive change. The system of penal discipline at the borstal was operated on a similar basis to that of the wider prison system in Ireland but with some important differences. This chapter will assess the key role played by the visiting justice in the apparatus of borstal discipline and the consultation process between the GPB and the institution in proceedings against inmates. The second half of the chapter will examine a series of actual cases where disciplinary procedures were taken against inmates of Clonmel borstal, to provide an insight not only into the daily operation and character of the institution itself, but also into the mechanism for punishing inmates who had transgressed. The analysis of these cases will underline the many weaknesses in the method of investigating borstal indiscipline, a process in which the inmates was almost always disadvantaged.

ORIGINS OF BORSTAL DISCIPLINE

The method of penal discipline that was applied at the original borstal institution in Kent, and five years later in Clonmel, had its origins in the Crofton system of the mid-nineteenth century. This system was described by Osborough as 'the single major Irish contribution to penal reform'.[2] The Crofton system, also known as the Progressive Stage System or the Intermediate System, consisted of four chronological phases through which the prisoners had to pass before release. The first stage was solitary confinement at Mountjoy prison. This was followed by a period of employment on public works at Spike Island in Cork. The third phase saw prisoners engaged in training in a variety of different trades either in Smithfield or in Lusk, in County Dublin. The final stage was the conditional release of prisoners.[3] Graduation through the stages was regulated by a mark regime whereby prisoners were rewarded for good conduct and industry. This principle of providing prisoners with a set of incentives to good behaviour became the cornerstone of the borstal system in the early twentieth century. Among the other elements of the Crofton system that transferred to the borstal was that of occupational training. The large-scale training and employment schemes that were pioneered by Crofton represented a complete break with previous practice and became an enduring feature of prison reform. The stages of the Crofton system were closely mirrored by those developed for the borstal. The four key elements were all featured: first, strict classification of inmates; second, 'firm and exact' discipline; hard work; and, finally, 'organised supervision' after discharge.[4]

Though the Gladstone report suggested a new penal reformatory for juvenile-adult habitually offending males, it did not stipulate much detail of the regime that was to be established or of the disciplinary methods that were to be imposed. The report stated that the proposed institution would be a 'half-way house between the prison and the reformatory', implying the maintenance of high levels of discipline but without the harsh and often unproductive regime of a prison. The comparison with the reformatory school sent an important message to those who would be charged with constructing this system. The penal reformatory should have 'penal and coercive sides', implemented according to the merits of each particular case.[5] The nature of the penal side of the reformatory was left to Ruggles-Brise and the Prison Commissioners to determine for themselves and the tone of the report suggests that the authors were aware that it was more desirable that such decisions were made by those operating the system on a daily basis, rather than by political élites. The system of discipline developed for the borstal was the product of careful negotiation, research and planning by Ruggles-Brise and his Prison Commissioners, with an array of international penal and psychological experts, and prison governors from various parts of England.

The inmates of the borstal institutions of Britain and Ireland were subjected to a system of penal discipline that was designed to be, as the Gladstone Committee suggested, both punitive and coercive.[6] The long-term goal was to inhibit the criminal habits of the inmates at their source and win them 'back into the ranks of industry and virtue'[7]. It became obvious to the boys that good behaviour and an attempt at self-improvement would be thoroughly rewarded, while misconduct and idleness would result in penalties and restrictions. In a sense, the inmates had a considerable degree of control over the quality of their lives in borstal. The system invited them to reform themselves but did not force them to do so. The entire inmate population of a borstal institution lived within a grade system; each inmate, depending upon various factors, was placed either in the penal, ordinary or special grade.

THE ORDINARY GRADE

The ordinary grade was the point of entry to borstal for all the offenders; time spent in that category decided their fate within the system and ultimately determined the speed of their release. When Clonmel borstal first opened as an experimental unit of the county gaol in 1906, it had only two grades, ordinary and special. All new borstal inmates entered the system through the ordinary grade, where conditions were similar to those of adult prisoners in local gaols. The principal difference between ordinary grade juvenile-adults and regular prisoners at that time was that the former had to do daily drill exercises, wore distinctive clothing and had certain other privileges including greater access to visitors and letter-writing. During the first three years of Clonmel borstal's existence, all inmates spent the first five months in the ordinary grade before promotion to special grade. This was based on a positive response during this phase, like whether or not they had earned enough merit marks for good behaviour and made progress in other aspects of their reformation. More often than not promotion was a good indicator of how a boy would respond to borstal treatment in the longer term.[8] A 1909 editorial in *The Nationalist* commented that the conditions of the borstal were 'altogether favourable for reclamation and reform'. The newspaper argued that the system was designed to bring to the surface all that 'is good in a boy'.[9] Over time the ordinary grade became a place for inmates who showed no great inclination to change, one way or another, and although more favourable than the penal grade, it nonetheless continued to represent a state of stagnation.

The ordinary grade was the period during which boys of a certain character were confronted with the challenge of reforming themselves. Such individuals were already accustomed to the harsh regime of a prison, which meant that introduction to borstal through the penal grade would have been counterproductive. On the other hand, entering the system through the special grade would have given inmates nothing to achieve – the ordinary grade was a type of no man's land where their future could go either of two ways. The ordinary grade also provided the managers of the institution with some time to identify and get to know their inmates as part of the process of individualisation. Promotion to the special grade was the ultimate reward for good behaviour and self-reformation became the principal concern of most new inmates.

The boys were dressed in different colours according to their grade. Those in the ordinary grade were clothed in brown.[10] Given how much more is known about the special and penal grades, it is safe to assume that inmates received no real privileges but neither were they subjected to any additional punitive measures. Some ordinary grade features can be gleaned, however, by examining the rules and regulations of the system as well as by assessing the evidence of an eyewitness to the scheme in operation at Borstal in Kent, where boys were, similarly, clothed according to their grade. In Kent, inmates in the ordinary grade were also dressed entirely in brown. Those in the special grade were dressed in blue, which was clearly regarded by the boys and their warders as symbolic of their progress. According to a first-hand account published in *The Treasury* in March 1910, inmates dressed in brown clothing had a visible tendency to hang their heads and avoid eye contact, while those in blue were upright and brisk in their approach to their work.[11] The brown uniform was regarded as a badge of shame, particularly in the presence of visitors to the institutions. The purpose was to make the boys *want* to wear the blue uniform.

Boys in the ordinary grade were to prepare for advancement to the special grade. In the records of the GPB there is no evidence that officers discriminated against inmates in order to prevent their promotion. Promoting inmates to the special grade was an indication that the governor and his officers were succeeding in their reforming task. An initiative aimed at preparing ordinary grade inmates for promotion was submitted by the governor of Clonmel, Major Dobbin, to the GPB in 1914. He felt that it would be advantageous to allow 'senior and meritorious' inmates from the ordinary grade to dine with each other rather than in isolation in their cells. Developing an idea he got from his counterpart in Kent, he proposed placing, in the hall outside their cells, a long table at which selected ordinary grade boys could dine together in preparation for 'mess room association', which would come with promotion. This experiment would require an investment of between nine and ten pounds and had the full support of the visiting justices and the medical officer.[12] The proposal was immediately accepted on a one-month trial basis by the GPB.[13] This was an obvious sign of the trust placed by officials in the abilities of Major Dobbin and the staff. Dobbin reported back to his superiors that the eighteen inmates selected for the experiment demonstrated 'in their general conduct and demeanour throughout the month, that the privilege is appreciated and were determined to do nothing to forfeit the distinction'. He went on to recommend the permanent adoption of the scheme.[14] It is not known if the GPB approved this suggestion but this communication suggests that the managers and staff of Clonmel borstal were anxious to place increasing levels of trust in those inmates that they felt were likely to respond positively.

Promotion was dependent on the number of merit marks an inmate collected during his initial period in detention. These were awarded and deducted by the institutional board for a variety of reasons.[15] If an inmate accumulated 2,200 merit marks within a five or six month period, he automatically qualified for promotion to the special grade. A joint decision was then made at this level as to the boy's suitability.[16] Promotion was not automatic, however, and a decision could be deferred if an inmate demonstrated 'idleness or misconduct'.[17]

Merit marks were distributed according to a very specific and explicit system. At Clonmel, marks were awarded by the ward officer, the party or trade officer, the drill instructor and the schoolmaster, all of whom held independent registers. Three marks were awarded when industry and conduct were deemed to have been very good; two marks when good; one mark when fair; and no marks for bad conduct or for inmates already under punishment. Boys could earn a maximum of twelve marks for each day of the week including Sunday. The registers were sent to the governor on a monthly basis and the marks were collated and entered into the inmate's record. These figures were monitored by the governor and the institutional board on an ongoing basis to assess the progress of each inmate and his response to reformatory treatment. Inmates in hospital were not disadvantaged by this system and were awarded marks based on the average of the previous week, with the approval of the medical officer. At its meeting, usually held during the first week of every month, the institutional board reviewed each case and had the right to award up to sixteen merit marks in addition to those already earned. Once the totals were compiled, inmates were given small financial rewards or gratuities. Ordinary grade inmates received one penny for every twenty-five marks earned; special grade inmates one penny for every twenty marks. This money was held in trust by the CDPAS (later by the BAI) and used to assist the inmate upon his release.[18] If an ordinary grade inmate earned the maximum number of marks possible within a six-week period he was eligible to write and receive a letter, as well as a visitor.[19] A decision was then made by institutional staff and the governor as to the boy's suitability for the higher grade.

SPECIAL GRADE

Life in the special grade brought many privileges for the inmates and the potential for a relaxation of some of the stricter regulations. Boys in this grade also received special letter-writing and visitation privileges. An inmate was allowed to write and receive a letter once he gained 400 marks. He was also allowed to receive a visitor for a period of up to thirty minutes. He had to earn another 400 marks in order to enjoy the same privileges again.[20] This was particularly useful for new inmates as it conditioned them into seeing not only the post-release financial benefits, but also such benefits as letters and visits as a privilege rather than an automatic entitlement. Borstal became a daily challenge where they could determine for themselves, by their adherence to the rules, how close they were to their next contact with family or friends. It should be remembered that, for the majority of these boys, their previous free lives were governed only by the laws of the street; the borstal system provided them with an early and important opportunity to modify their own behaviour.

Certain comforts were allowed in the cell, such as furniture and small pictures or photographs. Each boy in this grade was also permitted to have an 'iron bedstead', a 'looking-glass' and a 'strip of carpet'.[21] These could certainly have been deemed to be luxury items but, more importantly for the inmates, they were symbols of their achievement, their progress and their efforts at self-improvement. In the evening there could be limited fraternising with other special grade inmates. For each three-month period spent in the special grade, inmates received a good conduct badge, which brought with it a small payment. The first badge earned two shillings and the second and subsequent earned three shillings each. The money could be used to purchase extra food or could be reserved for discharge. Another important concession for those in the special grade was a thirty-minute visiting time, compared with twenty minutes for inmates in the ordinary grade.[22] Fahy quotes a document known as the 'Borstal Book', which states that 'the task is not to break or knead him [the offender] into shape, but to stimulate some power within to regulate conduct aright'.[23] The special grade acted as a tool, an incentive for inmates to regulate themselves and keep out of a somewhat harsher existence in the penal grade.

Special grade inmates were given certain dietary privileges, with a number of almost luxurious additions to their weekly food intake.[24] The privileges of the special grade did come at a cost to the inmates, however: each boy had to give something of himself by way of continuing to maintain a high standard of behaviour and to exercise restraint and self-control in the often fractious environment of a penal institution. The GPB argued that the system was designed to persuade each inmate that hard work and good behaviour would indeed be rewarded by increased freedoms and benefits within the institution, while raising the prospect of an early release. On the other hand, 'persistent idleness entailed prompt punishment, the withholding of privileges and a postponement of release'.[25]

Demoting an inmate from the special to the ordinary grade was highly unusual in Clonmel borstal. It was far more likely that a boy would be sent directly to the penal grade. During his time in charge at Clonmel, governor John Connor never sent an inmate from the special to the ordinary grade: he felt that it was more appropriate for a boy, if he had abused his privileges, to be subjected to the harsher conditions of the penal grade. A demotion of just one grade would have little effect, in his opinion, but the sudden loss of privileges, coupled with the many sanctions of the newly punitive regime, was likely to have a far greater impact.[26] The mobility of inmates between grades was a source of ongoing discussion between the management of Clonmel borstal and the GPB as both sides sought to arrive at a consensus as to how decisions should be made on the issue. In 1913 the Board pointed out to the new governor, Major Dobbin, that, although good conduct should be taken into account when punishing a special grade inmate, only boys who maintained the highest standards of discipline were to be retained at that level. Misdemeanours such as disobedience, not following orders or threatening an officer were grounds for automatic removal from the special grade.[27] In general, removal from this grade was wholly undesirable for staff and there is no evidence that officers and the governors were enthusiastic about demoting inmates. For an inmate, demotion represented not merely a theoretical device used by their superiors to exact change, but a radical and swift deterioration in their lifestyle, designed to shock them back into submission and self-control.

PENAL GRADE

An inmate was generally placed in the penal grade for 'idleness or misconduct' or if considered a bad influence over those in the higher grades. The regulation guiding the penal grade stated that an inmate should not be 'detained here longer than necessary in the interests of himself and others' but, while in the penal grade, he will be 'employed in separation at work of a hard and laborious nature, receiving no gratuity'.[28] The conditions of the penal grade could be considered harsh but they were designed to create an incentive for better conduct. As long as inmates remained in this grade they would receive no visitors or letters.[29] While the lack of contact with the outside world was considered to be in the boy's best interests, it was nonetheless a challenging stimulus for change. Osborough argues that a significant disadvantage for penal grade inmates was that, unlike other grades, they could not earn gratuities for good conduct.[30]

Penal grade inmates suffered further indignities. They were not permitted to associate with those in the higher grades and did not have access to the recreation room to play games in the evenings. Their cells contained minimal furnishings and none of the trappings afforded to those in the special grade. All of the boys shared a common diet but the special grade brought with it certain luxurious additions on specifically assigned days. Penal grade inmates were allocated the basic diet of the institution with no additions at all. Such treatment had a number of purposes. At a basic level it was the denial of luxury and a form of punishment for whatever reason. It also represented the setting apart of penal grade inmates from their peers – they had been rejected as unsuitable in character and behaviour and consigned to a lower class within the institution. The isolation of these boys was central to their punishment and, unlike some of those in the ordinary grade, they dined alone. This was partly to prevent the spread of their negative influence but was mostly a punitive measure. A 1913 inspection report recommended that penal grade inmates should be even further isolated and directed that the GPB and the institution make provisions in this direction.[31] The exact nature of the changes sought is not known but this report is indicative of the approach taken by the penal authorities to those in this grade. The denial of privileges and the restrictions to which the boys were subjected was a form of social control designed to remind them of their indiscretions at every juncture. This was further compounded by the fact that penal grade inmates were ordered, under the regulations of the Prevention of Crime Act 1908, to wear clothing that was deemed 'drab'.[32] The number of inmates held in the penal grade at Clonmel borstal cannot be fully determined but a 1912 inspection report does provide some data. In January of that year the special grade held fifty inmates, the ordinary grade thirty-five, while the penal grade held just three boys.[33] While this should not be taken to signify any wider trend within the institution, it does represent an insight into the state of penal discipline in Clonmel borstal at that particular time. It appears that at this point the staff were successful in maintaining discipline among the inmates, the majority of whom were aware of the benefits of good conduct.

APPARATUS OF PENAL DISCIPLINE

The method of responding to incidences of indiscipline within the borstal was on a par with that of the wider prison system. A number of different parties were involved and, when indiscipline occurred, a procedure to investigate and formulate a response was activated. An official with an ongoing interest in local prisons was the visiting justice, whose role was set down in legislation. Visiting justices were first appointed in England in 1877 with the nationalisation of prisons and were given powers to visit and inspect local prisons.[34] Under the Prisons Act (England) 1877 the visiting justice was described as being a justice of the peace whose jurisdiction was the area in which a prison was located. His remit was to enter the prison and inspect the condition of the prisoners and their surroundings. His observations and recommendations were to be entered in the gaoler's visitors' book and brought to the attention of the Prison Commissioners. The Act precluded the justice from visiting any prisoner facing capital punishment.[35] Visiting justices began work in Ireland with the foundation of the GPB two years after the Act. Radzinowicz and Hood describe the work of visiting justices in British prisons as 'weak'.[36] They were essentially members of the local judiciary and often visited as a committee. The Gladstone Committee advocated local participation in visiting committees and in prisons generally as this would inevitably be invaluable to the work of discharged prisoners' aid societies.[37] In the early years of the GPB it was found that visiting justices were largely ineffective and had little or no influence. In 1884 the Royal Commission on Irish Prisons concluded that the visiting justices were 'indifferent' in their public duty and were of little value in ensuring the proper treatment of prisoners. The result was that the public believed the justices contributed little or nothing to prison administration.[38] The Commission went on to call for 'the most entire feeling of co-operation' between visiting justices and prison authorities, in order to ensure the most efficient possible working of the prison system.[39]

The Gladstone Committee sought to redefine the role of the visiting justice and made a number of definitive recommendations in this regard. It proposed that the visiting committee should meet at least once a month and should be joined at their meeting by the prison governor or his representative. Justices were to be given the power to make representations to the prison authorities as they saw fit on the needs and requirements of the institution. They would also report on suggested repairs to the buildings or modifications to the system, the diet of prisoners, the requirements for prison labour and, significantly, on the state of prison staff.[40] Many of these functions already existed but were simply not carried out to their fullest extent and the hope of the Gladstone Committee was that the role of the visiting justice would gain a new momentum within the penal system. By the time the borstal institution was founded in Ireland, their role had indeed expanded. Visiting justices attended Clonmel in committee and individually. Their reports were often quoted when the governor, the BAI or the GPB needed support from the chief secretary or wished to influence public opinion. Several instances exist in the GPB correspondence where a complaint or recommendation on some matter arising from the visit to the borstal by a visiting justice triggered lengthy lines of communication to bring about a resolution. It appears that, by 1906, the visiting justice held greater sway in the Irish penal system or, at least, the borstal institution. When a visiting justice called at the borstal unaccompanied, it was usually because he was there at the request of the governor, to adjudicate on an incident of indiscipline.

At Clonmel borstal there was a considerable overlap between the visiting justices committee and the BAI. This was in keeping with the spirit of the Gladstone recommendations, which advocated strong local interest in the operation of penal institutions. The most prolific member of both bodies was BAI president Richard Bagwell. As a barrister, historian and politician, Bagwell was a highly influential figure and was held in high esteem in Clonmel. His activities in the BAI and as a visiting justice brought him into constant contact with the institution in the closing decade of his life. Another such individual was Alfred Fayle. Listed in the reports of the BAI as a justice of the peace, Fayle held the position of honorary treasurer of the association. The dual role of these figures was useful to the management of Clonmel borstal as their wide-ranging contacts ensured a greater knowledge of the daily working of the institution and a more hands-on approach to meeting the challenges of the system. There appeared to be effective collaboration between the visiting justices, the borstal management and the GPB. It should be remembered that each element had an agenda of its own and co-operation between all sides was paramount if the system, and ultimately those charged with working it, were to succeed.

BORSTAL DISCIPLINE

The structure of the grade system ensured that the borstal managers had a range of punishment options at their disposal when the need arose. The threat of the withdrawal of luxuries and privileges and the imposition of sanctions was exploited on an ongoing basis to induce the inmates to adhere to higher standards of behaviour. The hope was that this persistent good behaviour, coupled with all the educational benefits of borstal life, would somehow have a lasting effect on the boys. One of the disciplinary options that was not available at Clonmel borstal was physical punishment. In March 1912 Governor Connor sought guidance from his counterpart at Borstal in Kent on the extent of his powers to order a whipping.[41] His enquiry specifically referred to a certain category of juvenile-adults deemed 'incorrigible', who were usually sent to local prisons. It was not common for borstal inmates to be ejected on the basis that the institution found them too difficult but between 1906 and 1921 it did happen in a small number of cases. Governor Eccles of Kent replied to Governor Connor that it was regrettable that whipping was not allowed in borstal institutions as it could have meant 'the saving of many a lad'.[42] This non-violent approach to discipline was obviously in keeping with what *The Nationalist* described as the 'more humane and helpful treatment' that set the borstal institution apart from the rest of the prison system.[43] It is not clear what exactly, if anything, prompted this enquiry from Governor Connor. It may be an indication that he and his colleagues were encountering difficulty with certain inmates and had reached a point where they had exhausted all of their existing disciplinary options. Indeed the staff of Clonmel encountered many disciplinary challenges during this period and the response generally fell within a rigid framework that involved the GPB, the governor and the visiting justice.

The investigation of a breach of discipline at Clonmel borstal usually entailed a lengthy consultation process wherein every party to the incident was interviewed by both the governor and the visiting justice. It also led to a flurry of written communications. The dangers faced by the warders in their work at Clonmel were underlined by an incident at the institution in early March 1911. One of the officers, named by the governor as the shoemaker warder, Flannery, was supervising the inmates in the workshop when he was threatened and assaulted by two of the boys. According to Flannery, he was in the process of distributing tools to an inmate when another boy, Michael O'Dowd, left his seat and threatened him, before striking him in the face with his fist. The warder restrained his assailant before he was removed by another officer.[44] The second part of this attack took place when Flannery, in the process of restraining the boy, was threatened by another inmate, James Duffy, who approached him with a hammer and declared, 'By Christ Flannery if you do not let O'Dowd go I'll dash your brains out with this hammer.' According to Flannery, 'he then went for a rasp and punched me in the side with it'.[45]

When Governor Connor initially questioned O'Dowd, the boy took full responsibility and apologised. In his initial communication to the GPB, the governor described O'Dowd as 'a strong stubborn lad' who had been well behaved prior to this incident.[46] When questioned by Governor Connor about his attack on Flannery, Duffy apologised and claimed that 'people will do many things in the impulse of the moment and be sorry for it, as I am'. This inmate was already known as a troublemaker within the institution and had been punished on a number of occasions for other misdemeanours. Governor Connor recommended that the GPB call in the services of a visiting justice to deal with both cases.[47] The Board acceded and dispatched a visiting justice to Clonmel borstal, who ordered that both inmates be placed in the penal grade pending his ruling. Furthermore, it advised the governor to order the severest possible punishment to be imposed upon both inmates as it considered a physical attack on an officer to be among the most serious of crimes. The offence, according to the GPB, required that an example be made of both boys in order to maintain discipline.[48] The ultimate judgement in such cases, however, was left to the visiting justice.

While awaiting his arrival, the boys in question were placed as far apart as possible, to prevent them communicating prior to the judgement. They also exercised separately.[49] Two days after the alleged incident, the visiting justice, Alfred Fayle, attended Clonmel borstal. Inmate Michael O'Dowd was charged with assaulting Warder Flannery and admitted the offence. Inmate James Duffy was also charged with assault and with using threatening language against the warder. He also admitted the offence. Both boys were sentenced to fourteen days' number one punishment diet and close confinement.[50] The events of this incident are relatively straightforward and the evidence seemed to support the account given by Warder Flannery. The line of communications that detailed this incident does not, however, contain an account of the course of events from the point of view of the inmates. It did not reveal, for example, if any acts of coercion may have been brought to bear on the boys prior to their meeting with the visiting justice. There is also no further account of their relationship with Warder Flannery, although, in an apparent attempt at carrying out a balanced investigation, the GPB made a 'private' enquiry in a question to Governor Connor about the officer's work. The GPB sought clarification regarding the officer's efficiency, his popularity with other warders and his temperament.[51] The governor responded that Warder Flannery, who had begun working at Clonmel borstal two months earlier, having previously worked at Maryboro prison, had settled in well and seemed to be popular with the inmates. He appeared to be making a lot of effort with the boys and they seemed to be working well for him in return. Governor Connor assured his superiors that he would monitor the officer and report back to GPB if necessary.[52]

Not all of the inmates were successfully reformed and there were always new inmates, freshly removed from the local prisons where they had been awaiting trial. Immediately before that time they were on the streets, where they were governed by a different set of rules. This was clearly evidenced in the case of inmate Donald Hanly. In the summer of 1910 he was the subject of a serious controversy, which came to light during a routine inspection by the GPB. On 29 July the inspector visited the borstal and carried out his usual examination of buildings, staff and inmates. It was common for the inspectors to interview the inmates to ascertain whether they had any complaints or comments to make regarding their treatment or the conditions in which they lived and worked. During a conversation with Donald Hanly, the boy claimed that, on 14 July, Warders Meaney and Edwards entered his cell and beat him. He alleged that he was 'black and blue' when he was examined but that these marks were on his legs and buttocks and he did not wish to show these areas to the medical officer.[53] This allegation is somewhat unusual in that it came to light in a rather unconventional manner. It is also curious in that it was not immediately reported to the GPB at the time it allegedly occurred. The evidence here suggests that this inspection was the first time the matter came to the Board's attention.

In his report, Inspector MacDermot appeared to discount the boy's allegations. He pointed out that an inmate would not usually object to submitting himself to medical examination and that no other marks had been found on his body. He dismissed the allegation, reporting instead that the boy had been abusive and had used foul language on the day in question.[54] MacDermot made a more specific report on the matter to the GPB a few days later. It revealed that a charge of disobedience against the inmate had been investigated by the governor at the time but that the allegation of personal violence carried out by the warders was made for the first time during the inspection of 30 July. He reiterated the evidence of the medical officer, who had found no marks on the boy prior to him undergoing punishment for disobedience. His investigation had made clear that inmate Donald Hanly was one of the worst boys in Clonmel borstal at that time, 'one of the stunted prisoners by which is the product of Belfast slum life'.[55] Following this report the Board ordered that a visiting justice be sent to the borstal to make a ruling on the matter.

As was always the case in such situations, the visiting justice received oral and written evidence from all the parties to this alleged incident. According to Warder Meaney, he was on duty in the hall on the evening of 28 June when he opened the door of the inmate's cell to find him lying on the floor. When he asked him to get into his bed the boy rushed towards him and 'would have assaulted me had I not caught hold of him and prevented him'. At this point, Warder Edwards came to his colleague's assistance; all the while the inmate was using foul language towards them both. Warder Meaney denied using any form of physical violence against the boy but claimed that he simply restrained him in order to prevent an assault.[56] For his part, Warder Edwards supported the other officer's account of the episode, re-stating that Hanly had attempted to assault his colleague and that both men had sought only to restrain him.[57] The visiting justice also questioned the institution's medical officer, Dr O'Brien, who gave evidence of having been called to the inmate's cell on the evening of 29 June after the boy complained of having been beaten by two officers and of having swollen and bruised arms. Dr O'Brien found no marks on the boy's body and asked if he had any further complaints, to which he replied that he did not.[58] The inmate himself was questioned by the visiting justice, Mr Fayle, though to what extent is not clear. When asked why he did not get into bed when ordered, he replied that he would have done so if he had not been asked in such an insulting way. In any event he claimed, 'there's no use in I saying anything, but both of them beat me and I was black and blue after them'.[59] The charge of making a false allegation against the two warders was, in the opinion of the visiting justice, 'clearly proved' and inmate Donald Hanly was given fourteen days' close confinement on number one punishment diet.[60]

Such cases leave the GPB system of investigating misdemeanours at the borstal open to questioning. According to the inspector, the boy had a reputation for being troublesome. This could be construed as meaning that he had enemies among the staff. The minute details of the incident itself are excluded from the recorded evidence, which could be open to interpretation. For instance, what was the nature of the approach made by the officer? What was the tone used when addressing the inmate? Was he thought likely to be easily provoked into some type of violent reaction and was this the intention of the officers? Did the officers have an opportunity to devise a defence strategy prior to the arrival of the visiting justice? Why was the matter of an inmate seeking medical attention on the grounds that he had been assaulted not immediately reported to the GPB? These questions are not asked now to suggest that the officers or their superiors were engaged in any form of conspiracy. Instead, they highlight obvious deficiencies in the system. The investigation seems to have been unbalanced and the various parties could be open to the accusation of closing ranks to protect the integrity of the institution and its officers.

Disciplinary issues also seem to have been aggravated by loyalties. For example, on 10 June, Warder John Byrne filed a formal disciplinary complaint, again against inmate Donald Hanly. He was accused of running towards Byrne 'in a fighting manner' after the officer reprimanded him for not being at his place in the workshop. Hanly allegedly threatened the officer with his fists and told him that 'you're not fit to put me to my cell'.[61] When he was brought before Governor Connor (as was standard procedure), the inmate claimed in his defence that Warder Byrne threatened 'to stick the knife in him up to the maker's name'. The warder denied this allegation and was supported by the evidence of ten of the twelve remaining boys in the workshop, all of whom were interviewed individually by the governor. The two boys who supported the claims, Samuels and Peters, were both from Belfast, as was inmate Hanly.[62] As the incident had expanded beyond a minor incident in the workshop, it was decided by the governor to request the assistance of a visiting justice. Prior to his arrival, Hanly was placed in his cell under confinement while the other boys were allowed to continue in the workshop.[63]

On 15 June, the visiting justice, Randal K. Moore, a member of the BAI, called at Clonmel borstal to hear the charges against the three inmates involved in the accusation against Warder Byrne. Inmate Donald Hanly was given close confinement on number one punishment diet. Inmates Samuels and Peters, who supported the claim of assault against the warder, were admonished with a severe caution. This caused the GPB to question whether the inmates had actually been charged with conspiracy. The Board was also curious as to whether or not the inmates had been placed in the penal grade.[64] As in an earlier case, it was usually automatic for the governor to place offending inmates in the penal grade when the evidence against them appeared unambiguous but on this occasion Governor Connor did not take such action and this omission incurred the wrath of his superiors. In his own defence, the governor argued that the charge of making false statements was not serious enough for him, under his existing powers, to demote inmates Samuels and Peters to the penal grade, although that would have been his desire. In any event the visiting justice had disposed of the case and not recommended the penal grade for these boys. He went on to point out that there were five or six 'bad boys' from Belfast in the institution at that time and he would be removing them from the borstal were it not for the hope that he would be able to 'do something better with them' if he were given additional space for work and isolation.[65] Ultimately inmate Peters was removed to the penal grade for another offence and both boys remained unrepentant over their role in the accusation against Warder Byrne.[66]

This case brings to light a number of issues around penal discipline at Clonmel borstal. Firstly, it serves to highlight the sense of powerlessness felt by the governor and staff in responding to insubordination by inmates. The local management was often caught in a bureaucratic wasteland between the visiting justice and the GPB. The governor's powers were not so wide-reaching that he felt he could automatically dismiss an inmate to the penal grade without consulting his superiors. Secondly, this very problem did ensure that a system of checks and balances was in place and protected the governor and his staff from allegations of mistreatment of the inmates. The GPB monitored every step of the process of disciplining a boy, advising the governor and seeking explanations when it felt something was not clear. However, there was always room for collusion on the part of the warders, though it should be stated that no evidence of such behaviour has been found. Thirdly, the work of the institution was hampered from time to time by a lack of adequate space, which was of paramount importance in making a method of discipline such as the grade system function correctly. Governor Connor expressed his concerns on this issue to the GPB as early as 1908. The cells at Clonmel were so small and the windows so close together that it was difficult to maintain discipline and an even greater challenge trying to isolate those under punishment. When they were corrected for some indiscretion they immediately 'flare up with bad word made the first use of'.[67] The point was that it was difficult to

exploit the disciplinary procedures of the borstal system to their fullest
extent within the confines of the facilities at Clonmel.

A highly unusual breach of discipline, if it can be defined as such,
took place at the borstal in late 1912. The inmate involved, seventeen-year-old Peter Doyle, a native of Clonmel town, was under
borstal detention for stealing three bullocks. He had been known to
police for approximately eight years and had previously resided with
his father, who himself was of poor character and 'would be glad to
know his son committed theft provided he was not caught'.[68] At 4.15
pm on 11 November 1912, Warder Robert Neill visited the boy in his
cell to observe him at work at mat-making. He reported finding the
boy lying on the floor with a piece of yarn wound around his neck and
tied to one of the bars on the window. It was, in the opinion of the officer, 'a bogus attempt to commit suicide'.[69] The warder reported this
discovery to the governor, who sent for the medical officer, Dr
O'Brien. He examined the inmate and declared that in his opinion he
was 'shamming', recommending that he be placed under restraint.[70]

In his report on this incident, Governor Connor described the boy
as having been well behaved for a considerable length of time but that
he had recently become very troublesome. Doyle stated that he had
not intended to harm himself but nonetheless the governor requested
the presence of the visiting justice.[71] On 15 November, James Cahill
JP heard the case against the boy, who admitted the charge against
him, expressed his regret and assured the visiting justice of his good
conduct in the future. On this basis, Mr Cahill gave him close confinement and number one punishment diet for a period of seven days.
This was a lesser sentence than that usually handed down but the visiting justice considered this to be a relatively harmless 'crime' and the
inmate had not actually intended to physically harm himself.[72]

Not all of the instances of indiscipline at Clonmel borstal originated with acts of physical violence. On the morning of 16 February
1912, Warder Linton was carrying out his breakfast inspection of the
boys in their cells when he discovered inmate William Casey vandal-
ising a number of items with a shoemaker's knife. The matter was
immediately reported to the chief warder and both men entering the
cell provoked a violent reaction from the inmate. The articles
destroyed were a blanket, a rug, a pair of sheets, a pair of slippers, a
pillowcase and a slip.[73] According to the chief warder, the inmate,
who was employed in the shoemaker's workshop, displayed considerable violence while being placed under restraint within his cell; his

act of vandalism was apparently without provocation.[74] How an inmate might have a shoemaker's knife in his cell was a question addressed by the governor in his report on the incident to the GPB. Casey was one of a number of boys who worked both in the shoemaker's workshop and in his cell, thus explaining the presence of the knife. He was, apparently, 'one of the last lads in the institution that we would suspect of doing any mischief with it'. It was the opinion of the governor that the boy was trying to feign insanity as, when held in isolation for the day after the incident, he refused to communicate with the officers and his clergyman.[75]

James Cahill was summoned to deal with the matter as visiting justice. The inmate admitted the offence of causing damage to the institution's property but expressed no regret at having done so. He was found guilty of the offence and was given what appeared to be the standard punishment of fourteen days' close confinement with number one punishment diet.[76] The crime of vandalism or damage to property was not generally typical of the documented cases of indiscipline at Clonmel borstal, though it was not a completely isolated case.

One defence put forward by a borstal inmate against allegations of indiscipline was to respond with claims of assault or brutality by officers of the institution. Inmate Michael Howard was accused by Warder Kenefick of misbehaving in the bathroom by jumping in and out of the bath naked while throwing boots at other inmates. When threatened with report, the boy said that he would claim to the governor that he himself had been assaulted by the warder. According to the officer the boy had already mildly injured his own face by striking it against the bath during the course of his horseplay.[77] In his own written response to the officer's evidence, Howard stated that he was in the bath when Warder Kenefick 'threatened that he would drown me in the water and then he came in and struck me in the eye without any reason'.[78] Unsurprisingly, Warder Kenefick, for his part, roundly denied ever assaulting the boy or even attempting to do so.[79] In his report on the case to the GPB, Governor Connor repeated the boy's claim that Warder Kenefick assaulted him by striking him in the eye. Having inspected the inmate's right eye after the event, the governor found some redness. The following morning he found that the skin around the eye had broken and was bleeding but strongly believed that the injury was self-inflicted in order to strengthen his case against 'the oldest and best officer in the institution'. His submission to the GPB described the boy as a 'giddy erratic little fellow'.

He filed a charge of making a false accusation against an officer and requested the assistance of a visiting justice.[80] This was another case heard by Cahill, to whom the inmate denied misconduct in the bathroom and repeated his claim against Warder Kenefick. The case against the boy was deemed to be proved and he was given fourteen days' close confinement with number one punishment. Apart from finding the evidence of the institutional staff somewhat more credible, Cahill found that, as the mark on the boy's face had not turned into a black eye, it must have been a self-inflicted injury.[81] The counter-accusation formed a recurring resistance against charges of misbehaviour by inmates as it momentarily deflected attention away from their own alleged misdeed. It is not possible to determine the validity of their claims from the sources.

There is some evidence to suggest that the GPB closely monitored the warders' behaviour at Clonmel borstal and the inspectors constantly reported as to their suitability for work with juvenile-adult offenders. If an officer was deemed unsuitable for the institution, his removal to another part of the prison service was recommended by the Board's inspector. An officer could himself become a subject of investigation in much the same way as the inmates. One such case occurred in March 1914 during a routine GPB inspection. A group of inmates were working under supervision in the workshop when one, George Meehan, walked over to talk with another, James Boyle. The discussion was of an innocent nature: both boys were talking about the boot Meehan was making. At the time Meehan was sharpening his knife and, as he was walking away, he claimed to have playfully prodded the other boy in the stomach with it. It was not until several minutes later that Boyle realised that his shirt was wet and he was bleeding. A third boy asked an officer, Warder Stacey, for some cloth, saying that Boyle had merely scratched himself. Stacey, who was not actually on duty in that particular workshop, did not examine the wound and the matter was not brought to the attention of the GPB until Boyle's injury was discovered by the inspector.[82]

The incident sparked a stream of internal investigations as the management of Clonmel borstal sought to determine the exact circumstance of the incident. The injured party, Boyle, briefly outlined the events from his perspective in a short handwritten note. He described how he had been working on a shoe and went over to the other boy to ask a question relating to his work. Upon receiving the answer he walked away and, as he did so, the other boy, Meehan, struck him in the stomach with his knife.[83] This explanation is somewhat damaging to Meehan as it explains nothing of the playful exchange between the two boys, outlined by the inspector in his report. In further oral responses to specific questions from the (recently appointed) governor Major Dobbin, Boyle stated that he did not report the incident as he did not wish to 'get anyone into trouble'. He went on to confirm that the other boy did not stab him on purpose and that he himself was indeed 'quite well'.[84] For his part, the 'assailant' recounted the incident in much the same way and insisted that when he pointed the knife at Boyle it was purely in fun and that 'it slipped and went into him'.[85] The matter was first discovered by an officer of the institution at lock-up time that evening when Boyle attracted the attention of Warder Lilly and sought assistance. He reassured the warder that the stabbing was purely accidental.[86]

The main problem for the institution regarding this accident was that it was allowed to happen in the workshop and no warder appeared to notice what had taken place. It emerged in the subsequent internal investigation that, at the exact moment of the stabbing, the inmates were unsupervised. It was during the questioning of a Warder Stacey that the governor learned that the full-time shoemaker Warder Flannery had actually left his post to go to the storeroom. In doing so he left Warder Stacey, who was also supervising an adjoining workshop, in charge.[87] Warder Flannery admitted in his evidence that he was out of the workshop but provided a conflicting account as to how the matter was reported. He claimed to have found out at 12.45 pm and immediately informed the governor.[88] However, this statement made no mention of the question of whether Warder Flannery had permission to leave his post at this time. In his evidence, the medical officer, Dr O'Brien, outlined the extent of the injuries to Boyle. The wound did not penetrate his stomach or bowel and was not of a serious nature. Attached to Dr O'Brien's report was a summary report on the incident, probably written by the governor. It confirmed that there was no ill-feeling between the inmates concerned and that Boyle would be able to return to his work in a number of days, having been ordered to rest by the medical officer. Nonetheless the matter could not go unpunished; Meehan was mildly reprimanded and removed to the ordinary grade; he was 'penitent', however, and 'it was believed he had learned a considerable lesson'.[89]

In his assessment of the matter, the GPB inspector decided that, while Warder Flannery's absence was not 'a contributory cause to any great extent', the matter would have been discovered immediately, or possibly even prevented, had he been present. The inspection report reprimanded the warder for leaving his post without official permission from the chief warder and described his conduct as 'irregular'. It was not satisfactory to leave two classes under the supervision of just one officer, as Warder Flannery had done. The inspector concluded by stating that 'explicit' instructions had been issued to the institution to prevent such an incident from happening again.[90] The report made no mention of the fact that, when approached for some cloth to assist an inmate who had been scratched, Warder Stacey failed to investigate the matter fully for himself.

When an inmate entered Clonmel borstal, the governor and his staff were faced with a new challenge: another character that would have to be remoulded and brought into line with common standards of civilised human behaviour and decency. The disciplinary procedures of the borstal institution, with their roots in earlier ideas, were formulated into a unique grade system, providing a set of incentives designed to remedy the inmates' behavioural deficiencies. The discipline meted out to the boys was determined by a visiting justice, who was summoned to the institution by the governor or the GPB in the event of a suspected serious transgression of the regulations. A number of conclusions can be drawn. The procedure usually entailed a fairly thorough investigation whereby all of the parties to an incident were interviewed and provided written submissions to the visiting justice. In most cases, there was little or no opportunity for the accused inmate to state his case. Neither would the majority of borstal boys have had the articulacy to defend themselves before the imposing figures of the visiting justice, the governor and the warders. As it was an internal institutional inquiry, there was no legal representation for the inmate. A number of searching questions remain in all of these cases and it is possible that pressure could have been brought to bear on any inmate at the centre of a disciplinary procedure. The mechanism of this process was weighted in favour of the institution and against the inmate. This is reinforced by the fact that the visiting justices usually had strong links with the institution and its personnel through their work with the BAI. It was always in the interests of the borstal, the BAI and the GPB to identify, and stamp out, instances of poor discipline, as all three bodies were in some way dependent on public support. It must be stressed that there is no evidence of such irregular conduct but it should be noted that the documents recording the cases outlined in this chapter were all generated and maintained by the GPB or its agencies. There is, in a sense, no credible independent verification that the procedures were always followed fairly and that the rights and character of an inmate were protected.

NOTES

1. Sydney A. Moseley, *The Truth about Borstal* (London: Cecil Palmer, 1926), p. 34.
2. Osborough, *Borstal in Ireland*, p. 2.
3. Osborough, *Borstal in Ireland*, p. 2.
4. Hood, *Borstal Re-assessed*, p. 15.
5. NLI, *Report from the Departmental Committee on Prisons*, vi, 1 [C 7702-1], H.L. 1895, 3.
6. NLI, *Report from the Departmental Committee on Prisons*, vi, 1 [C 7702-1], H.L. 1895, 3.
7. *The Nationalist*, 31 May 1911.
8. NLI, *Twenty-ninth Report of the General Prisons Board*, x [Cd-3698], H.L. 1905–6, xi, 86.
9. *The Nationalist*, 26 May 1909.
10. NAI, GPB, CR, Borstal institution for males in Ireland; instructions for carrying out regulations under the Prevention of Crime Act 1908, 19 November 1909.
11. *The Treasury*, March 1910.
12. NAI, GPB, CR, Dobbin to the chairman of the GPB, 16 March 1914, GPB/2880/1914.
13. NAI, GPB, CR, GPB minute approving Major Dobbin's suggestion, GPB/2880/1914.
14. NAI, GPB, CR, Dobbin to GPB, 4 May 1914, GPB/2880/1914.
15. NAI, GPB, Clonmel Borstal Memoranda, Regulations with respect to Borstal Institutions for males in Ireland, May 1909, GPB/XB5.
16. *The Treasury*, March 1910.
17. NAI, GPB, Clonmel Borstal Memoranda, Regulations with respect to Borstal Institutions for males in Ireland, May 1909, GPB/XB5.
18. NAI, GPB, CR, Borstal institution for males in Ireland; instructions for carrying out regulations under the Prevention of Crime Act 1908, 19 November 1909, GPB/1825/1911.
19. NAI, GPB, Clonmel Borstal Memoranda, Regulations with respect to Borstal Institutions for males in Ireland, May 1909, GPB/XB5.
20. NAI, GPB, CR, Borstal institution for males in Ireland; instructions for carrying out regulations under the Prevention of Crime Act 1908, 19 November 1909
21. NAI, GPB, CR, Borstal institution for males in Ireland; instructions for carrying out regulations under the Prevention of Crime Act 1908, 19 November 1909.
22. NAI, Clonmel Borstal Memoranda, 1908–30, Regulations with respect to Borstal Institutions for males in Ireland, 29 July 1909, GPB/XB5.
23. Fahy, 'The boy criminal', p. 43.
24. NLI, *Twenty-ninth Report of the General Prisons Board*, x [Cd-3698], H.L. 1905–6, xi, 86.
25. NLI, *Thirty-fourth report of the General Prisons Board*, vii [Cd-6365], H.L. 1911–2, ii, 21.
26. NAI, GPB, CR, John Connor to Major Dobbin, 24 April 1913, GPB/1911/1835.
27. NAI, GPB, CR, GPB to Major Dobbin, 26 July 1913, GPB/1911/1835.
28. NAI, Clonmel Borstal Memoranda, 1908–30, Regulations with respect to Borstal Institutions for males in Ireland, 29 July 1909, GPB/XB5.
29. NAI, GPB, CR, Borstal institution for males in Ireland; instructions for carrying out regulations under the Prevention of Crime Act 1908, 19 November 1909, GPB/1825/1911.
30. Osborough, *Borstal in Ireland*, p. 14.
31. NAI, GPB CR, Inspection report, 29 March 1913, GPB/3680/1914.
32. NAI, GPB CR, Borstal institution for males in Ireland; instructions for carrying out regulations under the Prevention of Crime Act 1908, 19 November 1909, GPB/1825/1911.
33. NAI, GPB, CR, Inspection report, 27 January 1912, GPB/727/1912.
34. Radzinowicz, Roger Hood, *A History of English Criminal Law*, p. 570.
35. NLI, *Report from the Departmental Committee on Prisons*, vi, 1 [C 7702-1], H.L. 1895, 7.
36. Radzinowicz, Hood, *A History of English Criminal Law*, p. 571.
37. NLI, *Report from the Departmental Committee on Prisons*, vi, 1 [C 7702-1], H.L. 1895, 3.
38. NLI, *Second Report of the Royal Commission on Prisons in Ireland*, xxxviii [C-4145], H.L. 1883–4, v, 11.

39. NLI, *Second Report of the Royal Commission on Prisons in Ireland*, xxxviii [C-4145], H.L. 1883–4, v, 12.
40. NLI, *Report from the Departmental Committee on Prisons*, vi, 1 [C 7702-1], H.L. 1895, x, 3.
41. NAI, GPB, CR, Governor Connor to Governor Eccles, 6 March 1912, GPB/1835/1911.
42. NAI, GPB, CR, Letter from Governor Eccles to Governor Connor, 8 March 1912, GPB/1835/1911.
43. *The Nationalist*, 11 March 1908.
44. NAI, GPB, CR, Warder F. to Governor Connor, 2 March 1911, GPB/1835/1911.
45. NAI, GPB, CR, Warder F. to Governor Connor, 2 March 1911, GPB/1835/1911.
46. NAI, GPB, CR, Governor Connor to the GPB, 2 March 1911, GPB/1835/1911.
47. NAI, GPB, CR, Governor Connor to the GPB, 2 March 1911, GPB/1835/1911.
48. NAI, GPB, CR, GPB minute, 3 March 1911, GPB/1835/1911.
49. NAI, GPB, CR, Governor Connor to GPB, 4 March 1911, GPB/1835/1911.
50. NAI, GPB, CR, extract from Visiting Committee's minute book, 4 March 1911, GPB/1835/1911.
51. NAI, GPB, CR, GPB to Governor Connor, 6 March 1911, GPB/1835/1911.
52. NAI, GPB, CR, Governor Connor's response, 8 March 1911, GPB/1835/1911.
53. NAI, GPB, CR, Inspection report, 30 July 1910, GPB/1835/1911.
54. NAI, GPB, CR, Inspection report, 30 July 1910, GPB/1835/1911.
55. NAI, GPB, CR, GPB minute, 3 August 1910, GPB/1835/1911.
56. NAI, GPB, CR, evidence of Warder M., 11 August 1910, GPB/1835/1911.
57. NAI, GPB, CR, evidence of Warder E., 11 August 1910, GPB/1835/1911.
58. NAI, GPB, CR, evidence of Dr O'Brien, 11 August 1910, GPB/1835/1911.
59. NAI, GPB, CR, evidence of Warder E, 11 August 1910, GPB/1835/1911.
60. NAI, GPB, CR, W.H. Tyther to GPB, 11 August 1910, GPB/1835/1911.
61. NAI, GPB, CR, form for reporting a prisoner to the governor, 9 June 1910, GPB/1835/1911.
62. NAI, GPB, CR, Governor Connor to GPB, 9 June 1910, GPB/1835/1911.
63. NAI, GPB, CR, GPB minute, 21 June 1910, GPB/1835/1911.
64. NAI, GPB, CR, Governor Connor to GPB, 18 June 1910, GPB/1835/1911.
65. NAI, GPB, CR, Governor Connor to GPB, 21 June 1910, GPB/1835/1911.
66. NAI, GPB, CR, Governor Connor to GPB, 21 June 1910, GPB/1835/1911.
67. NAI, GPB, CR, Governor Connor to GPB, 14 July 1908, GPB/1834/1911.
68. NAI, GPB, CR, form of enquiry as to prisoner's eligibility for borstal treatment, 16 December 1911, GPB/9495/1912.
69. NAI, GPB, CR, Warder R.N. to Governor Connor, 12 November 1912, GPB/9495/1912.
70. NAI, GPB, CR, extract from medical officer's journal, 12 November 1912, GPB/9495/1912.
71. NAI, GPB, CR, Governor Connor to GPB, 12 November 1912, GPB/9495/1912.
72. NAI, GPB, CR, extract from visiting justice's book, 15 November 1912, GPB/9495/1912.
73. NAI, GPB, CR, Warder H.L. to governor, GPB/1584/1912.
74. NAI, GPB, CR, chief warder to governor, GPB/1584/1912.
75. NAI, GPB, CR, Governor Connor to GPB, GPB/1584/1912.
76. NAI, GPB, CR, extract from visiting justice book, 19 February 1912, GPB/1584/1912.
77. NAI, GPB, CR, Warder J.K. to governor, GPB/9616/1912.
78. NAI, GPB, CR, written evidence of inmate M.W., 16 November 1912, GPB/9616/1912.
79. NAI, GPB, CR, written evidence of Warder J.K., 16 November 1912, GPB/9616/1912.
80. NAI, GPB, CR, Governor Connor to the GPB, GPB/9616/1912.
81. NAI, GPB, CR, extract from Visiting Committee minute book, 19 November 1912, GPB/9616/1912.
82. NAI, GPB, CR, Inspector A.J. Owen Lewis to GPB, 7 March 1914, GPB/1511/1914.
83. NAI, GPB, CR, written evidence of inmate J.G., GPB/1511/1914.
84. NAI, GPB, CR, oral replies of inmate J.G. recorded by Major Dobbin, GPB/1511/1914.
85. NAI, GPB, CR, evidence of inmate J.C., 3 March 1914, GPB/1511/1914.
86. NAI, GPB, CR, evidence of Warder L., 3 March 1914, GPB/1511/1914.
87. NAI, GPB, CR, evidence of Warder S., 3 March 1914, GPB/1511/1914.
88. NAI, GPB, CR, evidence of Warder F., 3 March 1914, GPB/1511/1914.
89. NAI, GPB, CR, extracts from medical officer's journal, 3 March 1914, GPB/1511/1914.
90. NAI, GPB, CR, A.J. Owen Lewis to GPB, 7 March 1914, GPB/1511/1914

CHAPTER SIX

Improving the body: meeting inmates' daily physical needs

One of the basic aims of the borstal institution was to make the inmates feel as if they were not prisoners in a standard county gaol. To fulfil this, those charged with the daily operation of Clonmel borstal were required to show innovation and courage as they gradually constructed the system over time. The governors, the GPB and the BAI constantly devised new methods of bringing about tangible reform in the inmates' lives. The daily routine was an important weapon in the reform process and the object of borstal treatment was to fill each day with activities that would bring about much-needed physical improvements and enhance the development of the mind through stimulating recreational and educational activities.

This chapter will outline the ways in which the routine of the ordinary prison was adapted to meet the requirements of a treatment process for the boys. It will focus on how the institution met the physical needs of inmates on a daily basis. Juvenile-adult offenders were identified by the borstal founders as usually physically deficient and often malnourished. The physical dimension of borstal treatment was, therefore, crucial to the overall development of offenders. The ability of Clonmel borstal to meet its requirements in this regard will be examined. The chapter will also provide an analysis of the recreational pursuits that were available to the boys, tracing the evolution from draughts and dominoes to a full-scale institutional band. It will examine the dietary provisions for the inmates: the administration governed meticulously the amount of food that a boy consumed each day. In anticipation of an inmate's eventual release from detention it was essential that the boys were equipped to compete in the labour market of early twentieth-century Ireland. The very significant contribution of the medical officer will also be discussed, using a number of case studies to explain the various different aspects of his work.[1] This chapter will look beyond the theoretical aims of the borstal system and the high ideals of Ruggles-Brise and the founders to reveal something of the everyday existence for the inmates and staff at Clonmel.

DAILY ROUTINE

The daily routine included healthy physical development, something that had been envisaged as the first stage of reform by Ruggles-Brise. Before assessing the substance of the routine, it is important to take account of two factors. This regime emerged in the early years of a system that was still very much in an experimental phase. Secondly, it should be noted that the system was aimed at unruly young men who had offended more than once. At the core of borstal treatment was the idea that it 'was designed more particularly for rough and undisciplined boys of the lounging and hooligan types, who appear to be drifting towards a career in crime'.[2] The system was not suitable for first offenders or those without good physical strength.[3] On the contrary, it was designed to have the maximum impact on a young repeat offender. For such individuals, a harsh and repetitive regime was most likely to bring about a positive outcome.

The inmates of Clonmel borstal had an early start to their day, rising at 5.30 am. At 6.10 am, prior to breakfast, they had to do fifty minutes of gymnastics and drill. Breakfast was served at 7.00 am. At 7.40 am the various work or educational activities started and continued until 11.45 am. At that time, the boys went on parade until lunch at midday. At 1.00 pm they were again on parade before returning to work from 2.00 pm to 4.30 pm.[4] At 6.00 pm they were marched to the Roman Catholic chapel, where prayers commenced at 6.10 pm. They were marched back to their cells at 6.30 pm and, depending on the day, there were further classes, recreation or a bath.[5] The daily routine was almost identical for all the boys but the evening brought some relief for those in the special grade as they were granted an hour-long recreation period.[6] Boys were locked in their cells at 7.30 pm.[7] The lights were switched off at 8.30 pm for all inmates.[8] There was some variation to this routine at weekends. On Saturdays throughout the year the routine was the same as weekdays until midday. After Saturday lunch was choir practice before prayers in the chapel at 2.00 pm. From 2.15 pm the boys began 'general singing practice', except for special grade inmates, who marched to games. Inmates washed between 3.00 pm and 5.00 pm, at which time they commenced supper. The boys did not rise until 7.00 am on

Sundays, and were served breakfast at 7.30 am. At 10.30 am, and again at 3.00 pm, they were summoned to 'divine service'.⁹ Though the routine was often severe and always repetitive, it contained most of the essential elements of the new penal reformatory regime envisaged by Ruggles-Brise and the Gladstone Committee over a decade earlier.

A first-hand account from 1910 describes the daily timetable at the Kent institution. The boys of England's first borstal also rose at 5.30 am and at 6.00 am they began an hour of physical drill. At 7.30 am, they began to fulfil their various work or educational commitments and stopped for lunch at noon. From 1.30 pm they once again resumed training, classes or work, finishing at 5.30 pm, when they were given supper. Every evening the boys went to a service in the chapel, which was followed by an address. Lights were switched off at 8.30 pm; though this may seem a particularly early hour, it has to be remembered that these inmates awoke the next day at 5.30 am, winter and summer.¹⁰ The boys at the borstals in Kent and Clonmel were favoured with visits by various travelling lecturers and other assorted individuals deemed worthy of sharing their experiences with juvenile-adults. These activities usually took place in the evening time after supper. The strict repetitive routine of drill, work, education, training and prayer was designed to condition the inmates into a life governed by duty and responsibility, leading ultimately to self-discipline.¹¹

The distinctions between the daily routines of the three grades of offender are not very clear, though there were some divergences. Penal grade inmates were often excluded from some of the evening lectures and other events. As the system grew, a band was formed and participation in this activity was normally reserved for ordinary and special grade inmates. If there was no activity planned after supper, the boys of the ordinary and penal grades usually returned to their cells for the night, while those in the special grade were allowed to spend some time together in the recreation room. One of the key differences between the borstal system and the nineteenth-century prison was the amount of time that inmates spent in their cells. When juveniles were in convict or local prisons they did not necessarily spend much of their day in education and had much more time to absorb the negative influences of their older mentors. One of the intentions of the borstal system was to fill the day, and sometimes the evening, with useful and productive activities.

PHYSICAL PURSUITS

This study has, on a number of occasions referred to the scientific research carried out by the founders of the borstal system when deciding upon the age category and specific characteristics of the inmates that the reformatory set about treating. Many of their findings related to the physiological make-up of young male offenders, which was why the resulting system placed so much emphasis on physical activity such as drill instruction and gymnastics. Evelyn Ruggles-Brise outlined some of the reasoning behind this aspect of the borstal system in an address to the International Penitentiary Congress in Washington D.C. in October 1910. His initial argument was that the human body was not fully developed until it reached the age of twenty-one and, therefore, the brain would not gain full maturity until that time. The result, he claimed, was that character was intrinsically linked with physical development, meaning that the personality and mentality of an average man would not be fully developed before that age. Children of the poorer classes developed much later, some as late as twenty-five or twenty-six years of age.[12] This was the reasoning behind selecting twenty-one as the upper age limit for borstal admission. Ruggles-Brise went on to cite evidence from a study of young men discharged from Pentonville prison in 1888. This class of offender was two and a half inches smaller in height and weighed approximately fourteen pounds less than their non-criminal peers in the general population. Of the same group of prisoners, 26 per cent had some form of disease or physical deformity. Most of these offenders were from the same class of criminals that found themselves the subject of repeated short prison sentences,[13] the category that would later become known as juvenile-adults. The evidence was clear to Ruggles-Brise, who believed that physical neglect and indeed malnourishment were among the key problems that needed to be addressed among the juvenile-adult inmates. Physical decline was both a cause and an effect of their offending and its reversal through the borstal system would inevitably go a long way towards arresting and turning around the decline in their character.

After the 1910 conversion from prison status, Clonmel borstal employed a full-time drill instructor warder, often from the armed forces, perhaps an ex-officer experienced in training soldiers. There are also many examples throughout the GPB correspondence of how, when being moved about inside the borstal complex, or outside, the inmates were always marched in group formation. This was in keeping with the disciplinarian style of borstal treatment and was intended to focus a boy's mind on maintaining order and control at all times, even when he was not carrying out formal duties. Drill practice was the principal physical activity at Clonmel but the institutional staff would have preferred to bring the Irish borstal into line with its English counterpart in the provision of sporting facilities.

Sporting activities at the Clonmel borstal were severely curtailed by the lack of space. Writing in May 1913, Governor Dobbin requested permission from the GPB to allow the institution's thirty-six special grade inmates the opportunity to participate in sport. In fine weather and the long summer evenings, he considered that this grade should be allowed, for one hour after supper each evening, to play handball and football under the supervision of the officers on duty. The facilities for these sports seemed quite humble, described as 'a fair wall in the mess yard' for the handball and 'a limited space at the back of the new buildings where a ball could be kicked'. Pointing out that chess, dominoes and draughts were, at that time, the only games played at Clonmel, the idea of an outdoor sport after a long day of labour 'would be beneficial'.[14] It is not known if this request was granted and there is no record of the addition of any substantial sporting facility during the period under consideration. In 1921, Governor Dobbin again drew the Board's attention to the dire state of the sports facilities. He pointed to a recent newspaper report stating that England's borstal institutions had stretched themselves financially with a capital investment of £1,000 per acre for new football grounds. Meanwhile, at Clonmel, cricket matches on the little patch of ground in front of the workshop block had been suspended. A cricket ball had accidentally been batted through a window, resulting in the loss of inmate McMahon's eye.[15] The only available ground for the boys to exercise was described later on as wholly unsuitable; in 1940, 'games and sports do not exist' at Clonmel.[16] Dobbin's request to allow inmates to partake in limited sporting activities represents what can be described as a valiant (or desperate) attempt by a governor who must have been envious of the facilities of the borstal institutions of England. This situation is another example of capital under-investment in Clonmel borstal during these years.

In 1910 the English Prison Commissioners reported the addition of a fully equipped gymnasium with a qualified instructor to the borstal institution in Kent. The new facility, it was claimed, 'has done wonders in improving the general physique and fitness of the lads'. In the coming year the boys at that institution would enjoy the benefits of football and cricket, thanks largely to ongoing structural developments at the facility.[17] It must be remembered that there were between six and seven hundred inmates at the Kent borstal at any given time and the investment in facilities reflected that. During 1911 there were just sixty-eight committals to Clonmel borstal.[18] The fact remained, however, that the governors and staff at Clonmel were given the same remit as those in Kent of producing visible physical change in their inmates. The two regimes were given very different sets of tools with which to bring this about.

RECREATION

One of the features that set the borstal apart from the regular local or convict prison was the provision of a recreation room for the inmates. At Clonmel borstal, special grade inmates were allowed to meet in the recreation for an hour each evening to play chess, draughts or dominoes. The GPB claimed in 1907 that the boys 'thoroughly appreciate' the recreation room and that it had not been abused in any way.[19] The latter comment was significant as it was important that the Board presented the most positive account possible of this facility; otherwise it might be regarded as representing a soft approach to a group that, essentially, were criminals. The provision of the recreation room was linked to the reform process and could, therefore, be justified as necessary, should anyone decide to challenge its provision. The report of 1906?07 pointed out that the boys' good conduct in the room continued.[20] The language of these reports was important because adverse public opinion on this matter might lose the GPB public support for the idea and the BAI much needed financial support.

The evidence suggests that the inmates of Clonmel borstal had limited contact with the outside world. News of political developments was certainly prohibited but even this could not be completely controlled because of the arrival of new inmates, all of whom were only too willing to disclose the latest happenings to a receptive audience. The availability of newspapers increased with time but, even then, the material that could be accessed by the boys was heavily censored. The start of World War One presented both a challenge and an opportunity to Governor Dobbin regarding how, or whether, to communicate developments to the inmates. In August 1914, he highlighted a difference in the rules for the borstal institutions of England and Scotland, where daily newspapers were available to inmates, and those of Ireland, where they were not.[21] The non-availability of newspapers in the Irish institution was obviously a conscious decision made by the British administration in Dublin Castle in order to prevent the spread of subversive material or nationalistic sentiment among the boys. However, Governor Dobbin felt that the 'present crisis' warranted making available the daily reports of the war on the noticeboard of the mess room, where the special grade inmates dined. He pointed out that this action would not only allow the boys to keep in touch with external events at such an important time but would also strengthen his own position, as most of them would greatly appreciate the gesture.[22]

The BAI had suggested that, with the approval of the visiting justices, special grade inmates should be supplied with weekly copies of an illustrated newspaper, *The Sphere*, as well as *The Gardner* and *The Daily Mirror*. Dobbin requested that *The Sphere* be bound on a quarterly basis at the expense of the GPB.[23] It should be remembered of course that the visiting justices' approval of this scheme was not very significant as several of these individuals, including Richard Bagwell, were also members of the BAI. The scheme was approved by the GPB, who replied to Governor Dobbin that 'it is of course assumed that the Governor will as in all cases exercise care to exclude all matter unsuitable for boys who may have morbid tendencies'.[24] The information in this reading material, or indeed the daily reports of the events of World War One, was not restricted to the boys of the special grade. It would have spread amongst the whole inmate population in any event. Providing it exclusively to the special grade boys was yet another of their privileges.

As time progressed the management of Clonmel borstal and the GPB took increasing advantage of new developments in visual media to entertain and educate the inmates. Lantern slides were used from 1910 or 1911 onwards to accompany some of the lectures given by an assortment of visitors to the institution. Some of the lectures combined education and recreation; these occasions were attended not only by the inmates but also by the staff members and their families. In 1919, the BAI sponsored such an event when it invited Mr D. O'Brien of Cork to give a lantern lecture on the war. Described as 'illustrated entertainment', the session opened with a map of Europe on the screen while the speaker explained the 'objects of the enemy upon the outbreak of war' before going on to discuss key developments. He used slides to illustrate his commentary on the various land, air and naval engagements. This event was attended by fifty-five inmates as well as the staff and their families, all of whom, it was reported, 'enjoyed the whole thoroughly'.[25]

The arrival of the cinema signalled a new form of entertainment. This was particularly significant during the years of World War One, when there was sometimes shown film footage taken on the battle-fields of Europe. In November 1916, Mr Magner, the owner of the local 'Theatre of Variety', provided the film, the equipment and an operator for a cinematic presentation on 'The Battle of the Somme'. The governor later reported that fifty-three inmates and all the avail-able members of staff attended the showing; all took a keen interest because many 'had relatives in the great push'.[26] Exposing the inmates to such material had many purposes. At a certain level, it showed the same British forces that were occupying Ireland at that time, valiantly fighting an enemy that was seen as common to both islands. By 1916, many inmates of Clonmel borstal were discharged to fight in that very same army and allowing those still in detention to view this footage meant that they would see the ultimate in male bravery and honour. Young men, some of whom were taken from amongst their own ranks, were prepared to lay down their lives for a just and noble cause. The borstal system had always sought to instil such ideals into the minds of juvenile-adult offenders.

In the summer of 1914 Clonmel was visited by a Mr J. White, who lectured on his recent travels around Europe. Using photographs and a cinematic presentation, he recounted the story of his journey to Venice, the Dalmatian towns and Montenegro. The event was attended by ninety inmates, thirteen staff, the medical officer and the Roman Catholic curate. It was described by Governor Dobbin as 'a most prof-itable as well as pleasant evening'.[27] Providing juvenile-adults with lec-tures on subjects that entertained as well as informed was an integral part of borstal treatment. The system sought to provide the boys with the most rounded possible preparation for life beyond their detention. While these lectures of this type were indeed held in towns and cities throughout the country, it is unlikely that free juvenile-adult offenders would have taken time away from their criminal careers to attend them. At the borstal they were forcibly exposed to such subject-matter, which the authorities hoped would have an improving effect.

As the borstal system took root in Ireland, it was inevitable that philanthropic organisations became aware of its activities. One such body, the Pembroke Charities Fund, made a contribution to the BAI, on an unspecified date during 1914, for the purchase of instruments to form a band. This initiative marked the next step in moving the borstal away from the local or convict prison. However, as the band was not immediately formed, the GPB failed to appoint a warder qualified to give musical instruction. Some discussion on the issue took place in mid-1914, when a GPB inspector recommended the appointment of Colour Sergeant Mathews, a former band master of the Royal Irish Regiment. He was described as a competent music instructor and 'a good disciplinarian'.[28] It is unlikely that this appointment took place, though, as the institutional band did not become operational until December 1916. The likelihood is that the beginning of World War One meant that any such investment was not possible in the medium term. The BAI reported in August 1917 that the band had finally started using the instruments provided a number of years earlier by the Pembroke Charities. The Association provided a musical instructor at its own expense as well as supplementing the supply of instruments, and the initial results were 'very satisfactory'. The band members rehearsed from 5.30 pm to 7.30 pm three evenings per week. A vacancy arose only when a boy was discharged on licence or released to fight in the army.[29]

Following his visit to Clonmel in mid-1917, Lord Justice Moloney, an ardent supporter of the borstal system, singled out the band for special praise. He declared that, though the boys may 'not yet please the tuneful soul of a real musician', their progress in such a short space of time was admirable.[30] The band continued throughout the years of World War One, funded by the GPB but not expanded. In July 1919 the Visiting Justices suggested that representations be made to the Pembroke Charities for a further contribution to augment the supply of instruments. The boys and their instructor were praised for their enthusiasm and more instruments were deemed important for their advancement.[31] In his reaction to this suggestion, Governor Dobbin set out the status of the band and the effect it had on the inmates. The institution had just seventeen instruments but required almost double that number as there were thirty in the band. The BAI had spent over ten pounds on a clarinet from Hawkes and Son in London, which had exhausted their budget for that particular year. The borstal band was forced to borrow instruments from the local barracks because the 'effect produced by these seventeen instruments falls flat'. Governor Dobbin described the hugely positive influence that the band was having on the inmates: he believed that this had led directly to a reduction in instances of insubordination and, by extension, punishments had become almost non-existent.[32] It is not clear whether the GPB or the Pembroke Charities funded new instruments for the band; in 1920 the BAI reported that the 'borstal band has been quite good, but it is difficult to keep it up to a high standard'. The report did not explain why this was the case but under-investment in the system during these years was most likely an effect of the troubled political situation in the country. [33]

DIETARY PROVISION

While music, lectures and other forms of recreation were not necessarily tiring, there were aspects of borstal life that often involved physical exertion and it was important that inmates were well fed. Breakfast consisted of one pint of stirabout and one pint of new milk. (Stirabout was a porridge containing a combination of three and a half ounces of oatmeal and three and a half ounces of Indian meal, stirred into boiling water.) The dinner menu varied slightly each day though it always included four ounces of beef without bone. This was accompanied on Sundays, Wednesdays and Thursdays by sixteen ounces of potatoes and on Mondays, Tuesdays and Saturdays the meat was served with vegetable soup. New milk was provided with dinner on Wednesdays and Saturdays. Bread and soup was also a daily feature of this meal. Supper, served daily at 4.30 pm, consisted of ten ounces of bread and one pint of cocoa. Boys in the special grade enjoyed certain privileges on Sundays and Thursdays, when they were allowed two ounces of golden syrup or jam with their supper. All the inmates received one half pint of milk with biscuit at lockup time.[34]

There is little evidence to suggest that the inmates were ever treated to anything beyond this menu, although this cannot be completely discounted. In summer 1913 the governor and the medical officer lobbied the GPB for permission to allow certain inmates to have extra provisions once a week. It was hoped that on Sunday the special grade boys could have lettuce, radishes, mustard and cress placed on the mess table during the breakfast hour, as long as the vegetables were in season.[35] It is not clear what prompted this unusual request or if the Board consented. One reason why the governor and his colleagues may have chosen to let inmates have these particular vegetables is that they were grown in the borstal's garden and this may have been the only way to dispose of the amount produced.

TABLE 6.1
DIETARY FOR MALE INMATES OF BORSTAL INSTITUTIONS, 1913

Meal	Day	Content	Amount
Breakfast	Daily	Stirabout (consisting of 3½ oz Oatmeal, and 3½ oz Indian Meal)	1 pint
		New Milk	1 pint
Dinner	Daily	Meat Broth with 4 oz Beef without Bone	1 pint
Sunday Wednesday Thursday	Daily	Potato 16 oz	1 pint
Wednesday Saturday		Bread Vegetable Soup	16oz 1 pint
		New milk	1 pint
Supper	Daily	Bread Cocoa	10 oz 1 pint

Inmates in the special grade are in addition allowed 2 oz of golden syrup or jam at supper on Sundays and Thursdays.

Source: NAI, Clonmel Borstal Memoranda, 1908?30, *Dietary for Male Inmates of Borstal Institutions*, 1913.[36]

One of the most curious aspects of the administration of the borstal system in Ireland was the ability of a seemingly innocuous event or gesture to spark a lengthy set of communications between various bodies. In October 1914 the governor wrote to the medical officer seeking his advice as to whether the inmates should have an apple each on All Hallows Eve. Dr O'Brien replied positively: it would be particularly appropriate since the apples were provided by friends of the institution. Governor Dobbin reported to the GPB that the institution had recently received many offers of fruit for the inmates and sought permission to give 'one good eating apple to each inmate' except for those in the penal grade.[37] Each year between 1915 and 1919, and possibly beyond, the institution received apples for the inmates from the Duchess of St Albans. This annual gift probably began after a visit to the institution by the Duchess, along with her daughter, on 21 August 1915. The visiting party all 'expressed pleas-

ure at the cleanliness of the inmates and the institution and the discipline and physical training'.[38] These communications reveal two
important facts about the daily running of Clonmel borstal. Firstly, it
appears that no changes or additions were ever made to the inmates'
diet without the prior approval of the medical officer. Secondly, the
staff at Clonmel adhered very strictly to the dietary provisions laid
down by the GPB and only in exceptional circumstances did the boys
ever receive a 'treat'. It appears that the boys in the penal grade were
never given any kind of dietary privilege.

The stark differences in dietary provision between the borstal systems
of England and Ireland were laid bare in a 1912 communication from
Sydney Tippet, governor of Feltham, in Middlesex, to the GPB. Tippet
drew up a table comparing the food served in both institutions and it was
clear that Feltham was far more generous to its inmates than Clonmel.
While Clonmel provided the staple diet of bread, milk, potatoes and beef
outlined above, Feltham offered fat bacon, suet pudding, margarine
cheese and beans.[39] When the diets were compared, the boys at Clonmel
appeared almost deprived, while those at Feltham seemed to live quite
well. The letter pointed out how the Feltham borstal boy derived his necessary dietary fat from a greater variety of sources including fat bacon,
margarine cheese and suet pudding, while at Clonmel the main source
was milk. The Feltham diet also contained thirty-six ounces more potatoes than Clonmel. Governor Tippet outlined one of the main consequences of these differences, claiming that the physical condition of the
boys at Feltham was far superior to Clonmel. The much more varied diet
assisted in the acceleration of growth and a general enhancement in the
health and physical condition of the Feltham inmates. He also criticised
the timing of meals at Clonmel, pointing out that the time between supper and breakfast the following day was far too long. At Feltham, supper took place at 5.30 pm and the inmates were given breakfast at 5.50
am the following morning. The Clonmel timetable, he claimed, was
unwise for growing boys, who were often under-sized and under-fed at
the time of their admission. In a further reproach to the Irish system,
Tippet's letter pointed out that the borstal at Feltham provided special
cookery classes, of which the products were given to special grade
inmates, in addition to the diet already outlined. The cook at Feltham
had the power to obtain ingredients such as rice, tapioca, arrow-root,
cornflour, eggs, currants, sultanas, lime juice, sago or mixed herbs on
a given day and the best-behaved inmates benefited.[40] The information and advice in this letter was offered in a most courteous and

helpful manner but there is no evidence that any of the ideas were ever put into action in Clonmel borstal. The poor dietary provision there was almost a throwback to the reign of Du Cane over the English prison system. He had advocated the notion that providing anything more than the minimum diet would be akin to encouraging the offender to commit petty crimes and inevitably contribute to the creation of more habitual criminals.[41] It appears that the GPB had not progressed far from its 1880s mindset that the prison diet should not be 'agreeable' to the person in detention, thus suggesting that the Board had not fully grasped the main concepts or aims of borstal treatment.[42]

INMATE LABOUR

Convict labour was a common feature of Ireland's local prisons during the nineteenth century. Prior to the implementation of the Progressive Stage System in the mid-1850s, labour was often viewed by the prisoner as a punitive measure. Crofton used the Progressive Stage System to alter this view: after eight or nine months in the first stage, which was solitary confinement, the prisoner came to see the opportunity to work as a welcome break from imposed idleness.[43] The county gaol in Clonmel was no different in this regard. Prison labour involved many general tasks that required low levels of skill but kept the prisoners occupied nonetheless. During the 1880s and 1890s the men of Clonmel gaol were involved in an array of different projects ranging from fixing clothes lines to painting the governor's office.[44] Prison labour always involved essential maintenance to the physical structure of the gaol and it frequently eliminated the need to hire outside contractors. Contract labour was used for tasks it was not possible for prisoners to perform, like more professional ventures such as fitting a bathroom, laying gas pipes or repairing the plumbing of a building, within the walls of the complex. As expected, the nature of inmate labour at Clonmel changed when the institution was converted to a full-scale borstal.

Borstal inmates were also employed at mat-making, shoemaking, tailoring and carpentry. In the building sector they worked as carpenters, painters and glaziers.[45] All this work took place in the context of the training and education of the inmates, though the governor, the BAI and even the GPB did not actually believe that tailoring and mat-making were of value to a boy once he was discharged. A final category

listed boys as being employed at 'cleaning and jobbing work in and about the institution and institution yard'.[46] This, however, was exclusive of any kind of building work, which meant that, since the adult prisoners had been removed from Clonmel, this had to be contracted out. Inmate labour led to a high output of barrows, stools and tables for use in the institution. The chairman of the GPB, J.S. Gibbons, reported that boys employed in the shoemaking workshop for five to six months were capable of making new boots or slippers, while those engaged in tailoring became proficient in a short time. All of these boys, he claimed, were 'in a position to earn an honest livelihood'.[47] His position here somewhat contradicts the widely-held GPB position that tailoring was of little future use to inmates.

On the subject of inmate labour, the single issue of agriculture tended to dominate the public and private interactions of the various parties involved with the running of Clonmel borstal. The absence of government investment in land or even a small farm perplexed the governors, the BAI and even the GPB, all of whom were united in their calls for improvement. When the Gladstone Committee first suggested a penal reformatory in 1895, the report specifically stated that such an institution should be located in the country 'with ample space for agricultural and land reclamation work'.[48] As a means of circumventing Clonmel's lack of farm land, in 1917 Governor Dobbin implemented a new agricultural labour programme. A carefully selected group of inmates was allowed to leave the institution on a daily basis to work with local farmers. This was seen by the Board as useful to the development of the boys and acted as a means of training them for farm employment. The inmates left the institution at 8.00 am each day and returned at 5.30 pm During the day they worked 'strenuously' at harvesting and threshing, among other tasks, and were 'well-fed' by their employers. They were supervised at all times by an institutional warder dressed in plain clothes.

The initiative was open to inmates sentenced to three years' detention who had been well behaved during the previous eight months and, therefore, were seen as reliable and unlikely to transgress during their days of comparative liberty. Twenty-four boys were hired out during the first year of the scheme and paid at two thirds of the rate of local agricultural labour.[49] The institution was paid £111 for the provision of agricultural services, though it was not made clear if any portion of this money was passed on to the inmates upon their release.[50] This rate was arrived at after Governor Dobbin consulted with the Office of the Director of National Services in Dublin, who advised him that this would be a fair amount.[51] The BAI described the experience in wholly positive terms, pointing out that the boys were 'delighted' with the fresh air and freedom of their work expeditions. The Association's 1917 report claimed that the inmates were all well-treated and experienced a 'homely dinner of bacon with the usual vegetables, besides getting tea, with bread and butter and jam'. When they returned to the borstal at night they had a much better sleep thanks to the fresh air and exposure to country life. The work party usually conveyed their excitement about their experience on the farm to their less fortunate colleagues in the institution 'not to make them jealous, but to impress upon them that good conduct invariably receives its rewards'.[52] The Board's idealistic language and descriptions of the boys' work experience was inevitably addressing the real agenda, to highlight again the need for a farm, or at least a large field, to train the boys for agricultural work after discharge. The report concluded that, though the inmates sent out for farm work could not be described as having valuable experience, because they lacked essential training, but they were of considerable use in less skilled areas such as haymaking and weeding.[53]

The scheme was continued the following year and was once again deemed a success by the Board. Selected inmates were sent out in parties of six to twelve and earned over £219 for the institution during 1918–19. The Board repeated its assertion that the scheme could be only of limited benefit to the boys because it was practically impossible to teach them the necessary agricultural skills in the limited space within the walls of the borstal.[54] The BAI reported that the success of the second year of the scheme was underlined by all of the previous employers renewing their applications for inmates to work on their farms, and several new ones applied. The Association repeated its claim that the scheme had many advantages for the boys, including the fresh air and 'a diet quite different to that given to them when they were in confinement'.[55] It is not clear if this was a veiled criticism of the GPB-prescribed diet at Clonmel. By 1919, however, the scheme had to be discontinued owing to trouble in the local labour market.[56] The GPB report also highlighted a difficulty with placing discharged inmates in positions with farmers. Both problems could reflect the altered state of the economy and employment market following the end of World War One, as well as the political and social unrest in the country at the time. In October 1919 the BAI expressed regret at the decision, pointing out that the boys enjoyed working for the farmers, who were generally receptive to inmate labour and fed them well.[57] In 1917 a number of local farmers had contacted Clonmel requesting the assistance of inmates in saving their crops. The governor was unable to oblige, however, as the institution was short-staffed due to illness; he sought the appointment of an extra officer to aid helping the farmers.[58]

The boys at Clonmel borstal appeared to be at a disadvantage by comparison with their English counterparts yet again when it came to the number of hours worked. A comparative table commissioned by the GPB in 1911 showed that the inmates at Clonmel worked longer and indeed later hours than those in England. From 1 November to 15 February, English borstal inmates worked seven hours twenty-five minutes each weekday. Between 16 February and 31 October they worked eight hours twenty-five minutes each weekday. At Clonmel, the inmates worked nine hours and fifteen minutes per day throughout the year.[59] The Board sought to justify this difference by suggesting that, though the Irish hours were longer, the work was less intensive.[60] It was significant that in 1913 borstal inmate hours were on a par with hours worked by adult prisoners in local gaols and it is unclear why the GPB had taken over three years to address the issue. In a somewhat cynical attempt at a cosmetic change to borstal conditions, the Board went on to suggest that the borstal labour hours should be shortened 'if only for the sake of making them different from the local prisoner hours'.[61]

MEDICAL CARE OF INMATES AND STAFF

The overall responsibility for the health of prisoners fell to the medical representative on the three-person GPB. This position was established following a recommendation in 1884 by the Royal Commission on Prisons in Ireland.[62] The 'medical member' of the Board oversaw the formulation of general medical policy for Irish prisons. He was consulted in the event of any divergence from this policy or any unusual or unprecedented medical event at local level, such as an epidemic.

The medical officer had long been an important figure in the Irish prison system. Locally, he looked after the health of prisoners. The role was usually filled by a local doctor who was approved by the GPB. In a complaint to the Royal Commission investigating Irish prisons in 1884, the medical officers argued for better pay on the basis of the many duties they were required to fulfil. First among these was the obligation to visit the prison to inspect all the prisoners on a daily basis, and more frequently if necessary. They were also required to approve the diet of prisoners and regularly inspect the implements used in food preparation. As well as preparing medicines himself, the medical officer carried out sanitary inspections of the premises occupied by the prisoners and staff. He was also required to provide medical care for the families of prison staff who resided on, or within half a mile of, his institution. This particular duty excluded the provision of care for long-term or serious illness, as well as midwifery. Finally, the medical officer himself had to perform the many and often painstaking clerical duties connected with the job.[63] The medical officer attached to Clonmel was Dr O'Brien. The records of that institution show that his professional life was very active and the volume of written material indicate that clerical duties occupied a great deal of his time.[64]

A key function of the borstal medical officer was to ascertain the fitness of each inmate for the regime he would face during detention. Each boy was medically assessed prior to the sentencing phase of his trial and would be sent to Clonmel only if he was deemed fit. One of the recommendations of the Gladstone report was that inmates of the penal reformatory should be of sound physical and mental health.[65] An inmate needed to be strong enough to endure the early mornings, long hours of work and relatively poor dietary provisions. Upon his arrival at Clonmel, a boy would again be assessed as part of the regular procedure of Irish prisons. On rare occasions an inmate with a physical defect was approved for borstal detention. An undated letter shows an enquiry from Dr O'Brien to his superiors in the GPB regarding the procedure for an inmate who was admitted with heart disease. The medical officer was concerned about the boy's ability to participate in a number of aspects of the borstal's daily routine. The reply stated that Dr O'Brien should take personal responsibility for the boy, including the regulation of his work and physical drill.[66]

The inspection aspect of Dr O'Brien's work occupied just a small portion of his time. A typical report covered the general cleanliness and sanitary condition of the complex, also referring to the state of the bedclothes and food, before coming to a conclusion on the health of the inmates and staff. One factor that could account for such sparse reporting is that Dr O'Brien was in the institution with such regularity that he most likely monitored conditions on an ongoing basis and ensured that everything was up to its required standard. The evidence suggests that he was particularly vigilant and his inspection of the building complex was of special importance during the warm summer months. In July 1914 he reported that an offensive smell had now been removed thanks to repairs to the sewer in the ball alley yard. In very hot weather he ordered that a pane of glass be removed from the window of each cell, to improve ventilation.[67] The medical officer could be summoned to the borstal at very short notice in the event of injury of an inmate or a warder. His report on these specific incidents was always taken into account in the event of an investigation by the visiting justice and was sometimes crucial in making a determination of the culpability of an inmate. It was inevitable, of course, that accidents were frequent in a busy and highly physical institution such as the borstal. Some of these incidents were quite serious, though the majority were not of huge significance.[68]

Work-related accidents were commonplace. On the evening of 5 March 1912, inmate David Rogers was employed breaking down an arch over an old cell in order to make room for a new wall and chimney breast. In the course of his work he accidentally stepped backwards off his plank and fell onto a rubbish heap, hitting his head against a wall. The supervising warder reported that the boy did not pass out but appeared to be in shock.[69] As the boy complained of a pain in the back of his head, it was decided by Governor Connor to summon Dr O'Brien. The governor stated that inmate Rogers appeared to have made a good recovery the next day.[70] For his part, O'Brien reported that the boy suffered concussion to the back of his head and confined him to his cell.[71] Three days later Rogers was deemed to have made a full recovery from his injury and was allowed to resume his duties.[72]

Dr O'Brien was concerned not only with the physical state of the boys; his responsibility also extended to their mental care. An example of a mentally unstable inmate came to his attention in November 1917. The episode began at 1.00 pm on 20 November when the boy concerned, John Francis, refused to eat his dinner. Now under observation by the warders, he also refused his supper that day as well as his milk and biscuit at 7.30 pm. He took no breakfast the following morning and after being sent out to work at 9.30 am he requested to be returned to his cell. This was refused, he returned to work and again failed to eat his dinner. When questioned by warders he declared that he would not eat because he was not being given enough food. He threatened that, unless he was given more food at breakfast, he would stop eating altogether.[73] Dr O'Brien was called by the governor and questioned Francis about his refusal to eat. He repeated his assertion that he was not being given sufficient food and so the medical officer persuaded him to eat if more food was provided. An extra pound of bread was ordered for his dinner as a temporary measure. Dr O'Brien reported that Francis' 'mental condition appears to me not quite normal'.[74] The following day the doctor reported that the inmate had resumed eating on the basis that he was receiving the extra amount of bread, and passed him fit for working in the garden; he was kept in his cell at meal times. He again stressed that the boy seemed to be in an abnormal mental condition.[75]

With the food issue under some degree of control, Francis was closely monitored by the warders and Dr O'Brien over the following weeks. The boy's mental condition appeared to the medical officer to have deteriorated and he sought permission to consult with the medical superintendent of the district asylum. A case conference took place on 10 December when Dr O'Brien met with local asylum's Dr Harvey. No definite action was taken at that time and instead it was decided to keep the inmate under close observation.[76] John Francis was again placed under strict observation after a further incident on 27 February of the following year. Governor Dobbin reported that the boy threw a spade over a high boundary wall into the neighbouring police barracks, risking serious injury to the men, women and children who were there. Francis was removed from the garden to the tailor's workshop but the governor wrote that the officers felt distinctly uncomfortable having an inmate of such unstable character in their midst. Dr O'Brien declared that the inmate's responsibility for his actions appeared to be 'questionable'.[77] The records of the borstal and the GPB provide no further evidence as to the fate of John Francis but the institution's prison register shows that he was discharged by order of the lord lieutenant on 4 June 1918.[78] No reason was given. This incident serves to highlight not only the volatile nature of some juvenile-adult offenders but also the extent of the human and professional resources needed by the medical officer in dealing with such boys.

Dr O'Brien also held responsibility for the health of the staff. In the majority of cases the individual was examined by the medical officer and returned to work when he was deemed fit. The doctor was also occasionally challenged by the arrival in the institution of potentially contagious illnesses. Such an event took place in early 1914 when a mild case of scarlet fever was detected among Governor Dobbin's family. The governor's house was located within the borstal complex and he resided there with his family at the expense of the GPB. Dobbin was on leave in Waterford when his daughter was diagnosed with scarlet fever. Upon his return to Clonmel he travelled straight to the doctor's surgery and was advised not to return to the institution until the Board was fully acquainted with the situation.[79] This development raised a number of problems for all parties concerned. Dr O'Brien was not only concerned with the health and recovery of Governor Dobbin's daughter but with protecting the inmates and staff of the institution from infection. If Governor Dobbin were allowed to return home and run Clonmel as normal, he would be putting his colleagues and the inmates at risk. It was suggested that he live outside the institution at his own expense until the infection was cleared. He indicated to the Board, however, that this would be a financial strain for him. The Board replied that it was not in a position to supplement his income with an accommodation allowance for the period of his daughter's illness and offered to transfer him to another position in a local prison elsewhere.[80] It is not known how this issue was resolved, though there is no record that Governor Dobbin was ever temporarily transferred from his duties at Clonmel.

Another example of infection that threatened to penetrate the walls of Clonmel borstal was the influenza epidemic in 1918. Dr O'Brien sought to protect the inmates and requested Governor Dobbin to seek a supply of vaccines urgently from the GPB. The governor forwarded the request to the Board, describing the outbreak in the Clonmel area as 'acute'. The Board pointed out that before such a vaccine could be administered the consent of the boys and/or their parents would have to be sought by the medical officer. It was argued that the medical profession had not yet reached a definitive opinion on the effectiveness of the vaccine and in these circumstances the request was turned down.[81]

As the influenza epidemic gripped the town during the first week of November 1918, the local authorities came under enormous pressure to maintain the supply of food and other aid to the suffering. Over 2,000 of the poorer inhabitants of the town were struck down, with entire families incapacitated and lacking warmth and nourishment. As the local doctors and the Red Cross mobilised a relief effort, some of the more noteworthy residents, including Richard Bagwell and William Casey of the BAI, approached the borstal for assistance. Dobbin agreed to open the cookhouse, where the officers and inmates prepared over fifteen gallons of Bovril over four days. The soup was collected by the women of the local Red Cross, who distributed it throughout the region. Governor Dobbin concluded that there was no doubt that the actions of the borstal had led directly to the saving of lives in Clonmel that week and he retrospectively sought the Board's approval for his actions. Approval was granted unconditionally.[82] This incident marked one of the only occasions when the borstal institution had this level of interaction with the town and people of Clonmel. The following year the BAI singled out Dr O'Brien and Major Dobbin for special mention, crediting both men, along with the borstal staff, for keeping the institution free from influenza during the crisis.[83] Indeed, it is an indication of Dr O'Brien's dedication and professionalism that the infection did not spread to the borstal, given the daily movement of staff and others in and out.

THE INSPECTION PROCESS

The responsibilities of the GPB prison inspectors were formally laid out in the Board's *First Annual Report* in 1879. Each inspector was required to visit each prison in his district at least once every six weeks, to ensure that it was clean and well maintained. He was required to draw the attention of the governor to the necessity of ensuring the security of the prison at all times. The inspector viewed the officers on parade and ascertained whether they had an accurate understanding of their duties. He was obliged to hear any complaint or representation from an officer of the institution and deal with the matter at the time or refer it to the GPB. The inspector dealt with complaints against officers with regard to any aspect of their work. These were often made by prisoners, or indeed borstal inmates, all of whom had an opportunity to meet with the inspector in their cells or at work. It was also the responsibility of the inspector to ensure that inmates were given work within the institution that was entirely appropriate to their disciplinary ranking. Finally, the inspector was obliged to examine the records of the institution, including the journals kept by the governor, medical officer and chaplains. The financial records were also subject to similar scrutiny.[84] The inspector's powers, however, could not be described as sweeping or all-powerful and certain limitations of his position within the prison system were reaffirmed by the Royal Commission of Prisons report in 1884. Prison inspectors were not empowered to punish either prison staff or prisoners, nor were they permitted to give direct orders to a governor or any warder. Any such order could come from an inspector only as a result of a directive from his superiors at the GPB. The inspector was, in a sense, simply required to 'serve as the eyes of the board'.[85] At Clonmel borstal, the functions of the inspector were very much in line with those outlined in the two reports. The evidence suggests nevertheless that on many occasions the inspector had a direct effect on the daily operation of the institution.

The borstal inspection reports provided the GPB with an account of the inmates in detention on the day of the visit. Each report usually indicated whether the rules of classification were being correctly followed and, where appropriate, commented on the nature of the work or education in which the boys were engaged. For example, an early report criticised the method by which the boys were taught arithmetic. The inspector, on this occasion Mr MacDermot, considered that a blackboard should be introduced because the present method of giving the inmates sums to do on their slates 'unaccompanied by explanation is quite too lazy and abstract a way of teaching'. He also criticised the absence of sponges to clean slates, having witnessed the 'filthy' way in which the boys spat on their slates and then wiped them clean with their handkerchief or coat sleeve.[86] This was a prime example of the way in which the inspection system was utilised to raise the standard of the institution. The inspector was not only concerned with the wider and sometimes more dramatic issues of borstal life, but also in the minute detail of the sort outlined here. It should be remembered that this particular report was filed in October 1910, less than a year after the county gaol was converted into a full-scale borstal institution, so the system was still in its infancy.

The evidence from the borstal inspection reports shows that the GPB inspector required a good deal of understanding of the system. The borstal was clearly different from the regular adult prison. Borstal inmates had an altogether different daily routine and the intended outcomes were not the same as those of a local or convict prison. There were many elements of an inspection report, however, that were the same for the borstal and the local prison. For example, both reports outlined details of the inspection of staff and prisoners or inmates. Both gave details of examining the institutional financial accounts and required the most up-to-date cash balance. The reports differed in that for the borstal there were references to various aspects of treatment such as the training of inmates. One such example arose in January 1913, when the GPB inspector, A.J. Owen-Lewis, recognised that the borstal was lacking in any form of gymnastic equipment. To that end, he suggested that the Board acquire a number of gymnastic appliances such as a vaulting horse and parallel bars on an experimental basis. If the equipment proved successful, the Board should, in the longer term, give serious consideration to the construction of a gymnasium.[87] It is not clear if the suggestion of providing equipment was actually enacted at the time but in 1917 the BAI announced that in the previous year a gymnasium had been added to the complex. It claimed that the development served the dual purpose of providing the boys with a new source of amusement as well as contributing significantly to their physical development.[88] Owen-Lewis continued to show a keen interest in the physical fitness of inmates. In April 1918, he highlighted the need for the appointment of an experienced drill and gymnastic instructor. His report stated an intention to contact the Discharged Soldiers Employment Association, which might suggest a suitable candidate to join the borstal as a temporary instructor.[89]

The inspection process had a very real influence over the boys' lives. If the inspector felt that some aspect of their condition was lacking or could be improved, a recommendation was written into his inspection report and usually acted upon. In March 1913, for example, Owen-Lewis observed the inmates at work and during exercise in the borstal and was surprised to see that their clothing was 'threadbare and ill-fitting'. He acknowledged that the borstal routine meant that the boys' clothing was subject to much more severe treatment than the uniforms of local prisoners. The inspector's wider knowledge of the prison system came into play in this instance with his suggestion that a batch of clothing that had been purpose-made for borstal inmates several years earlier at Maryborough prison should be sent to Clonmel immediately.[90] The inspectors were not afraid to criticise anything they witnessed at the borstal: a good example can be seen in an inspection report from April 1914. Owen-Lewis was highly critical of the state of the inmates' kitchen. A batch of discarded utensils awaiting disposal were stored on shelves, many alongside implements that were still in daily use; many of these, in turn, were in a poor condition. The general cleanliness and hygiene of the kitchen were very poor.[91]

The inspector also had a certain degree of influence over the selection of staff, though this did not necessarily extend to the power to appoint or dismiss. In 1913 Owen-Lewis drew the Board's attention to the performance of Warder Fenton, a man he described as conscientious but 'somewhat slow-witted'. Fenton was a member of the original Clonmel prison staff and did not have the relevant personal experience for dealing with juvenile-adult offenders. The inspection report recommended that he be transferred to a prison more appropriate to his experience.[92] The same inspector took a serious approach to striking the correct balance of experience in staff working at the borstal and in his following inspection report he recommended two further staff changes. Neither Warder Linton nor schoolmaster Warder Brogan could be deemed ineffective in their work but did not have the right temperament for dealing with the boys 'over whom they have very little authority or control'. The report recommended the transfer of assistant schoolmaster Warder Ballam from Mountjoy and Colour Sergeant Rowlands from Limerick to Clonmel as replacements.[93] This was another example of the need to appoint inspectors of a perceptive nature and with a good knowledge of the requirements of the borstal system. On 24 February of the following year Owen-Lewis again recommended the transfer of warders Fenton, Linton and Brogan. The inspection report possessed a greater sense of urgency and was more critical of Warder Linton, describing him as 'a very unsatisfactory officer for a Borstal Institution, he has very little idea of discipline and is most unsuitable to be in charge of boys'.[94] These interactions were an indication that the GPB was taking seriously the need to staff its borstal with a different type of warder. The records of the institution show that, over time, the profile of the staff evolved and came more into line with the needs of the juvenile-adult offender.

A visit by a GPB inspector did have the potential to precipitate a stream of correspondence between the borstal and Dublin Castle. In January 1912, Inspector MacDermot reported that the boots worn by many of the boys were in 'a disgraceful state of repair'.[95] The remainder of that inspection report was entirely positive and indeed highly complimentary of the work carried out by the governor and his staff. Two days later Governor Connor received a terse follow-up letter from the controller of industries at Dublin Castle, demanding an immediate explanation for the state of the inmates' boots.[96] The governor explained that the inmates' boots were in poor condition because the institution had recently received a large consignment of officers' footwear from Castlebar and Waterford prisons that had to be repaired. This resulted in the borstal's own boots being left in repair. He apologised and assured his superiors that the problem ..ad now been remedied and the Board would not find grounds for complaint in relation to boots in the future.[97] This exchange, along with the incident involving the lack of sponges for slates outlined earlier, illustrates the vigilance of the GPB inspectors and the usefulness of the process in helping to raise the overall standards of the borstal by identifying and remedying seemingly small problems.

When the first juvenile-adult offender arrived at Clonmel in May 1906, the structure of daily life had not yet been fully established. The GPB and the borstal's first governor had the advantage of being able to take their lead, to a certain extent, from the already established borstals in Kent, and later Feltham. One of the fundamental challenges for the authorities was to structure a daily routine that was far removed from what the same boy would have experienced in the local and convict prisons just a few years earlier. The overriding concern was that this daily routine should be structured in such a way as to allow the staff to concentrate on bringing about all the required changes of the borstal treatment process in a humane yet disciplined manner. To this end, the borstal day forced the juvenile-adult offender to adhere to a strict routine where he was not only compelled to submit to authority through education, training and work, but was also exposed to a range of recreational and cultural activities designed to broaden his mind.

The average day for an inmate was usually the same as the one before. Each day was intentionally repetitive and the intended effect was to bring about a sense of habit and order to the lives of the boys, many of whom had never adhered to any manner of timetable. The evidence strongly suggests that, in promoting the physical fitness of its inmates, Clonmel was severely hampered by a lack of capital investment and unable to compete with its counterparts in Kent and Feltham. However, the development of recreational provisions gathered pace at a quicker rate at Clonmel, mainly because it required less financial input from the GPB. The BAI was largely responsible for the many and varied lectures that were a feature of borstal life and inmates gained from exposure to a range of subjects that they would surely not have encountered either in an adult prison or outside. The evidence of the GPB's own records show that, while Clonmel borstal provided a strictly controlled diet for its inmates, even in this regard the institution lagged behind England. The commitment of the governors and staff at Clonmel to fulfilling the aims of borstal treatment is perhaps best exemplified by the 1917 farm work scheme, an initiative originating with Governor Dobbin. Along with the governor, the medical officer was a key member of the borstal staff and the evidence shows that Dr O'Brien's contribution to the institution often went beyond that of a regular medical practitioner. As the sole medical officer for the borstal he not only attended to the wide variety of different and unusual problems that arose from inmate population but participated voluntarily in many of the daily recreational events. The GPB inspector was another key figure in the maintenance of high standards at Clonmel. His influence wrought many adjustments in the lives of the inmates that over time moved the institution ever closer to fulfilling its intended purpose. While the inspection reports were often critical of Clonmel borstal, they failed to take account of the conditions under which the staff were forced to labour, a result of GPB under-investment.

NOTES

1. Among the most revealing sources of information on the daily life of Clonmel borstal institution are the six-weekly reports of the GPB inspectors. These reports will be utilised, not only to outline the inspector's role in maintaining high standards at the institution, but also to show some of the many problems and improvements that occurred over time.
2. NAI, GPB, Clonmel Borstal Memoranda, 1908–30, *Memorandum on the Prevention of Crime Act 1908, received by the Governor of Clonmel borstal institution,* 10/11/09, GPB/XB5.
3. NAI, GPB, Clonmel Borstal Memoranda, 1908–30, *Memorandum on the Prevention of Crime Act 1908,* GPB/XB5.
4. NAI, GPB, CR, Borstal Institution bell scale, GPB/2132/1911.
5. NAI, GPB, CR, Borstal Institution bell scale, GPB/2132/1911.
6. Osborough, *Borstal in Ireland,* p. 64.
7. Osborough, *Borstal in Ireland,* p. 64.
8. NAI, GPB, CR, Borstal Institution bell scale, GPB/2132/1911.
9. NAI, GPB, CR, Borstal Institution bell scale, GPB/2132/1911.
10. *The Treasury,* March 1910.
11. *The Treasury,* March 1910.
12. NLI, *Proceedings of the International Penitentiary Congress,* vi [Cd-5286], H.L. 1909–10, xxxix, 12.
13. NLI, *Proceedings of the International Penitentiary Congress,* vi [Cd-5286], H.L., 1909–10, xxxix, 12.
14. NAI, GPB, CR, Major Dobbin to GPB, GPB/1835/1911.
15. NAI, GPB, CR, governor's letter, 29 October 1921, GPB/8683/1921.
16. Fahy, 'The boy criminal', p. 47.
17. NLI, *Report of the Commissioners of Prisons and the Directors of Convict Prisons in England,* iv, [Cd-1278], H.L. 1900-1, xx, 214.
18. NLI, *Thirty-fourth Report of the General Prisons Board,* vii [Cd-6365], H.L. 1911–2, viii, 13.
19. NLI, *Twenty-ninth Report of the General Prisons Board,* x [Cd-3698], H.L. 1906–7, ix, 86.
20. Reported in *The Nationalist,* 26 May 1909.
21. NAI, GPB, CR, governor to GPB, 17 August 1914, GPB/8333/1918.
22. NAI, GPB, CR, governor to GPB, 17 August 1914, GPB/8333/1918.

23. NAI, GPB, CR, Governor Dobbin to GPB, 18 June 1916, GPB/2219/1916.
24. NAI, GPB, CR, Governor Dobbin to GPB, 18 June 1916, GPB/2219/1916.
25. NAI, GPB, CR, Governor's report, 21 February 1919, GPB/5632/1920.
26. NAI, GPB, CR, Governor's report, 24 November 1916, GPB/5632/1920.
27. NAI, GPB, CR, Governor's report, 27 January 1915, GPB/5632/1920.
28. NAI, GPB, CR, Inspection report, 06 June 1914, GPB/3680/1914.
29. NAI, Clonmel Borstal Memoranda, BAI, *Seventh Annual Report*, 14 August 1917, GPB/XB5.
30. *The Nationalist*, 15 August 1917.
31. NAI, GPB, CR, extract from visiting justice journal, 11 July 1919, GPB/5253/1919.
32. NAI, GPB, CR, response of Governor Dobbin, 26 July 1919, GPB/5624/1919.
33. *The Nationalist*, 20 October 1920.
34. NAI, Clonmel Borstal Memoranda, 1908–30, *Dietary for Male Inmates of Borstal Institutions*, 1913. See Table 6.1.
35. NAI, GPB, CR, governor letter to GPB, GPB/8333/1918.36. NAI, Clonmel Borstal Memoranda, 1908–30, *Dietary for Male Inmates of Borstal Institutions*, 1913.
36. Ibid.
37. NAI, GPB, CR, governor to GPB, 17 October 1914, GPB/7856/1919.
38. NAI, GPB, CR, governor's report on the visit of the Duchess of St Albans, 21 August 1915, GPB/4452/1915.
39. NAI, GPB, CR, Tippet to GPB, 23 September 1912, GPB/4879/1919.
40. NAI, GPB, CR, Tippet to GPB, 23 September 1912, GPB/4879/1919.
41. McConville, 'The Victorian prison: England, 1865–1965', p. 148.
42. MacDonnell, 'Review of some of the subjects in the Report of the Royal Commission on Prisons in Ireland', p. 617.
43. Putney, Putney, 'Origins of the reformatory', p. 438.
44. NLI, *Twenty-second Report of the General Prisons Board*, x [Cd-9123], H.L. 1899–1900, x, 121.
45. NLI, *Thirty-second Report of the General Prisons Board*, v [Cd-5286], 1909–10, ii, 40.
46. NLI, *Thirty-second Report of the General Prisons Board*, v [Cd-5286], 1909–10, ii, 42.
47. NLI, *Proceedings of the International Penitentiary Congress*, vi [Cd-5286], H.L., 1909–10, xxxix, 14.
48. NLI, *Report from the Departmental Committee on Prisons*, vi, 1 [C 7702-1], H.L. 1895, 7.
49. *The Nationalist*, 15 August 1917.
50. NLI, *Fortieth Report of the General Prisons Board*, iii [Cm-42], H.L. 1917–8, ix, 9.
51. NAI, GPB, CR, GPB to office of the director of national services, 6 August 1918, GPB/2939/1919.
52. *The Nationalist*, 15 August 1917.
53. *The Nationalist*, 15 August 1917.
54. NLI, *Forty-first Report of the General Prisons Board*, vi [Cmd-687], H.L. 1918–19, x, 101.
55. *The Nationalist*, 28 August 1918.
56. NLI, *Forty-first Report of the General Prisons Board*, vi [Cmd-687], H.L. 1918–19, x, 81. The report did not elaborate on the nature of this trouble.
57. *The Nationalist*, 1 October 1919.
58. NAI, GPB, CR, Governor's request for further staff, 18 October 1917, GPB/4219/1917.
59. NAI, GPB, CR, Comparison of hours of labour in borstal institutions in England and Ireland, GPB/2132/1911.
60. NAI, GPB, CR, GPB minute, GPB/2132/1911.
61. NAI, GPB, CR, GPB minute, GPB/2132/1911.
62. NLI, *Second Report of the Royal Commission on Prisons in Ireland*, xxxviii [C-4145], H.L. 1883–4, v, 15.
63. NLI, *Second Report of the Royal Commission on Prisons in Ireland*, xxxviii [C-4145], H.L. 1883–4, v, 16.
64. NAI, GPB, CR, medical reports, GPB/1835/1911.
65. NLI, *Report from the Departmental Committee on Prisons*, vi, 1 [C 7702-1], H.L. 1895, x, 32.
66. NAI, Clonmel Borstal Memoranda, 1908–30, Medical Officer enquiry on fitness of inmate for work and physical drill, GPB/XB5.

67. NAI, GPB, CR, Medical Officer's quarterly inspection, 2 July 1914, GPB/4305/1914.
68. NAI, GPB, CR, disciplinary reports, GPB/1291/1918.
69. NAI, GPB, CR, account of Trades Warder Martin, 5 March 1912, GPB/1925/1912.
70. NAI, GPB, CR, account of Governor John Connor, 6 March 1912, GPB/1925/1912.
71. NAI, GPB, CR, account of medical officer, 6 March 1912, GPB/1925/1912.
72. NAI, GPB, CR, Final report of Medical Officer, 9 March 1912, GPB/1925/1912.
73. NAI, GPB, CR, Report of Chief Warder, 21 November 1917, GPB/1722/1918.
74. NAI, GPB, CR, Report of the Medical Officer, 21 November 1917, GPB/1722/1918.
75. NAI, GPB, CR, extract from medical officer's journal, 22 November 1917, GPB/1722/1918.
76. NAI, GPB, CR, Report of Medical Officer, 10 December 1917, GPB/1722/1918.
77. NAI, GPB, CR, Joint report of the Governor and Medical Officer, 27 February 1918, GPB/1722/1918.
78. NAI, GPB, Clonmel prison and borstal institution, register of inmates, 1903–23, GPB/1/7/14.
79. NAI, GPB, CR, Medical Officer's report, 6 January 1914, GPB/719/1914.
80. NAI, GPB, CR, GPB minute, 19 March 1914, GPB/719/1917.
81. NAI, GPB, CR, extract from medical officer's journal, 1 November 1918, GPB/6886/1918.
82. NAI, GPB, CR, Governor Dobbin's report, 8 November 1918, GPB/7063/1918.
83. Reported in *The Nationalist*, 1 October 1919.
84. NLI, *First Annual Report of the General Prisons Board*, ix [Cl-1121], 1878–9, iii, 31.
85. NLI, *Second Report of the Royal Commission on Prisons in Ireland*, xxxviii [C-4145], H.L. 1883–4, v, 15.
86. NAI, GPB, CR, Inspection report, 21/10/1910, GPB/7244/1910.
87. NAI, GPB, CR, Inspection report, 29 January 1913, GPB/3680/1914.
88. *The Nationalist*, 15 August 1917.
89. NAI, GPB, CR, Inspection report, 29 April 1918, GPB/3472/1919.
90. NAI, GPB, CR, Inspection report, 29 March 1913, GPB/3680/1914.
91. NAI, GPB, CR, Inspection report, 14 April 1914, GPB/3680/1914.
92. NAI, GPB, CR, Inspection report, 30 September 1913, GPB/3680/1914.
93. NAI, GPB, CR, Inspection report, 17 November 1913, GPB/3680/1914.
94. NAI, GPB, CR, Inspection report, 24 February 1914, GPB/3680/1914.
95. NAI, GPB, CR, Inspection report, 12 January 1912, GPB/727/1912.
96. NAI, GPB, CR, controller of industries to Governor Connor, 29 January 1912, GPB/727/1912.
97. NAI, GPB, CR, Governor Connor's response, 31 January 1912, GPB/727/1912.

CHAPTER SEVEN

Improving the mind: meeting inmates' educational, training and spiritual needs

The challenge faced by the governor and staff of Clonmel borstal was immense. Their mission was far greater than the day-to-day management of a penal institution. Legislation and precedent handed them the task of repairing the broken morals of a class of offender that had previously not existed in the field of penal science. The intention of the founders of the borstal system was to transform each boy by attacking and eliminating all of his negative external and internal characteristics and turning him into what the attorney-general for Ireland in 1911 called 'a useful member of society'.[1] Correcting the physical deficiencies in an offender, such as his appearance and his bearing was already a well-practised routine in the penal system but the borstal made additional demands of the institutional staff. The governor, teachers, instructors and chaplains were charged with examining and improving the moral fibre of each boy through a process of firm but kind treatment. The system sought to encourage the boy to reform himself from within and in the process improve his demeanour, outlook and sense of self-worth. Using three of the main pillars of borstal treatment, education, training and religion, the staff set about exerting the strongest and most positive moral influences over each individual offender.

This chapter is concerned with the ways in which Clonmel borstal sought to improve the mind of the juvenile-adult offender. It was only by addressing the fundamental weakness in his character that real and lasting change could be brought about. In this regard, the school, the workshop and the chapel became the other three key weapons in the battle to bring about the moral transformation of each boy. As prison education expanded during the nineteenth century, it followed that the schoolroom would have a central function in the new penal reformatory proposed by the Gladstone Committee. The chapter will examine the school at Clonmel that not only educated the boys, but aimed to broaden their outlook on life and the world with an ongoing series of lectures on carefully selected topics. It will also consider the effectiveness of the school, with a review of the educational success rates as presented each year by the GPB. The borstal system approached the task of preparing their inmates for employment by training them in various useful trades. The training facilities that existed at Clonmel borstal between 1906 and 1921 will be assessed not only for their effectiveness in preparing the boys for employment but also for their ability to evolve over time. The workshops and training fields of the borstal faced many problems during this period, and this chapter will evaluate the responses of the government and the various interested agencies to such challenges. As with education, the place of religion had gained greater significance in the penal system during the century leading up to the foundation of the borstal. Using anecdotal evidence, extracts from various annual reports and the words of the chaplains themselves, the chapter will examine the role of religion and spirituality in the moral improvement of borstal inmates. Further to this, it will assess the dual function of the chaplains, not only as spiritual and moral guardians but as key figures in the BAI. Religion and education were built into the structure of the system in order to further strengthen a boy's moral fibre and advance his academic abilities. According to Moseley, after these practical elements were put in place, they needed to be supported by the personal influence of those charged with looking after the inmates. 'It was', he argued 'to meet these moral and physical needs and to grapple with a real social peril', that the system was originally set up.[2]

DEVELOPMENTS IN PRISON EDUCATION

Prison education had been an established feature of the Irish penal system since the 1820s. It emerged as a force for change in the context of the growing view that prison should be seen as an opportunity for improvement and not merely a place where society takes its revenge. This thinking developed during the second wave of reform and was accompanied by a greater focus on the prisoner as an individual with certain rights. Education was part of this individualisation process and was seen as key to the moral and physical reformation of prisoners. The first report, in 1819, of the Association for the Improvement of Prison Discipline claimed that the principal causes of crime were ignorance and lack of education among the poorer classes.[3] Reading, writing and arithmetic were taught as prison education took hold. Controversy arose in 1850 with the visit to Pentonville prison of the inspector of Irish government prisons, Henry Martin Hitchins, part of an investigation laying the groundwork for the system to be established at Mountjoy. Hitchins was highly critical of the provision of education at Pentonville and condemned the extent of the influence afforded to the teachers.[4] His dictatorial style ensured high levels of tension among staff at Mountjoy, resulting eventually in the resignation and dismissal of the teachers.[5] Despite these setbacks, education at Mountjoy, led by the chaplains, was quite successful, with 90 per cent of inmates apparently able to read and write by the end of their sentence. There was, however, some resistance within the mainstream press in England, where a number of commentators were suspicious of the progressive reforming methods of education and training, and leaned more towards the traditional values of punishment and repression.[6]

The use of education as a bridge to reform became so fixed in prisons during the nineteenth century that it was an obvious candidate for inclusion in the penal reformatory system proposed by the Gladstone Committee and developed by Ruggles-Brise. In making its recommendations on the institution that eventually emerged at Borstal in Kent, the committee provided a clear account of the central purpose of the treatment process that would be applied to inmates. The institution would be staffed by individuals 'capable of giving sound education, training inmates in various kinds of industrial work'. Furthermore, these people should be 'qualified generally to exercise the best and healthiest kind of moral influence'.[7] But the notion of education as a tool for imparting strong moral values did not originate with the borstal system. As Carey pointed out, the nineteenth-century Irish prison was constructed on a strong moral basis.[8]

The role of education in reform was raised to a new level by Ruggles-Brise, who moved education from the margins of the prison system to become one of the foundations on which the borstal programme was built. This came about for a number of reasons. Ruggles-Brise was first and foremost an enlightened thinker whose ideas were out of step with his Victorian civil service training and those of his predecessor, Edmund Du Cane. Secondly, the recommendation by the Gladstone Committee cited above provided him with official sanction to embrace education-based methods. Thirdly, he gained his greatest influence as a result of his visit to the Elmira Reformatory in New York. Though critical of some of the extravagances of the Elmira system, he was impressed overall with its principles, including the idea of implementing 'special measures' for the training of inmates.[9] Elmira possessed a vast array of training workshops and educational facilities on a scale unlike anything in Europe at that time. Amidst this lavishness, Ruggles-Brise identified something that could be applied to his own penal reformatory.

From the inception of the borstal institution, first at Bedford in 1900 and a year later on a more permanent footing at Borstal in Kent, education and training were central to the methods of reform being applied to juvenile-adults. The system pioneered at both locations included the classification of inmates, the imposition of discipline, hard work and post-release supervision. The regime was built around strict rules: physical drill, training and basic education.[10] The purpose of this repetitive daily routine was to reinforce positive values in the inmates, and present them with opportunities to reform themselves from within. The idea was to arm them with the dual-purpose weapon of self-discipline and education. A first-hand insight into the borstal in Kent, published in *The Treasury* in 1910, illustrates the importance of the classroom in that institution and the apparent esteem in which it was held by the inmates. The author of the account, H. George, witnessed twenty boys working on arithmetic independently of each other at separate desks: 'The progress of each class,' he pointed out, 'is not that of its dullest scholar.' This was an example of the process of individualising the inmates and setting each one apart from the group to identify his strengths and weaknesses. The schoolmaster was described as a man of good humour and great experience.[11] This account fits with the intention of the founders of the borstal system ,who decreed that the institution should not be completely punitive but a place where staff were firm, coaxing and coercive, rather than harsh and authoritarian. It was a system that the GPB called 'reforming by kindness' and it still had currency later on.[12] British home secretary Reginald McKenna declared in the House of Commons that the borstal should neither be called a prison nor seen as such. Instead it should be regarded as a school where inmates are subjected to 'severe discipline with a strict industrial training'.[13] Despite his enthusiasm for the system, his concern with its public perception emerges. The borstal was not formally constituted as a place of education but remained a penal reformatory under the administration of the prison system. In Ireland, in what was undoubtedly a reflection of its image as a place of education, it was frequently referred to as the 'borstal school', in both the national and local newspapers. It would be an overstatement, however, to claim that Clonmel borstal fully achieved this goal of actually being first and foremost a place of education. Though it styled itself as such, in reality it very much retained many of the features of a traditional penal institution. Nevertheless, like its English counterpart, Clonmel was greatly concerned with the education of the boys and the GPB went to great lengths to fulfil its obligations in this regard.

EDUCATIONAL PROVISION IN CLONMEL BORSTAL

In assessing educational facilities at Clonmel borstal, it should be remembered that the complex in which it was located was originally constructed as a prison. The physical structures of the county gaol were very much grounded in their nineteenth-century origins when the borstal experiment was launched in May 1906. Among the physical changes to the prison was the addition of a schoolroom for the purpose of educating the juvenile-adults. The GPB appointed a schoolmaster warder to teach the boys, many of whom had serious problems with reading, writing and numeracy. In 1913 the BAI reported that a number of 'large and well-ventilated schoolrooms and a gymnasium' were added to the complex.[14] This development can be viewed as a vote of confidence in the progress of the system at Clonmel by that stage and its capacity for educating inmates. A brief insight into the inner workings of the school is seen in a 1909 requisition from Governor Connor to the GPB for necessary educational equipment and stationery. This list included various levels of reading, arithmetic, and table books, as well as slates, pencils, inkstands and other types of writing material.[15] The record provides evidence of a small, but fully functioning and well-equipped school. To enhance the visual impact of teaching upon the inmates, the GPB ordered the governor to acquire a set of Philip's 'School Gardening Diagrams', to be hung on the walls of the schoolroom.[16] Soon after the arrival of the first juvenile-adults in Clonmel, the institution also obtained a set of maps, which were mounted in the schoolroom. The 'Johnston's Small Wall School Maps' included images of North America, the British Isles, Ireland, the Eastern and Western Hemispheres and Europe.[17] The impact of the provision of such facilities on this class of offender should not be underestimated. The majority of the boys were poorly educated and had long since graduated from formal education to delinquency and social deviance. The imposition of daily education was a deliberate tactic of the borstal founders, who sought to promote not only a greater degree of learning in the boys, but also to impress a sense of self-discipline through the repetitiveness of the routine.

This basic education was supplemented throughout the year by lectures from individuals such as visiting justices, chaplains, doctors and the governor. This was usually facilitated by the philanthropy of the BAI. In one example, the inmates received a lecture on electricity, accompanied by lantern slides and practical demonstrations. This event was organised by 'gentlemen not connected with the prison'.[18] The importance and social standing of BAI members ensured that they had little difficulty in attracting those qualified to lecture the boys in this way. An example of their ability to attract local philanthropic support was shown by the donation by Archdeacon Warren sometime in May 1910 of a magic lantern.[19] The device was utilised extensively at the institution over the following years.

In 1913–14, Randall K. Moore, a visiting justice, gave a lecture on 'his travels in far-off lands', while his wife accompanied him with songs and music on a piano.[20] The details of this particular event were also reported in *The Nationalist*. The presentation was described as 'an interesting illustrated geographical lecture' attended by eighty inmates, as well as members of staff, chaplains and the medical officer. The magic lantern that provided visual images to accompany the lecture was operated by Mr Webster, while a piano was loaned for the event by Mr Hyatt. As if to reinforce the usefulness of the event, at the end of the evening, Mr Fayle, a member of the BAI, read out a letter from a former inmate. The boy was now living in Queensland, Australia, working as a carpenter and credited his success to his experiences in Clonmel borstal.[21] Exposure in this manner to such a wide range of issues was considered by the BAI to be useful in lifting the spirit of the boys during the long winter evenings of their detention and also in enriching their knowledge and stimulating their appetite for further learning. A visiting justice from Belfast prison, W.H. McLaughlin, gave the inmates an oral and visual presentation about his visit to South Africa. Lectures were also given by F.E. Hackett of the Royal College of Science on 'Electricity', Professor Carpenter of the Zoological Gardens on 'Animal Life' and Dr P.J. McGinnis on 'Anatomy'.[22] During that same year, the borstal's medical officer, Dr O'Brien, along with other members of staff, delivered a number of lectures on 'First Aid'.[23] No other such lectures are specifically referred to in the various reports and correspondence of the GPB and BAI but it is known that they took place on an annual basis, though it is likely that these events were disrupted during the First World War. In the mid-nineteenth century, geography lessons had been provided to prisoners by the penal authorities in a calculated effort to encourage them to emigrate.[24] Years later, the GPB were driven by altogether different motives with the programme of education it approved for juvenile-adult offenders. The combination of basic education and carefully selected lectures was designed to equip the boys not merely with the faculties necessary for independent survival, but also with the moral fibre to lead good lives.

The frequency of the lectures depended purely on the availability of lecturers. The evidence shows that the borstal and the BAI took full advantage of the presence of visiting lecturers in Clonmel town. In late November 1914, the borstal's medical officer, Dr O'Brien, began a series of lectures on the subject of first aid (as mentioned page 144). This lecture series continued until late January 1915 and Dr O'Brien was assisted in his demonstration by Nurse O'Brien. In his first lecture, the doctor demonstrated the various uses of triangular bandages, incorporating a skeleton and diagrams into his presentation. All of the boys of the special and ordinary grades attended this class, along with various staff members.[25] Among the topics were first aid to the injured, the proper procedure for bandaging injuries, and how to respond to a drowning person and to someone 'who was hanging by the neck'. The material for the practical demonstrations during the lectures was provided by the local St John's Ambulance Association. The governor reported that one of the most important results of the lecture series was that a large number of officers and inmates were more competent in the practical administration of first aid. The medical officer received particular praise for his talents in conducting the lectures, on a voluntary basis, in a way and in a language that ensured they were 'understood by the youngest inmate'.[26] The first aid theme continued at the borstal with the visit of Sergeant Hammer of St John's Ambulance Brigade in December 1915. On this occasion, again sponsored by the BAI, the boys were presented with a first-aid lecture. Sergeant Hammer had given the lecture in the town's theatre earlier in the week and was particularly keen to repeat it for the boys. He had previously given the same lecture at Wakefield borstal. At Clonmel it was attended by fifty-four inmates (special and ordinary grades), along with members of staff and their families. Governor Dobbin later described the event as 'the best illustrated programme we have had'. Afterwards, the boys were each instructed to write an essay summing up what they had learned.[27]

An important element of the learning environment at Clonmel borstal was the provision of a library, not only as part of the educational process, but for recreational use as well. The maintenance of the library was one of the ongoing priorities for all parties involved in the management of the institution. The library was originally founded after the GPB made an appeal to prison governors throughout the country to donate, after careful consideration, any surplus books that might be useful to juvenile-adults at Clonmel.[28] Initially the books were of an educational nature, covering subjects such as science, geography, arithmetic, carpentry and agricultural chemistry. Many of the books selected covered agricultural matters, reflecting the determination of the GPB, the BAI, and indeed the founders of the system, that the boys should receive a broad theoretical and practical education in farming methods. There were also several volumes relating to gardening, an area in which Clonmel borstal was able to provide satisfactory practical training for inmates. A number of works dealt with some of the practical subjects taught at the borstal, such as shoemaking, woodwork and basic building. The library also included many non-educational works of fiction and biography. Their titles suggest books espousing the highest moral values, with tales of heroism, bravery and great achievement. Among the books sent to Clonmel and included in the library were *The Boy Voyager* by Annie Bowman, *Station Life in New Zealand* by Lady Barker and *Boy's Book of Travel and Adventure*.[29] The availability of appropriate reading material was 'one of the most important influences in the reformatory treatment of the Borstal Institution', according to the GPB chairman.[30]

EFFECTIVENESS OF EDUCATION

An accurate assessment of education at Clonmel borstal is only possible from 1912 onwards. Prior to that time the GPB did not provide any data on the educational attainment of inmates. In its 1912 report the Board began the practice of providing a detailed breakdown of progress in reading, writing and calculating. For the sake of the reports, the inmate population was divided into four categories (i) 'wholly illiterate' (ii) 'number of those able to read' (iii) 'number of those able to read and write' (iv) 'number of those able to read, write and calculate'.[31] Within each of these categories there were different levels of achievement in numeracy and literacy. In total, the reports between 1912 and 1921 examined the progress of 1,206 inmates.[32] A number of interesting trends may be drawn from this data.

Between 1912 and 1921, a total of 98 inmates were deemed 'wholly illiterate' on admission. Of these, 75 (76 per cent) had learned to read, write and calculate. Twelve inmates in this category learned to read and write, while five learned to read. Over 6 per cent of these inmates 'remained wholly illiterate'.[33] This allowed the Board to claim a success rate of 94 per cent. The failure rate in this category is fairly low, though it must be pointed out that the quality of reading, writing and calculating referred to in these reports cannot be measured by statistics alone.

TABLE 7.1
EDUCATIONAL PROGRESS OF INMATES IN DETENTION, 1912–21

(A) Number of wholly literate	Total between 1912 and 1921[34]
Who learned to read	5
Who learned to read and write	12
Who learned to read, write and calculate	75
Remaining wholly illiterate	6
(B) Number of those able to read Who learned to write	3
Who learned to write and calculate	56
Remaining unable to write or calculate	5
(C) Number of those able to read and write	
Who learned to calculate	25
Remaining unable to calculate	4
(D) Number of those able to read, write and calculate	
Who have improved in one or more of these subjects	997
Who have not made any progress	18

Source: NLI, GPB, annual reports, 1912–21

The second category evaluated the success of those sixty-four inmates already able to read. Fifty-six boys (87 per cent) also learned to write and calculate. Three of the boys just learned to write, while five (7.8 per cent), remained unable to either write or calculate. The third category assessed the numerical abilities of the 29 boys already able to read and write. Twenty-five inmates in this category learned to calculate while four did not.[35] It is not clear if the boys had no numerical skills whatsoever (i.e. they were unable to count), that they lacked basic mathematical skills.

The fourth and final category in the Board's annual educational report was perhaps the most vague. It was entitled the 'number of those able to read, write and calculate' and it included 1,015 inmates. The report, when totalled, claimed that 997 (98 per cent) of inmates in this category had improved in one or more subjects, while just eighteen inmates were deemed to have made no progress.[36] While the apparent success rate in this category would be enviable for any penal institution, it raises more questions than it answers as no criteria are established for improvement.

In 1911, Governor Connor pointed out that, upon committal to the institution, many inmates had a very poor understanding of geography but the borstal school had allowed many of them to locate the rivers and mountains of their own native regions. Inmates who had passed out of the third class of the national board of education 'were well able to read any secular book' and the results of teaching overall were 'satisfactory'.[37] In the clearest indication of the extent to which some boys had improved, he argued that the third class was too low a level for them to cease their schooling and that provision should be made for them to continue. The governor took it upon himself to visit each one in his cell on a daily basis, where the inmate would have prepared a written transcription from one of his books, as well as some mathematical exercises. This was, according to the governor, 'in order they would not forget what they have learned'.[38] This type of initiative by institutional staff conformed to the ideals of Ruggles-Brise and the founders, who felt that such individual attention would set the borstal apart from other juvenile penal institutions. However, despite being enriched in many different ways through the provision of education, the problem remained that the boys were not gaining adequate exposure to appropriate training for work, the one area that would most benefit them on leaving the institution.

THE ORIGINS OF BORSTAL TRAINING

By the second half of the nineteenth century, the Irish prison service displayed a considerable enthusiasm for training inmates in a trade in order to give them increased employment opportunities upon their release.[39] Prison staff for the new penal reformatory therefore, had to be able to teach the inmates and train them 'in various kinds of industrial work, and [be] qualified generally to exercise the best and healthiest kind of moral influence'.[40] The use of the words 'moral influence' in this context is highly significant, expressing the essence of the borstal system as a reformatory process. This was in line with the Victorian attitude that, by keeping offenders occupied and giving them the means to find employment, their criminal inclinations would have less time to flourish.[41] The intention of the founders was that the treatment programme developed for these young offenders should seek to improve their morals using a number of different but associated methods. Training was essentially another methodology in the process of reforming juvenile-adults. The Gladstone Committee did not provide any specific detail as to how the reformatory should approach the question of training but instead gave a fairly broad remit to those charged with implementing its recommendations. For Ruggles-Brise, the borstal system, complete with its training provisions, provided the best 'chance for the weak, and feeble and unfortunate to make a fresh start and take their place in the great industrial army'.[42] He relied heavily on the training methods he witnessed at Elmira, though his resulting ideas were not replicated in the English institution on the same grand scale.

He later wrote of being impressed at the fact that underneath 'the elaborate system of moral, physical, and industrial training' of inmates, a very obvious 'human effort' was underway to bring about the reform of juvenile offenders in certain US states.[43] A number of years after his American trip, Ruggles-Brise set up the pre-experimental reformatory at Bedford prison, which was staffed by carefully selected officers who would work on the 'exhortation and moral persuasion of inmates'. The prison commissioners adapted the existing prison day by introducing the use of physical drill, gymnastics, technical and literary education and a grade system as part of the new venture.[44] England's borstal inmates were subjected to a 5.30 am start and their routine thereafter was governed by work, education and training.

The founders of the system placed an emphasis on work for two reasons. Firstly, juvenile-adult offenders tended to have little or no employment experience due to the vicious circle of their offending. A routine of hard work was designed to instil good habits and efficiency. Secondly, their work was combined with teaching them a trade in order to make them competitive in an often over-crowded labour market.[45] These ideas were summed up by an unnamed officer of an English borstal institution in 1926. Once the physical health and development of a boy have been addressed, there followed a need to equip him with a trade or occupation in order to make him 'self-supporting and self-reliant'. It was believed that his tendency towards committing crime would inevitably be greatly reduced by this stage. Training a boy in what the officer described as 'a healthy atmosphere, away from the home (or lack of home) environment', created an opportunity that he would not otherwise have been afforded. In the natural order of things 'his criminal career comes to an end'.[46]

In his 1926 profile of England's borstal institutions, Sydney A. Moseley outlined the development of training in the system during its first twenty-five years. Juvenile-adults were trained as bricklayers, farm-workers, gardeners, cooks, carpenters, painters, smiths, shoe-makers, launderers, poultry and pig-keepers, dairy-workers and domestic workers.[47] Prior to 1926, however, some controversy existed in England about the quality of training that was provided for the inmates. Radzinowicz and Hood claim that the Prison Commissioners gave the less-than-accurate impression that boys were employed at 'skilled trades' when this was not the reality. Instead, they claim, boys learned the elements of a trade and were employed, in the main, in manual labour. This caused judges to have an inaccurate impression and led to a general misunderstanding on this aspect of the institutions.[48] Ironically, the system was often known, both in England and Ireland, as borstal training. Controversies around the issue of training were not restricted to the English borstal system, however. One of the most heavily debated and criticised aspects of Clonmel borstal between 1906 and 1921 was the extent to which it was able (or indeed unable) to provide appropriate training to its inmates.

TRAINING AT CLONMEL BORSTAL

It is fair to say that the prison authorities in Ireland promoted the idea of training as one of the most important features of Clonmel borstal. Among the physical changes to the county gaol complex in 1906 was the addition of a 'large and commodious carpenter's shop'.[49] A plan of Clonmel prison, commissioned by the GPB in 1909 in anticipation of the conversion to a full borstal institution, shows that a number of small gardens were set aside for use by the juvenile-adults. These would have been the only facilities in for gardening, agricultural training and physical exercise. In 1940, Dublin barrister Edward Fahy described the exterior of the complex in some unflattering detail. He noted that a small patch of ground, no bigger than the average residential lawn, lay inside the main gates. It was dusty in the summer and muddy in

Owing to a printing error on this
page the Borstal plan has not
appeared. We apologise for this
and direct the reader to the back
of the cover where a copy of the
same plan can be seen.

Plan of Clonmel prison and borstal inastitution, 1909.

the winter and was the only available space for the inmates to exercise. A further piece of ground was described as a small and narrow garden, whose soil was depleted as a result of repeated and frequent cultivation.[50] A small field owned by the prison but outside its walls was also used for the purposes of the agricultural training of borstal inmates. This initial review of the institution's training facilities immediately reveals a serious deviation from the intention of the borstal founders. The recommendation of the Gladstone Committee was that the penal reformatory should be located in the countryside with ready access to land on which to teach agricultural skills to inmates.

In theory, the juvenile-adults at Clonmel borstal had to attain a prescribed standard of elementary education before they were permitted to engage in any form of training for a trade. Initially the inmates at the borstal were taught the skills of carpentry, gardening and horticulture. By 1908 the list of trades had increased to include shoemaking, tailoring and painting.[51] The boys worked at these under the guidance of 'competent instructors' but it is not clear if they were being trained to become fully qualified in a craft or merely to become experienced labourers. In 1910, the GPB chairman J.S. Gibbons indicated that some inmates worked in the areas of carpentry, gardening, laundry, painting, whitewashing, shoemaking and tailoring. There was a high level of production of timber products from the carpentry workshop.[52] A 'commercial class' was assembled at the institution whereby 'twenty of the more intelligent inmates' were educated in basic secretarial skills including 'the preparation of invoices, the addressing of letters, the writing of telegrams, etc.'[53] This represented a considerable expansion of the range of training options for inmates, coming as it did in the initial period after the conversion of the complex to a full borstal institution. The creation of this commercial class would not have represented a serious drain on the physical facilities of the borstal as such a subject could be taught in an existing classroom. Beyond the addition of new classrooms in 1913 there is no record of any expansion of the training facilities up to and including 1921. By 1920, the borstal staff included instructors in gardening, tailoring, carpentry and shoemaking.[54]

In order to support the facilities for training boys in practical trades, the borstal provided a library. Alongside the volumes that espoused the positive human characteristics of heroism and charity there were *Carpentry Workshop Practice* or *Woodworkers Handbook*.

Among works given to the borstal by prisons around the country were books on subjects that were clearly beyond the capacity of the borstal to teach to their fullest extent, including Webb's *Elementary Agriculture*, Johnston's *Catechism of Agri Chemistry* and Wright's *Pictorial Practical Fruit Growing*.[55] While agricultural work and training were part of the daily routine at Clonmel borstal, the institution was ill-equipped to train inmates to their maximum ability. There is a sense that, in providing such a wide range of reading on these subjects, the institution's management was attempting to compensate for the borstal's shortcomings.

At every juncture, the punitive aspects of the scheme were played down and a heavy emphasis was placed on the individualisation of inmates. In its annual report for 1914–15, the GPB declared that its remit of converting would-be criminals into decent members of society was 'not only a humane but profitable work'. The Board confidently claimed that, if many of the repeat offenders now costing the government large amounts of money on an annual basis had benefited from borstal training, their criminal careers would have ended early in life.[56] To this end, the Board publicly sought to treat borstal inmates in a fair and equitable manner. Their training facilities should be practical, and no more or less comfortable than the conditions in which they would be expected to live following discharge.[57] According to the Board's own pronouncements, the initial response of inmates to the training programme offered at Clonmel was good. In its first report on the borstal institution, the GPB claimed that the boys were working 'most industriously' and many had already developed noticeable skill in carpentry.[58] In 1911 the governor reported a positive reaction to the commercial class referred to earlier, with a high level of competition between the boys.[59]

Although they continued to have many concerns, prison authorities in Ireland were determined to accentuate everything that was positive about their training provisions in Clonmel. To underline the beneficial effects of their work, the Board published accounts of ex-borstal inmates in its 1918 report. These are extracts from letters sent to the institution by discharged inmates serving in the British army during the First World War. Two of them make special reference to the training received in the borstal and were obviously published by the members of the GPB because of their own agenda in seeking increased government support for the institution's training capacity. Nonetheless, their previous borstal training obviously made quite an important impact upon these two soldiers. The first letter expressed gratitude for the training received. The author points out that in his current role as a soldier he would be 'a complete duffer' were it not for the training and drill procedures he had been shown. The second boy described how his training had saved both him and his army instructor a great deal of time and energy. His abilities were so obvious to his military instructor that the senior officer asked the boy if he had received training elsewhere and the young soldier admitted that he had been trained at Clonmel borstal. The instructor responded that 'he had a good many lads from that place under him, and that they were no trouble to him'.[60] While the selective publication of these words may have amounted to a propaganda exercise by the GPB, it was only for the purpose of pressuring the British government, through the office of the chief secretary, for greater funding for training.

TRAINING PROBLEMS

As early as 1911, the BAI and the governor of Clonmel were actively engaged in attempting to acquire further land for the institution. A letter from Governor Connor to the GPB outlined three different expansion options available in that year. The first piece of land was described as a 'large garden' and was at the time rented by a local shopkeeper from a hotel owner in Jersey. It was deemed by the governor to be the most suitable of the three. Rent on the land would be paid to the head landlord, Richard Bagwell, also president of the BAI. Bagwell was also head landlord of the second suggested plot, another one-acre field. It was used by his tenant on fair days 'for the purpose of trying horses, for amusements, also for grazing two cows which supply his hotel with milk'. The third plot was held by the Roman Catholic chaplain of the borstal, Canon Flavin, and directly joined the number one prison, where adult inmates were previously held.[61] It is known that the GPB did acquire a field adjoining the borstal institution for the purposes of training inmates in agricultural skills but it is unclear which of these plots it was.

The need for greater facilities at Clonmel borstal was raised in the 1912 report of the GPB. It outlined how the Board had commenced the process of obtaining a field for the purpose of instructing the boys in 'high class gardening'.[62] Nothing came of this approach and in its 1913 report the GPB pointed out that there was limited space within the walls of the institution to facilitate training in basic farming practices such as the care and feeding of livestock or the milking of cows. The report described the existing trades of shoemaking and tailoring as 'blind alley' employments in that they were not very helpful in preparing the boys for work upon their discharge.[63] The problems facing the institution came to national attention in the same year when it drew support from the *Freeman's Journal*. The newspaper called on the government to ensure that borstal inmates would be provided with the type of training that would 'produce intelligent and skilful farm labourers, who will obtain not merely certain employment but good wages'.[64] This rhetoric was part of a concerted effort by the GPB and BAI, united in their goal of persuading the government to purchase a substantial tract of land for agricultural training. William Casey, the honorary secretary of the BAI, wrote to Alderman Condron, East Tipperary MP, in July 1913.

> I suppose Mr Birrell [chief secretary of Ireland] will readily admit the absurdity of trying to teach ninety boys farm work on three acres of land without a cow! and I may say the ability to milk cows is considered a very important matter when boys are being sent out on licence to farmers.[65]

This summed up some of the most obvious failings of Clonmel's training facilities. The agricultural labour market was the most likely first destination for borstal-age young men in Ireland (and England). It followed, therefore, that the three main groups charged with operating the system, the GPB, the BAI and the institutional staff, placed a strong emphasis on training in farm work. All parties saw this type of training as the best hope for post-release success. In a sense, everything that happened to the boys *inside* the institution was in preparation for that time. The challenge for the system was the inadequacy of facilities to support that.

The issue came to a head in 1913 when a farm was identified by the management and the BAI as being ideal for use by the institution. This view was supported by the GPB. In a detailed appeal to Augustine Birrell, the chief secretary for Ireland, William Casey of the BAI argued in favour of agriculture as the most suitable occupation for borstal inmates. A 'healthy outdoor occupation', he pointed out, would 'improve and strengthen them physically and morally, removing them from their original vicious surroundings and the slums of the towns and the cities'.[66] This had always been the intention of the borstal system as the founders recognised early on that most of its inmates should not return to the cities, if at all possible. Casey went on to list the deficiencies of the facilities in Clonmel and argued that most of the boys departed the institution unfit for the only type of work in which they were likely to find employment. While carpentry, tailoring and mat-making were honourable trades, the boys could not become sufficiently qualified in them to support themselves in this work. In any event, he argued, the trades unions would not recognise workers trained in a borstal as qualified. The letter concluded by appealing to the chief secretary to consider purchasing the 136-acre farm, a half-mile from the borstal, on sale at four thousand pounds.[67] Casey had made clear that the future of the borstal system in Ireland hinged on the resolution of this issue.

As part of the same campaign, Max Green, the chairman of the GPB, repeated many of the points made by Casey. In another letter to Birrell, he pointed out that the borstal systems of England and Scotland operated on a different level to that of Ireland. In England, the borstal institutions housed 752 inmates and had 132 acres of land available for agricultural training. In Scotland, there were 30 acres available for just nineteen inmates. The comparative figure for Ireland was 3 acres for eighty-seven inmates, even though Irish agriculture remained the predominant source of employment. The agricultural sector was not the dominant employer in England, where discharged inmates had many opportunities of work in large manufacturing cities. He argued that the one and a half acres within the walls of Clonmel borstal were wholly inadequate for training the boys in skills such as haymaking, ploughing, sowing, reaping, care of livestock and milking. In a final effort to sell the idea to his political and administrative masters, Green pointed out that, apart from providing cost-price provisions for the institution, there would be actual monetary profit from the farm.[68]

Many of the arguments made by both Green and Casey were repeated in further lengthy communications to the chief secretary's office. None were successful. So anxious were the BAI and GPB to resolve the issue that, later in 1913, a fresh appeal was made. Max Green drew Birrell's attention to a 170-acre farm at Lusk Common in County Dublin, enclosed in 1856 for use by juvenile offenders. A group of adult convicts had been employed at the farm to prepare it for use as a juvenile prison. This first stage of the project was so successful that the idea of a juvenile prison was abandoned in favour of retaining the adults as part of the Intermediate System. It would be their final stage of detention prior to release. In 1888 the land was taken over by the military authorities, in whose possession it remained. Green and the GPB felt that, by 1913, with the borstal system now having proven its worth, it would be fitting to return the land to the penal system for its original use as a farm for juvenile offenders.[69] It is not clear whether Green was suggesting the transfer of the entire borstal institution to Lusk but in any case the idea was rejected by Birrell and indeed the War Office in London.

Despite this failure, the members of the BAI took up the issue of relevant practical training publicly in their *Third Annual Report* published in 1913.[70] While there were a large number of enquiries from potential employers of discharged inmates, the lack of agricultural training was a constant impediment to future employment. The Association argued that the type of training received at Clonmel, such as carpentry or tailoring, would be of minimal use to the boys once they had left the institution. The report was unrelenting in its criticism of what the Board believed had become a major shortfall in the system. The Association, in a less than subtle lobbying exercise, called for equal status with borstal institutions in England, which by this time were being allocated the resources to provide proper training in farm work. One year later it was still making the same demands but highlighted a worrying consequence of the unchanged situation. When discharged, inmates were sent to work on farms as unskilled labourers but they were forced to accept a wage reduction. When they became aware that others of their own age, engaged in similar work in the area, were earning more, they became agitated and often violated the conditions of their early release. The Association was critical of the lack of progress on the land issue six years into the system and rebuked the government for its rejection of the farm proposal.[71] In a 1915 editorial, *The Nationalist* denounced the lack of land for the borstal as 'deplorable' in light of the 'splendid, fruitful reform work' that was ongoing there.[72] The situation also came to the attention of the British press in the form of an article in the *Times Educational Supplement* in 1917. In a profile of Clonmel borstal, the newspaper pointed out that many discharged inmates were destined for a life in the army because the necessary agricultural training was so poor. The article alleged that the blame for this situation lay firmly with the government.[73] The land controversy continued unabated throughout the second decade of the twentieth century. In 1920, BAI member A. Fayle JP commended the institution for turning out well-trained inmates who nonetheless faced difficult circumstances because of their lack of this experience.[74] These concerns not only serve to highlight the proactive role of the Association but also draw attention to the fact that, even after more than sixteen years in operation, the institution remained under-resourced.

THE ROLE OF RELIGION

Spirituality, religion and the chaplain had all been used as tools for the moral improvement of prisoners for many decades before the foundation of the borstal system. Moral regeneration was the sole reason for the chaplain's role in the lives of the juvenile-adults in the borstal. The prison chaplain had come to great prominence in the mid-1850s with the establishment of Mountjoy and the Crofton system. In fact, the director of convict prisons in Ireland explained that one of the purposes of building Mountjoy was 'to induce religious principles into the hearts of convicts'. The presence of a chaplain in prison was not a new phenomenon but his function did take on a renewed significance under the Crofton system. For a prisoner incarcerated under the system, one of his many visits from the chaplain served to interrupt the tedium of a day often spent separated and isolated. Isolation was a well-considered element of the Intermediate System, designed to keep convicts apart from the influences of the wider prison population, to leave each alone with his thoughts and to engage with his spiritual side. Paradoxically, this system set up to allow greater space for religious influence was often resisted by the chaplains. Both the Roman Catholic and Presbyterian chaplains of Mountjoy felt that long periods of time alone were detrimental for convicts as this created room for highly immoral feelings, particularly among uneducated men with no interest in reading.[75] Some Roman Catholic chaplains confined their work to purely spiritual matters, while others engaged with prisoners at a more practical level, providing them with the necessary resources to succeed after their discharge.[76]

In assessing the influence of religion on the borstal system it should be remembered that it was actually the evidence of a prison chaplain that brought about the establishment of the Gladstone Committee in 1894, which in turn recommended the foundation of a new penal reformatory for juveniles. G.P. Merrick was the chaplain of Holloway and Newgate prisons and in 1893 presented a serious indictment of the English penal system under the leadership of Edmund Du Cane.

Merrick's evidence led to the establishment of the Departmental Committee on Prison Reform in 1894 under the chairmanship of Herbert Gladstone. While the Gladstone Committee recommendations on the penal reformatory made little mention of the place of religion and the role of the chaplain, it did frequently refer to the need 'to exercise the best and healthiest kind of moral influence'.[77] Ruggles-Brise later interpreted this by designing a system that he believed should focus on the 'individualisation of the prisoner, morally and physically'. The new arrangements should include a system of rewards that would motivate the inmates to good behaviour, self-discipline and self-respect.[78] The use of the chaplain in this regard does not appear to have been the subject of much public debate at the time of the foundation of the borstal system, either in England or Ireland. It seems that it was taken for granted that the churches would have a place in the new system, though not the all-powerful role they exercised in other juvenile penal institutions.

A number of religious denominations were represented in the population of Clonmel borstal. Mirroring the country as a whole, inmates came from the Roman Catholic community (the highest number), and also the Protestant Episcopalian and Presbyterian churches. Their spiritual needs were served by chaplains representing the Roman Catholic Church and the Church of Ireland. They were drawn from the clergy already working in the Clonmel area and their commitment to the borstal was not full-time. The first Catholic chaplain was the Very Rev. C.J. Canon Flavin, an elderly and highly influential local parish priest who was elevated to the position of archdeacon in 1911.[79] Rev. Flavin was supported in his borstal work by his curates, Rev. P. Doocey, C.C. and Rev. N. Walsh, C.C.[80] Flavin was also a founding member and influential figure within the CDPAS (later to become the BAI). The names of the Church of Ireland chaplains are not listed in any official documents but members of both faiths were represented on the committee of the BAI and were most likely active in the institution on a daily basis. It is most likely that the first Church of Ireland chaplain was Rev. Mr Burke, supported by Rev. Mr Smith and Rev. Mr Nebitt, all of whom were members of the BAI.[81] While the local clergy had an important function both within the institution and in the Association, it must be remembered that this was the full extent of their influence. As this book will later show, the BAI was very much influenced by the clergy, though it presented itself as a non-denominational body. The borstal, on the other hand, was clearly managed by government through its agency the GPB, and at local level by the governor. Consequently, there was a very clear demarcation between the clergy and the lay management of the borstal: there is no evidence of conflict between the two groups in this regard. There was, however, some confusion among the wider population as to the identity of the institution.

The annual reports of the GPB made frequent mention of the chaplains of Clonmel borstal but reported little of their actual daily and weekly work there. When the borstal experiment first began in Clonmel prison the Board made only passing reference to the chaplains, pointing out that they, along with the governor and the schoolmaster, would pay 'special attention' to the boys.[82] This was part of the individualisation process espoused by Ruggles-Brise but it should be remembered that, in their first three years in Clonmel, the borstal inmates were part of a much wider prison population for which the chaplains also had spiritual responsibility. Apart from officiating at the daily and weekly religious services of their respective congregations, the chaplains also gave lectures to the boys in matters of a spiritual nature. Both sets of chaplains visited the inmates in their cells to provide religious counsel on a regular basis and sometimes met with groups of boys collectively.[83] The chaplains also had some input into the selection of reading material for inmates and occasionally requested the GPB to provide religious books. For example, in 1908, Canon Flavin submitted a requisition for 150 books to the Board's headquarters in Dublin Castle. The titles included *The Children's Mass: Prayers and Hymns with Music*, *Catholic Piety* and *Roman Catholic Catechisms* by Dr James Butler.[84] In 1913 the GPB approved a request from the Church of Ireland chaplain to provide each member of his borstal congregation with a copy of *The Irish Churchman's Almanak* at a cost of two pence per book.[85] The limited surviving evidence suggests that members of both churches approached their work with great enthusiasm and their duties extended beyond the realm of providing spiritual support.

The moral improvement of juvenile-adults was a key element of borstal treatment. The chaplains gave lectures to the boys, not just on religious themes but on issues of etiquette, hygiene and disposition.[86] This approach was seen by those working in the system as an important part of the borstal detention process. It was one of the civilising influences over the young men, most of whom had previously been completely devoid of any of the accepted norms of social behaviour or personal bearing. The CDPAS claimed that the appearance and personal behaviour of many inmates were enhanced following their period of detention.[87] This aspect of the borstal process was specifically designed to turn juvenile-adult offenders into what the attorney-general, Lord Justice Cherry, termed 'useful members of society'.[88] However, the chaplains formally affiliated with the borstal were not the only clergy to make a contribution to its spiritual development and the institution was regularly visited by various church denominations.

The earliest recorded external clerical involvement with the borstal came on 25 May 1908. The Roman Catholic bishop of the diocese of Lismore and Waterford, the Most Rev. Dr Sheehan, administered the sacrament of confirmation to six inmates, an indication of the early success of the chaplaincy.[89] As the institution was still predominantly a county gaol at this time, it is unclear whether the visit of the bishop would have taken place with or without the presence of the borstal system. A further such visit took place on 21 May 1911, when Dr Sheehan administered the same sacrament to eleven inmates.[90] These are the only surviving records of visits paid by a serving Roman Catholic bishop to Clonmel but, in light of the further expansion there, it is not likely that they were the last. Also at this time the Sisters of Charity visited the borstal each Sunday to teach the catechism to the inmates, 'the backward boys receiving the most attention'.[91]

A number of visits to the borstal by different orders of priests took place intermittently. In early October 1910, the Redemptorist fathers began a mission in the parish local to the borstal. On 3 October, they visited the institution and lectured the boys. The group also heard the confessions of Roman Catholic inmates and held Mass the following day and on each Sunday of the mission.[92] In 1914 the BAI reported how the Jesuits had visited Clonmel during the previous year. Accompanied by Archdeacon Flavin, they provided spiritual instruction to the inmates.[93] These events were important to the borstal institution on two levels. Firstly, they represented an affirmation of the work of the borstal and recognition of its identity as an established penal institution. Secondly, they acted as a welcome diversion for the inmates.

The response of the boys to such events and their general interactions with the chaplains is not fully clear. The chaplains claimed that, for the most part, the inmates reacted positively and sometimes quite enthusiastically to the different religious ceremonies and related events. Unsurprisingly, the first published appraisal of the borstal system from the Church of Ireland chaplain gave it a highly positive seal of approval. In praising the first year of work in Clonmel, he went on to discuss one discharged inmate who had written to him and appeared 'to be doing well'. The inmate expressed a strong desire 'to lead an upright life'.[94] In 1912 the Roman Catholic chaplain wrote of the participation of the inmates in religious ceremonies, particularly highlighting the good conduct of the boys during such events as Mass and the various lectures given by the chaplains. He also praised their involvement in the institutional choir and their reverence in the presence of the 'Holy Sacrament'.[95] In the same year, the Church of Ireland chaplain reported good levels of participation by his borstal congregation. The response of the inmates to the individual and collective attention given during his weekly visits was 'very hearty and encouraging'. The Presbyterian chaplain wrote of the positive response from his inmates after they left the institution. All of them, he claimed, wrote to him after leaving, to express their gratitude for the kindness received in the borstal. He found all the inmates under his spiritual care to be 'exceedingly attentive and respectful'.[96] It should be noted that these thoughts were reproduced in the various annual reports of the GPB and are, in a sense, selective extracts, making it impossible to identify the wider views of the clergy regarding their borstal work and the boys.

The singular purpose of Clonmel borstal institution in the minds of the agencies charged with its operation was to arrest the declining morals of the inmates using a number of carefully considered and not necessarily new strategies. The class of offender that was housed in Clonmel was not equipped with the necessary social, educational and emotional skills to enable them to make a worthwhile contribution to society. The borstal founders identified what was positive and progressive about the existing prison system and transferred those ideas to their penal reformatory. The practical uses of the school, the workshop and the chapel were adapted for the inmates and a spirit of individualisation set the borstal apart from previous penal institutions. The school was modest and grew in stature as the borstal expanded. The provision of elementary education in tightly controlled circumstances was of benefit to inmates who had entered with low levels of achievement in reading, writing and mathematics. The inmates enjoyed certain educational benefits that were not available to ordinary schoolboys. A well-stocked library advocated the values such as heroism, charity and self-reliance that the borstal system sought to promote. The training programme for inmates at Clonmel was lacklustre and generally deficient, however. An inexplicable absence of government investment in agricultural facilities meant that the institution fell behind its English counterparts. There is evidence, albeit limited, to suggest that the inmates responded positively to the training provisions at Clonmel, something that might be attributed to the enthusiasm of staff. The fact that training did not evolve to meet the needs of the changing labour market remains one of the key failures of the borstal during this period. Among the part-time staff of the borstal were the chaplains, representing the Roman Catholic Church and the Church of Ireland, who provided spiritual and moral guidance for the inmates. With an altogether different role in the borstal from that adopted in other juvenile institutions, they formed a powerful body within the BAI, whose influence was felt on a daily basis.

NOTES

1. Cherry, 'Juvenile crime and its prevention', p. 436.
2. Moseley, *The Truth about Borstal*, p. 24.
3. Quoted in Carey, *Mountjoy: The Story of a Prison*, p. 25.
4. Carey, *Mountjoy: The Story of a Prison*, p. 52.
5. Carey, *Mountjoy: The Story of a Prison*, p. 55.
6. John-Paul McCarthy, 'In hope and fear: the Victorian prison in perspective', in Joost Augusteijn, Mary Ann Lyons (eds), *Irish History: A Research Yearbook* (Dublin: Four Courts Press, 2002), p. 125.
7. Hood, *Borstal Re-assessed*, p. 2.
8. Carey, *Mountjoy: The Story of a Prison*, p. 104.
9. Hood, *Borstal Re-assessed*, p. 7.
10. Hood, *Borstal Re-assessed*, p. 15.
11. *The Treasury*, March 1910.
12. *The Nationalist*, 11 April 1906.
13. Quoted in Hood, *Borstal Re-assessed*, pp. 23–4.
14. NAI, Clonmel Borstal Memoranda, 1908–30, BAI, *Third Annual Report*, 1912–13, GPB/XB5.
15. NAI, GPB, CR, requisition form, 31 March 1910, GPB/1909/7880.
16. NAI, GPB, CR, Douglas to Connor, 23 March 1907, GPB/4478/1913.
17. NAI, GPB, CR, GPB/1913/4478, list of approved books, 14 June 1906, GPB/1913/4478.
18. *The Nationalist*, 26 May 1909.
19. *The Nationalist*, 1 June 1910.
20. NAI, Clonmel Borstal Memoranda, 1908–30, BAI, *Fourth Annual Report*, 1913–1914, GPB/XB5.
21. *The Nationalist*, 13 September 1913.
22. NAI, Clonmel Borstal Memoranda, 1908–30, BAI, *Fourth Annual Report*, 1913–1914, GPB/XB5.

23. NLI, *Thirty-seventh Report of the General Prisons Board*, vii [Cd-8082], H.L., 1914–5 xiii, 44.
24. Carey, *Mountjoy: The Story of a Prison*, p. 105.
25. NAI, GPB, CR, Governor's report, 25 November 1914, GPB/5632/1920.
26. NAI, GPB, CR, Governor's report, 27 January 1915, GPB/5632/1920.
27. NAI, GPB, CR, Governor's report, 27 January 1915, GPB/5632/1920.
28. NAI, GPB, CR, GPB minute, GPB/4478/1913.
29. NAI, GPB, CR, list of library books, Maryboro, GPB/4478/1913.
30. NAI, GPB, CR, minute applying for a Treasury grant, GPB/4478/193.
31. NLI, *Forty-third Report of the General Prisons Board*, xiv [Cmd-3304], H.L. 1920–1, v, 34.
32. NLI, *Forty-third Report of the General Prisons Board*, xiv [Cmd-3304], H.L. 1920–1, v, 34. This figure is the combined total of inmates under instruction for each year, meaning that most inmates are counted more than once. A specific breakdown for each year is not possible because, for example, the 1916 report would have counted inmates also included in the 1915 report and not just new committals for the past year.
33. NLI, *Forty-third Report of the General Prisons Board*, xiv [Cmd-3304], H.L. 1920–1, v, 79.
34. An overall total is not possible because some inmates are counted multiple times as most were detained in the borstal for longer than one calendar year.
35. NLI, *Forty-third Report of the General Prisons Board*, xiv [Cmd-3304], H.L. 1920–1, v, 80.
36. NLI, *Forty-third Report of the General Prisons Board*, xiv [Cmd-3304], H.L. 1920–1, v, 34.
37. NAI, GPB, CR, governor's minute to GPB, GPB/1911/1835.
38. NAI, GPB, CR, governor's minute to GPB, GPB/1911/1835.
39. McCarthy, 'In hope and fear: the Victorian prison in perspective', p. 121.
40. Quoted in Hood, *Borstal Re-assessed*, p. 2.
41. McCarthy, 'In hope and fear: the Victorian prison in perspective', p. 124.
42. *The Daily News*, 26 August 1908.
43. Ruggles-Brise, *The English Prison System*, p. 91.
44. Ruggles-Brise, *The English Prison System*, p. 93.
45. Hood, *Borstal Re-assessed*, p. 97.
46. Moseley, *The Truth about Borstal*, p. 22.
47. Moseley, *The Truth about Borstal*, p. 28.
48. Radzinowicz, Hood, *A History of English Criminal Law*, pp. 394–5.
49. NLI, *Twenty-ninth Report of the General Prisons Board*, x [Cd-3698], H.L. 1906–7, x, 86.
50. Fahy, 'The boy criminal', *The Bell*, 1940, 1, 2, p. 47.
51. NLI, *Thirtieth Report of the General Prisons Board*, v [Cd-4253], 1907–8, xx, 13.
52. NAI, GPB, CR, Gibbons address to International Penitentiary Congress, 1910, p. 55.
53. NLI, *Thirty-fourth Report of the General Prisons Board*, vii [Cd-6365], H.L. 1911–2, ix, 43.
54. *The Nationalist*, 20 October 1920.
55. NAI, GPB, CR, file on borstal library, GPB/4478/1913.
56. NLI, *Thirty-seventh Report of the General Prisons Board*, x [Cd-8082], H.L. 1914–5, x, 12.
57. NLI, *Thirty-fifth Report of the General Prisons Board*, i [Cd-6996], H.L. 1912–3, i, 63.
58. NLI, *Twenty-ninth Report of the General Prisons Board*, x [Cd-3698], H.L. 1906–7, viii, 44.
59. NLI, *Thirty-fourth Report of the General Prisons Board*, vii [Cd-6365], H.L. 1911–2, xiv, 67.
60. NLI, *Fortieth Report of the General Prisons Board*, iii [Cm-42], H.L. 1917–8, xi, 19.
61. NAI, GPB, CR, Letter from Clonmel borstal institution, GPB/1832/1911.
62. NLI, *Thirty-fourth Report of the General Prisons Board*, vii [Cd-6365], H.L. 1911–2, xiv, 15.
63. NLI, *Thirty-fifth Report of the General Prisons Board*, i [Cd-6996], H.L. 1912–3, i, 11.
64. *Freeman's Journal*, 18 August 1913.
65. NAI, CSORP, Casey to Alderman Condon, 1A/81/1/1913.
66. NAI, CSORP, William Casey to Augustine Birrell, March 1913, 1/A/81/1/1913.
67. NAI, CSORP, William Casey to Augustine Birrell, March 1913, 1/A/81/1/1913.
68. NAI, CSORP, Green to under-secretary for Ireland, 26 April 1913, 1/A/81/1/1913.
69. NAI, CSORP, Green to under-secretary for Ireland, 1 August 1913, 1/A/81/1/1913.
70. NAI, Clonmel Borstal Memoranda, 1908–30, BAI, *Third Annual Report*, 1912–13, GPB/XB5.
71. NAI, Clonmel Borstal Memoranda, 1908–30, BAI, *Fourth Annual Report*, 1913–14, GPB/XB5.

72. *The Nationalist*, 25 August 1915.
73. Reproduced in *The Nationalist*, 5 September 1917.
74. *The Nationalist*, 20 October 1920.
75. Carey, *Mountjoy: The Story of a Prison*, pp. 70, 71.
76. McCarthy, 'In hope and fear: the Victorian prison in perspective', p. 126.
77. Hood, *Borstal Re-assessed*, p. 2.
78. NLI, *Proceedings of the International Penitentiary Congress*, vi [Cd-5286], H.L., 1909–10, xxxix, 13.
79. *The Nationalist*, 8 March 1911.
80. *The Nationalist*, 19 May 1906.
81. *The Nationalist*, 19 May 1906.
82. NLI, *Twenty-ninth Report of the General Prisons Board*, x [Cd-3698], H.L. 1906–7, x, 12.
83. NLI, *Thirty-fourth Report of the General Prisons Board*, vii [Cd-6365], H.L. 1911–2, xiv, 14.
84. NAI, GPB, CR, order sheet submitted to GPB, 12 February 1908, GPB/1522/1908.
85. NAI, GPB, CR, Church of Ireland chaplain's memorandum, 2 October 1913, GPB/7430/1913.
86. NLI, *Thirtieth Report of the General Prisons Board*, v [Cd-4253], H.L. 1907–8, xx, 10.
87. Quoted in NLI, *Thirtieth Report of the General Prisons Board*, v [Cd-4253], H.L. 1907–8, xx, 10.
88. Cherry, 'Juvenile crime and its prevention', p. 439.
89. NAI, GPB, CR, Governor Connor to GPB, GPB/6317/1908.
90. NAI, GPB, CR, Governor Connor to GPB, GPB/3744/1911.
91. NLI, *Thirty-fourth Report of the General Prisons Board*, vii [Cd-6365], H.L. 1911–2, xiv, 15.
92. NAI, GPB, CR, Canon Flavin to Governor Connor, GPB/6731/1910.
93. GPB, Clonmel Borstal Memoranda, BAI, *Fourth Annual Report*, 1913–14, GPB/XB5.
94. NLI, *Twenty-ninth Report of the General Prisons Board*, x [Cd-3969], H.L. 1906–7, v, 86.
95 NLI, *Thirty-fourth Report of the General Prisons Board*, vii [Cd-6365], H.L. 1911–2, xiv, 14.
96. NLI, *Thirty-fourth Report of the General Prisons Board*, vii [Cd-6365], H.L. 1911–2, xiv, 14.

CHAPTER EIGHT

'Passing into the rights of citizenship'[1]: discharge and aftercare, 1906–21

The emergence of a young man from the borstal institution did not imply that his treatment was completed, merely that it had moved into a new phase. It was this feature that distinguished borstal treatment from other branches of the juvenile penal system. Unlike the industrial and reformatory school systems, the state had a legally defined role in the lives of former borstal inmates after their sentence was served. The majority of boys were released on licence before the end of their sentence. An inmate's release was assured only after he had satisfied a number of conditions during his detention. The decision to release an inmate on licence was taken following a number of carefully choreographed procedures, carried out by the institutional authorities and the locally based national aftercare body, the BAI. It was into the care of this philanthropic group that a young man was placed after his sentence was completed. The idea of prison aftercare was not new and was not exclusive to the borstal system. It took on a new importance in this context, however, as the state sought to utilise the resources of such groups to assist and guide a young man to a more promising future. The BAI was established in 1906 under the name of the Clonmel Discharged Prisoners' Aid Society (CDPAS). Despite serving discharged borstal inmates from all parts of the country, the group was almost entirely reliant on local financial support. Though the Association did have some input into the daily life of the borstal, its principal concern was to care for the needs of discharged inmates. To this end, it provided a number of support mechanisms, which included locating suitable employment and accommodation. Perhaps an altogether more important function of borstal aftercare was to ensure that the discharged boy complied with the terms of his release. There is evidence to suggest that many former inmates did in fact adhere to these conditions and most, though not all, went on to live industrious and respectable lives.

This chapter is an account of the transition from borstal incarceration to relative freedom. It will examine the background to prison and borstal aftercare, particularly the benevolent societies that first started working in that field in Ireland in the early nineteenth century, outlining the foundation and evolution of the BAI, from its humble origins in the town hall in Clonmel in County Tipperary to its role in the national fight to reform juvenile-adult offenders. The chapter will also consider the redefinition of the role of the BAI following the enactment of the Prevention of Crime Act 1908. It will explore whether the Association had an altogether more powerful influence over the lives of inmates than any of the discharged prisoners' aid societies upon which it was modelled. The daily operations of the BAI will be assessed in the context of the many financial, bureaucratic and infrastructural obstacles with which it was confronted. The chapter will discuss the circumstances through which a juvenile-adult offender was allowed, first, to leave the borstal, effectively on probation, and with the support of the BAI, and second, to begin the process of constructing a new and hopefully more productive life than the one lived prior to his incarceration. Also considered will be the discharge of more than four hundred inmates on licence to enlist in the British armed forces, the progress of some who survived the war and those those who paid the ultimate price for their freedom. Finally, the chapter will assess the various rates of success that were claimed for Clonmel borstal by the GPB and the BAI, while attempting to weigh up the reality of the return to society for the juvenile-adult offender.

THE BACKGROUND TO BORSTAL AFTERCARE

Among the first aftercare bodies established was the Sheriff's Fund Society, set up around 1807 'for the relief of necessitous prisoners discharged form Newgate Gaol'. An Act of Parliament in 1823 empowered the judiciary to order that any newly discharged prisoner without adequate means should be paid a moderate sum.[2] This set in motion a new movement towards a more caring approach to those in that situation. A number of organisations emerged, including the Birmingham Discharged Prisoner's Aid Society, which 'took its rise in the conviction of its founders that crime is to a considerable extent the result of external circumstances'. The Birmingham society engaged the services of an agent, who searched for employment and accommodation for discharged inmates. It even provided certain guarantees to employers that they would be compensated for any loss they suffered at the hands of a former prisoner.[3] This compassionate new approach marked a recognition that a criminal was more often than not the result of his environment. These sentiments were echoed by the founders of the Borstal Association in England more than three quarters of a century later.

The first borstal association originated as the London Prison Visitors' Association, founded by Ruggles-Brise in 1901. The report of the Gladstone Committee six years earlier did not make significant reference to the necessity for such a body, merely pointing out that 'special arrangements' should be made for inmates discharged from the penal reformatory.[4] The method that Ruggles-Brise employed to activate this part of the borstal project was typical of his character and his sometimes unorthodox approach. In 1901, he invited about twenty carefully selected but unsuspecting acquaintances to a dinner party at the home of a colleague, Gilbert Johnstone. The group included a bishop, an actor, a journalist, a soldier, a barrister, a stockbroker and an ex-convict. All were invited on the pretence that the chairman of the Prison Commission was going to address them about an exciting new development in the penal system. After the meal ended, Ruggles-Brise spoke for an hour without pause, describing the plight of the young male offender between the ages of seventeen and twenty years, and the fledgling borstal system that was being devised to deal with him. He went on to describe the need to find a group of well-disposed philanthropists who would visit these boys, win their confidence and help to keep them on course when they were discharged. Ruggles-Brise then arrived at the crucial point in the evening: he casually announced the purpose of the dinner party, asking 'Who will volunteer?' One of the guests, Haldane Porter, described the reaction to the question as being 'one of those dreadful pauses which often follow a direct question involving personal exertions'. To his own surprise, it was Porter who first raised his hand, declaring, 'I will have a shot at it.' He went on to become the first honorary secretary of the London Prison Visitors' Association and later the first holder of the same position in England's first Borstal Association.[5] According to Ruggles-Brise, the entire success of the borstal system rested on the work of an aftercare body such as this.[6]

Initially, the London Prison Visitors' Association was primarily concerned with the adult convict prisons at Pentonville, Wandsworth and Wormwood Scrubs. It was 'also charged with giving special attention' to the juvenile male adults at England's two experimental penal reformatories at Bedford and, later, Borstal. This organisation evolved over the following years and in 1904 its name was changed to the Borstal Association.[7] This was a model for the society that would later be founded in Clonmel in Ireland. This first Borstal Association was by no means an inconsequential organisation and, for the most part, it was concerned with 'helping and keeping in touch with discharged Borstalites'. Initially it received an English government grant of one hundred pounds per year, but it was chiefly reliant on the benevolence of the public.[8] Ruggles-Brise later described the moment of an inmate's discharge as the point where the duty of the state ends and the role of charity and benevolence takes over.[9] Those charitable and benevolent functions were fulfilled by the Borstal Association.

In the Irish context, the key functions of an aftercare organisation were set out by Dublin barrister James Alcorn in 1881. He believed the aftercare society should first provide help to discharged prisoners by finding suitable accommodation upon their release from prison and, second, render some financial assistance to those actively seeking employment or returning to their home. Such a body would also help discharged prisoners in their search for employment. Alcorn pointed out that one of the great forces in raising the fortunes of such individuals was the moral and personal influence of those charged with looking after their welfare.[10]

The Irish penal system fell far behind that of continental Europe in embracing the idea of the prison aftercare body. One of the earliest known examples of such an organisation was the refuge for discharged women based in Harcourt Road in Dublin. It was founded in 1821 by two female members of the Society of Friends (Quakers). By the 1880s, the 'Shelter', as it had become known, was confined to Protestant women, of whom just four or five remained in residence. A similar refuge for Roman Catholics was also opened at Golden-bridge and by 1880 was home to around fifty discharged women.[11] In November 1879, the chief secretary for Ireland certified the Belfast Prison Gate Mission as a discharged prisoners' aid society for Protestant convicts. Even so, in March 1880 the GPB criticised the lack of philanthropic efforts by individuals in this cause, comparing the lack of participation to the already well-developed aftercare system in

England.[12] In response to this criticism, two further organisations emerged in Dublin during 1880. An aid society for discharged Roman Catholic females began operating from premises in North Great George's Street, while a similar institution for male and female Protestants was situated in the Christian Union Buildings at Lower Abbey Street.[13] Walsh describes how middle-class Protestant women waited outside prison gates at dawn to help newly released prisoners. At other times they patrolled the streets seeking individuals for their various shelters and refuges.[14] Nevertheless, throughout the 1880s and 1890s, the GPB continued its annual criticism of the poor performance and lack of duty of Irish philanthropists towards newly discharged prisoners. In 1896, it reported a slight improvement in the number of societies present throughout the country. Three bodies now existed in Dublin, two in Belfast and one in Limerick. The societies in Dublin were affiliated to one or other of the main churches, while the Limerick Prisoners' Aid Society was non-denominational.[15] These organisations would provide further models for the BAI: the CDPAS adopted the rules of the Limerick Prisoners' Aid Society as its model.[16]

Aftercare was fundamental to the success or failure of the borstal method. Some commentaries have given the misleading impression that the BAI was little more than an employment agency. Indeed, one of the primary concerns of committee members was to locate suitable employment but the Association's role extended further than that. Prior to the prisoner's release, it carried out a careful investigative process to gather all details about him. When the time for release came, the BAI acted as a 'go-between', assisting the boy with his transition to freedom. Beyond this, it was the Association's responsibility to monitor him and ensure that he adhered to the terms of his licence. If there was a problem, for example between a boy and his employer, officers of the Association had the power to mediate. While the borstal aftercare bodies were developed in parallel with the institution itself, the idea of modern prison aftercare organisations originated in nineteenth-century England.

THE FOUNDATION OF THE BORSTAL ASSOCIATION OF IRELAND

The BAI began life as the Clonmel Discharged Prisoners' Aid Society (CDPAS) at a meeting in the town on 18 May 1906. (The first juvenile-adult arrived at the prison a few days later.) At that time the GPB reported that there were twelve such bodies operating in Ireland. Along with those already established in Dublin, Belfast and societies emerged in Waterford, Londonderry and Cork.[17] The first chairman of the CDPAS in Clonmel was Richard Bagwell, DL, and Lord Donoughmore was elected vice-chairman. Other founders included local magistrates, merchants, clergy and professionals.[18] Bagwell indicated that his involvement arose out of a sense of guilt about the absence of such an organisation to serve the existing gaol in the town.[19] In a way, the CDPAS had a particular advantage in that it evolved along with the borstal and so did not have to make the same level of adjustment as the existing penal authorities. At a political level, the GPB created the rules of this new system, which was implemented at 'ground level' by the staff of the existing county gaol at Clonmel. For both bodies, the arrival of the borstal system involved a considerable change, not only in practice but also in attitude.

The first meeting of the CDPAS was attended by many prominent figures from the town as well as a number of individuals who would ultimately play a key part in Ireland's first borstal. The most senior members of the local Roman Catholic and Protestant clergy were in attendance, including the chaplains, Canon Flavin and the Rev. Mr Burke. Many of the attendees expressed their opinions on the state of crime in Ireland and the benefits of the experiment that was about to be undertaken in their county gaol. One such voice, Dr Hewetson, hoped that the 'drink evil' that had been the cause of so much crime in the country would soon be done away with, thus reducing the number of criminals. The first committee of the CDPAS included Richard Bagwell, Lord Donoughmore, Canon Flavin, Count De la Poer, Alderman Skehan (the mayor of Clonmel), Dr Hewetson, Mr F. Tydd, Colonel Watson, John Grubb and William Casey, plus John Connor and Dr O'Brien, the governor and medical officer of the prison. Among the members of the committee were individuals who held a high profile in the town. One such was John Grubb, himself a member of a prominent local Quaker family. At one time or another, Grubb held positions as a town commissioner in Carrick-on-Suir, a member of South Tipperary county council, a governor of the local asylum and, significantly, a magistrate and member of the visiting committee of the county gaol at Clonmel.[20] The first honorary secretary of the society was Clonmel's town clerk, William Casey, who went on to become a dominant and very active figure in the BAI. (Although the members of the CDPAS were some of the most noteworthy figures in local society, their profile paled into insignificance when compared with the English Borstal Association. Its president was the home secretary and amongst its patrons were the archbishop of Canterbury, the bishop of London and the lord chief justice.[21] Only one other member of the committee in Clonmel had a higher local profile than the clergy, Casey or Grubb: Richard Bagwell was elected the first chairman of the society and held the position until his death in 1918.

Richard Bagwell was born in 1840 in Marlfield House in Clonmel and was the son of an MP for the area. He was educated at Christ Church in Oxford and became a barrister in 1866, though he never practised as a lawyer. He returned to Clonmel in 1883 and inherited Marlfield House from his father. Upon his return to Ireland he began work on his most noted historical writing, *Ireland under the Tudors*. An ardent supporter of the union of Ireland with Britain, Bagwell was active in public life both at national and local level.[22] His high local profile in Clonmel and position as chairman of the visiting committee for the county gaol made him the natural choice to lead the CDPAS. The records of the GPB show that Bagwell played an active daily role in the operation of the borstal and the BAI. He wrote many letters on some of the more mundane aspects of the life of the borstal and the surviving body of correspondence shows him to have been an enthusiastic, hands-on leader of his organisation. This chapter will later show him to be a most passionate defender of Clonmel borstal and its inmates in the face of some of the controversial matters that often consumed the public discourse on the institution. Bagwell appeared to have a good working relationship both with the GPB and the borstal personnel, with whom he often had daily contact. In a letter to the Board reporting his death dated 4 December 1918, Governor Dobbin confirmed that Richard Bagwell had been a visiting justice at Clonmel prison and later the borstal since 1878.[23] In a mark of the high esteem in which the borstal held Bagwell, Governor Dobbin attended his funeral at Marlfield House on 7 December 1918 with no less than eight warders and twenty special grade inmates. The borstal party walked in procession behind his body from Marlfield to the gates of his final resting place at Lisronagh churchyard.[24] This level of participation in an external event by borstal inmates and staff from Clonmel was unmatched during the period 1906?21.

The CDPAS progressed largely along the same lines as the borstal itself. Between 1906 and 1910, when the institution was just a part of Clonmel prison, it did not adopt the borstal as part of its name. But in 1910 the county gaol became a borstal institution and the Society evolved accordingly, reconstituting itself as the BAI in the same year. From the beginning, the Society styled itself as non-denominational, a factor that worked to its great advantage in later years as it was able to attract the attention of a range of unique individuals and organisations to its work. Between 1906 and 1909 the CDPAS' work was very much in line with that of similar bodies in Ireland. The committee visited the boys in advance of their discharge. If his anticipated domestic situation was seen as undesirable, they sought employment and a home for him elsewhere. During these years the Society's reports consisted largely of accounts of the system that was emerging in the borstal wing of Clonmel prison, with shorter portions devoted to its own aftercare work. This was mainly due to the fact that, like other such societies, it did not have any real legal power over the lives of the juvenile-adults. This changed with the passing of the Prevention of Crime Act in 1908, when the CDPAS became unique among aftercare bodies in Ireland; after this time its work was put on a statutory footing. For the first time, an Irish aftercare body now had considerable power over those in its care, including the right to seek their return into custody.

The main consequence of the 1908 Act was that it brought statutory recognition for the CDPAS. Although the Act did not mention the Society by name, the closeness of its relationship with the state authorities was clearly expressed by the annual grant it received towards its work from the Irish exchequer. The BAI summed up the nature of the link in 1911 by pointing out that it was acknowledged but not supported by the state.[25] This statement should not, however, be misunderstood – the Association meant that the government did not *fully* fund its work. In reality, the government, through the agency of the GPB, very much needed a society such as the CDPAS/BAI in order to make the borstal system work. Ruggles-Brise described the borstal aftercare body as the 'corner-stone' of the entire scheme, highlighting the necessity for 'earnest, philanthropic and benevolent men' who were willing to visit the inmates in detention, and follow this up by devoting much of their time to their supervision on discharge. In a glowing commendation of the work of the English borstal association he went as far as to claim that the entire future success of the system was largely dependent on its work.[26] Hood argues that the relative independence of the borstal associations suited both the government and the aftercare bodies themselves. From a governmental standpoint, a voluntary organisation was always much more capable of generating public enthusiasm than a fully state-funded venture. For a borstal association it was easier to attract the support of voluntary organisations and philanthropists if it remained an independent entity. Both of these positions further strengthened the image of the borstal as an exciting new departure in the treatment of juvenile offenders.[27]

Borstal aftercare worked effectively as a type of parole system. Inmates were frequently discharged on licence from the institution, having fulfilled the normal requirements and earned a sufficient number of merit marks. Prior to 1908, discharge was possible after six months. The period of the licence was six months: if an inmate gave no cause for concern during that period, his licence expired and his sentence was complete.[28] This process was supervised by the CDPAS, although its functions had not yet been placed on a statutory footing. After the Prevention of Crime Act 1908 came into effect, the CDPAS had a legally designated role in the lives of discharged inmates. Not only would the Society provide the usual aftercare services but it would act in a supervisory capacity until the boy's licence expired. No inmate would leave the borstal without undergoing a rigorous process leading to the aftercare body's determination of where he would live for the period of his licence. In the economic climate of early twentieth-century Ireland more often than not boys were placed in an agricultural setting. Members of the committee would maintain contact with him and his employer for the licence period and held the power to recommend his return to the institution in the event of a transgression. Under the 1908 Act the power of recalling an inmate to the institution was set at four months.[29] This was usually a last resort, however. This function placed the BAI in a unique and powerful position among Ireland's discharged prisoners' aid societies.

DAILY FUNCTIONS OF THE BORSTAL ASSOCIATION OF IRELAND

As described previously, certain members of the BAI had various roles within, or contacts with, Clonmel borstal, though not always in their capacity as members of the Association. As visiting justices, chaplains and medical officers they held key positions that informed their work in aftercare of discharged boys. If a visiting justice was called in to adjudicate on a matter of alleged indiscipline, his contact with the inmates involved would provide invaluable insights for his work with the BAI. Association members' day-to-day contact with the borstal and its detainees often related to such matters as providing recreational facilities or lectures. Whether it was the formation of an institutional band or the installation of a borstal cinema, the Association, despite its limited resources, sought to maximise the potential of the borstal scheme.

The Prevention of Crime Act 1908 gave legislative standing to aftercare bodies such as the BAI, thus paving the way for financial support from the Irish exchequer.[30] For its day-to-day operations, however, it was dependent on the charity of ordinary individuals.[31] The BAI annual reports listed the various contributors and their donations. The problem faced by the Association in Clonmel was its dependence on local financial support at a time when it served a national purpose. Boys were sent to the borstal from many parts of the country; their aftercare was almost exclusively provided by the philanthropic endeavours of the community in the Clonmel area.[32] Indeed, an editorial in the *Irish Times* in July 1910 highlighted the work of the Association and pointed out that 'those who really desire to help the poor when they most need it could not do better than support the work of the association'.[33] It was a clear endorsement for an organisation that, as Osborough implies, battled to stay in existence in the early years.[34] Its annual reports were usually reported in one of South Tipperary's most popular newspapers, *The Nationalist*. Each time a BAI annual report was featured, it was usually accompanied by an editorial espousing its work. The newspaper repeatedly spelled out the argument for greater national financial support because all but one inmate (in 1909) came from outside of Tipperary. The association was assisting boys from many other counties but getting little support in return.[35]

Indeed, resources were a thorny issue with the BAI. Apart from limited government funding – the Association received small payments for the care of each discharged inmate, was added to the gratuity he earned while at work in the institution – it also had financial and other support from a number of charities. The BAI worked in co-operation with the Discharged Prisoners' Aid Societies of Dublin, Belfast and Cork, as well as the Society of St Vincent de Paul, the Salvation Army, the Pembroke Charities Fund and the Prison Gate Mission in Belfast.[36] The assistance of these groups was particularly significant in the early years because the Association's lack of resources often meant that its members could not travel to certain locations to organise employment or a home for a discharged boy. In

1908 William Casey addressed a meeting of presidents of the Society
of St Vincent de Paul (SVP) in Dublin, which was attended by 101
members from 94 branches from around the country. After explaining the mechanics of the two-year-old borstal and aftercare process,
he made an impassioned appeal for support for the BAI. The purpose
of aftercare, he argued, was to take the boy and treat him with some
sympathy and encouragement, perhaps preventing him from re-
offending in the future. No other organisation, in his opinion, was
better equipped or positioned to carry out such work, as the SVP. He
suggested that the various conferences of the Society would be given
every support by the GPB and could communicate with and advise
each other in the care of discharged inmates. He envisaged an
arrangement whereby the CDPAS would forward monetary grants to
the SVP, which would use the payment in a boy's best interests. He
went on to express his dismay at the fact that, though he had written
many letters to other likely organisations, most did not even favour
him with a reply.[37] The SVP was thanked for its assistance in many
subsequent BAI annual reports so a certain level of co-operation in
response to this entreaty can be assumed. Monitoring a boy from a
long distance was difficult during the early years and so any physical
as well as financial help rendered by other organisations allowed the
BAI to outsource some of its functions. A similar call was made by the
GPB in its annual report for 1911. The cities of Dublin and Belfast
were again targeted as they contributed the highest proportion of
inmates ? whose aftercare was funded almost entirely by the inhabitants of Clonmel.[38] In an editorial published in 1911 *The Nationalist*
criticised the populations of these cities for their failure to provide
adequate support for the Association.[39]

The difficulties in funding the work of the BAI were put directly to
the GPB in a letter from William Casey in 1909. Still known as the
CDPAS, the organisation called for an increase in funding from the
Treasury. The Treasury grant was made on the basis that it would not
exceed twice the amount raised through subscriptions and charitable
donations. Casey called this system unworkable in light of the paltry
sums that had been raised thus far. He pointed out that assisting discharged prisoners of any category did not excite general sympathy
and the public tended to recoil from criminals. They might approve
of the efforts of the Association in theory but, because of its nature,
they will 'do nothing either by purse or personal effort to help in the
work'. Casey declared that, unless there was increased government

funding for the BAI, the borstal system in Clonmel would fail.[40] This was why it was essential that the Association link up with other organisations throughout the country. An increase in donations during the year 1911–12 allowed the BAI to provide a greater degree of support to discharged inmates. For example, a fifty-pound donation from the Pembroke Irish Charities Fund or ten pounds from Lord Iveagh permitted the Association to buy better clothing and footwear for the boys as they went into employment.[41] Such contributions took on a greater significance in the absence of wider support from around the country. The Treasury did eventually sanction a higher level of funding for the BAI but not until 1913. The GPB reported that the increased expenditure would permit the purchase a 'proper outfit' for each inmate upon his discharge.[42]

Between 1906 and 1921 the BAI acted almost as a lobby group for the Clonmel and its inmates. Funding was not the only problem to confront the Association as its work was also greatly handicapped by the lack of a farm for training the inmates (see Chapter 7). The campaigning nature of the BAI was fully exposed during the decade-long crusade to force the government to acquire land for this purpose. In 1913, William Casey pointed out, in a letter to the chief secretary for Ireland, Augustine Birrell, that the Association was forced to send boys to work for farmers where they had to learn almost everything from the beginning, including the proper way to handle a spade. Their fellow farm labourers were more skilled so better paid, so the boys often became discontented and unsettled, with some eventually returning to 'their original undesirable haunts'.[43] This scenario raised the stakes for the BAI because first, it not only caused them the inconvenience of having to deal with inmates had transgressed but, second, any boy who fell back into criminality was deemed a failure and adversely affected the joint appeals of the BAI and the GPB for greater funding from the public. Generally though, the Association was more concerned with influencing borstal policy than interfering to a large extent in the daily running of the institution. Its reports contain pieces on a number of issues, including sentencing policy, training of inmates and family life. In this respect it acted almost as an advisory body, both to the government and the judiciary.

DISCHARGING BORSTAL INMATES

Clonmel prison became a fully-fledged borstal institution in August 1910. Some evidence exists to suggest that, prior to this changeover, the authorities were uncertain about the correct way to discharge inmates. On 22 February 1910, the Borstal Association in London wrote to the governor at Clonmel about the appropriate steps to be taken. It was stated that 'the date of discharge of inmates of Borstal Institutions is fixed by the Institution Board and not at the request of the Association'.[44] This indicates that the governor had sought confirmation of exactly which body held the power to discharge inmates. (There is no suggestion that the advice of the local branch of the Association was sought first.) Along with this letter, the governor was furnished with a memorandum explaining the correct procedure for discharge.

The 1909 Regulations with respect to Borstal Institutions for males in Ireland identified the criteria used to select inmates suitable for discharge. Eligibility was based on the perceived progress and conduct of a boy during his borstal detention. If it was felt that he would lead a worthwhile and diligent life, free of his old criminal ways and capable of gaining employment, he was considered for discharge on licence. Additionally, he must have earned six months' worth of merit marks. If these conditions were fulfilled, the institutional board (comprising officers of the borstal selected by the GPB) could initiate the procedure that might lead to discharge.[45] At this juncture the BAI entered the scene: the extent to which it became a powerful force in a boy's life should not be understated.

The discharge process was, therefore, a joint undertaking between the institution board and the BAI. During the first week of every month, the board met to compile a list of those inmates 'who are expected to be fit for release on licence during the next month but two'.[46] (This meant that the board would meet in February to select inmates for discharge in May.) The first two pages of form 740 were filled in for each inmate at the borstal and forwarded to the BAI. The assessments of individual officers were filled in later. On receiving these forms, the Association then began a process of visiting the home and family members of the inmate, as well as his previous employers. Towards the end of the first month, the officers of the borstal recorded their opinions on form 740 and returned it to the BAI. On the second Tuesday of the second month, members of the Association visited the inmate. On the third Tuesday of the following month, the BAI presented its report to the Visiting Committee of the GPB, who examined 'the inmate as to his adherence to the arrangements proposed'. The Visiting Committee, in turn, passed on its recommendations to the Prison Commissioners for a final decision.[47] If the boy was recommended for release on licence, he was discharged to the care of the BAI.

The primary concern for the Association was that an inmate would be relatively financially secure, well clothed and have a home in which to live, whether it was with his family or an employer. Members of the committee would then pay occasional visits to the boy at his selected location for the duration of the period of his licence. He was not allowed to change his residence or leave his employment during that time without the permission of the BAI. If he did so without permission, he would have to put up a very strong argument to avoid being sent back to Clonmel to serve out the remainder of his sentence. Beyond the period of his licence, the Association had no legal right of intervention in the life of an inmate. Once a licence expired, any information-gathering efforts on its part only succeeded because of the goodwill of an employer or an inmate. In the days leading up to the release of a juvenile-adult offender, the borstal governor would write to Dublin Castle and inform the GPB of the specific provisions in place for his aftercare. A number of examples survive within the Board's correspondence register.

On 9 July 1913, Governor Dobbin reported that inmate George Gubbins would be released within the next four days on his second licence.[48] The prison register for Clonmel borstal shows that this inmate was sentenced at Castlebar assizes in July 1911 to two years' penal discipline larceny. His father was listed as his next-of-kin and was of no fixed abode.[49] With his obviously dysfunctional family background it was incumbent upon the BAI to locate a suitable situation for him. The governor outlined how the Association had secured him a position with a Mrs Ryan of New Inn, in County Tipperary, who promised him employment at £8 per year.[50] She was interviewed and considered 'a suitable person to exercise good influence over him'. As was the practice for discharged inmates, the honorary secretary of the BAI would maintain communications with Mrs Ryan, while Governor Dobbin would write to the local police to inform them of the boy's presence in the area (purely for monitoring purposes). Inmate Gubbins was also recommended for the standard Treasury grant of three pounds, which would be used by the Association to provide him with a new outfit. This money was in addition to any gratuity he earned while at work in the institution.[51] Another inmate, Robert Gray, was scheduled for release on the same day. Gray was convicted for breaking and entering at Belfast city assizes in July 1911 and received a sentence of two years' detention in Clonmel borstal. His next-of-kin was his father, who had an address in Belfast.[52] Gray's discharge process indicates that an inmate did have some input into his own living conditions after his release. A situation was not necessarily imposed on a boy but was sometimes a negotiated compromise. Gray was granted the usual stipend of three pounds for use by the BAI, as well as his earned gratuity. Governor Dobbin reported that Gray refused employment in the agricultural sector, preferring instead to return to his parents in Belfast, where he would seek work for himself. The Association promised to make contact with the Society of St Vincent de Paul in Belfast and request its assistance in monitoring and supporting Gray.[53] This is a good example of the importance of other charitable organisations such as SVP to the work of the BAI. In the case of this particular inmate, it is likely that his domestic environment was considered suitable for his return.

As the borstal system took root in Clonmel, the BAI built up a system of locating employment for the boys. The committee gradually built up a network of contacts among the agricultural community around the country as it sought potential employers. By 1912, it reported that it was having little difficulty placing discharged borstal inmates in employment. The Association noted that the reputation of the scheme was enhanced when one boy went to a locality and proved to be a worthy employee; the institution subsequently received many applications from farmers in that same area.[54] In 1913 it reported that the number of applications from farmers was 'enormous' and finding employment was no problem.[55] While the BAI annual reports tended to emphasise, with great enthusiasm, the apparent popularity of discharged inmates with the farming community, there were many issues that were not addressed. For instance, they made no reference to the treatment of discharged inmates by their employers, which could have been abusive. It should be stressed that there is no evidence from the GPB for this, although there were problematic issues. The fact remains that in many respects the BAI annual reports were tailored to make the Association's work appear as fruitful and positive as possible; the information and arguments presented within their pages should always be viewed in this regard. There was no benefit to be gained by overplaying the negative for an organisation largely reliant on public subscription for its very survival. The GPB's own records, however, do show evidence of workplace discontent among some newly discharged inmates and it is the written testimony of these boys that provides the most reliable, and sometimes raw, account of life immediately after borstal.

On 10 January 1919, Michael Desmond, a farmer from Cashel in County Tipperary, wrote to Governor Dobbin seeking the return of one of his employees, an inmate on licence named James Dowling. Desmond claimed that he had allowed Dowling to take four days' holiday at Christmas but he failed to come back, along with the money he was given for his transport costs.[56] Dowling had been convicted of malicious damage at the Munster winter assizes in Cork in December 1916. He was listed as a carpenter and his father was named in the prison register as his next-of-kin.[57] Dowling's explanation for his disappearance from his place of work reveals something of the frustration experienced by discharged borstal inmates. The boy revealed that since he had left his employer he had been working at his trade at an aerodrome in Gormanstown, County Meath. That work was now finished and Dowling had returned home but would soon be taking up a new position in Dublin. He explained to Governor Dobbin that he could no longer tolerate farm work as it was too difficult and he felt he was not capable of it. During his time as a farm labourer he often wished he were back at the institution.[58] This inmate appears to be a victim of the government's under-investment in Clonmel borstal and his words seem to justify all of the BAI and GPB arguments for additional land.

In the process of figuring out how to respond to Dowling's predicament, the GPB and the governor realised that their attitude was coloured by their reaction to the case of another discharged inmate. Robert O'Dea was sentenced to three years' penal discipline in Clonmel borstal at the Munster winter assizes in Cork in December 1916. His father Patrick, with an address in Tralee, County Kerry, was listed as his next-of-kin. O'Dea was convicted of causing malicious damage to property to an amount exceeding five pounds.[59] Obviously he was involved in the same incident as Dowling. At an unspecified date in 1919, O'Dea also absconded from his employment while on licence. In his explanation to Governor Dobbin he alleged that his employer treated him very badly, locking him out of the house the previous Sunday night. This was the second time he had been shut out, he claimed, and he was forced to sleep in the cow-house on both nights. He appealed for Governor Dobbin's assistance and claimed that the farmer had no grounds for treating him in that manner.[60] On 2 March 1919, the governor received a letter from O'Dea's father seeking mercy for his son. Patrick O'Dea supported the claim that his son had been victimised by the farmer but did not provide further details. He asked that his son be allowed to remain at home with him in Tralee as he was now an elderly man and the breadwinner of the family. He promised to provide employment for his son and gave an undertaking that the boy would not be keeping bad company in the future.[61] The police in Tralee succeeded in returning O'Dea to his employer temporarily but he remained there just a few days.

At a regular meeting of the BAI committee on 4 March 1919, William Casey recommended that both inmates be returned to the borstal to serve out their sentences. He was over-ruled by his colleagues, however, who felt that the boys were capable of earning a good wage and 'were sinned against by neglect of proper training for the work on a farm which proved distasteful to them'. It was agreed that both Dowling and O'Dea would be placed in the custody of their respective fathers for the remainder of their licence.[62] These problems were commonplace and not unexpected, given the varied backgrounds and circumstances of Clonmel's juvenile-adults. While no allegations of cruelty against these farmers appear to have been investigated or proven, these incidents show the sometimes difficult readjustment of these offenders to life after borstal and brings into sharp focus the need for the intervention of the Association. It should be noted that all the potential employers of discharged borstal inmates were subject to a vetting procedure to determine their suitability.

As the profile of the borstal discharge scheme was raised amongst the agricultural communities of Tipperary and beyond, the institution received an increasing number of requests for boys to be sent to work with farmers. One such request, received by Governor Dobbin in March 1919, was from James Cunningham, a farmer from a rural district close to Thurles, who enquired whether it would be possible to hire a 'man or boy' to work on his farm.[63] Following the usual procedure, Governor Dobbin wrote to Cunningham's local RIC branch to make enquiries as to whether the farmer was a suitable 'person to exercise good influence over the young man in the event of his being released on licence'. Cunningham promised Governor Dobbin that he would keep the boy in constant full-time employment, give him good advice and 'keep him under friendly supervision'.[64] In an example of why this process was not only useful but essential, a reply was received at the borstal a number of days later. The local RIC sergeant advised the borstal authorities that Cunningham was 'a man very much addicted to drink' and wholly unsuited to the task of employing and supervising a discharged inmate.[65]

CLONMEL BORSTAL INMATES AND THE FIRST WORLD WAR

The beginning of the First World War had the effect of expediting the release of hundreds of inmates. Juvenile-adults volunteered to join the British military forces on the battlefields of Europe in exchange for their early release. In fact, the war had the effect of 'emptying' the prisons of Britain and Ireland.[66] This practice was common in Ireland's prisons and was not limited to the inmate population. Warders who had been reservists in the army or navy left their institutions to rejoin their regiments. In some prisons, the practice of sandbag-making was introduced as a new and useful form of labour.[67] In 1915 the GPB acknowledged the necessity for financial prudence in a time of war but argued that the potential benefits of reforming juvenile-adult offenders were so great that a cut in the already small expenditure of the borstal would not be a 'real economy'.[68] Indeed, there is no evidence to suggest that Clonmel borstal suffered any major cutbacks during the war years. In financial terms, the main effect of the war was that the system failed to receive any increased investment. If Clonmel was seen by the government as succeeding, it would almost certainly have been in line for greater funding by 1914. The fact that there appeared to be no cut in expenditure can be taken as a small gesture of political and official confidence in its work.

In its first report published after the outbreak of the war, the GPB revealed that forty-three of Clonmel borstal's inmates volunteered and were accepted for duty with the British army. To be accepted for service an inmate first had to obtain the consent of his parents or guardians. He then had to seek the approval of the visiting justices and the BAI before being put forward for consideration. Apart from the forty-three boys who enlisted for the war, a number of other discharged inmates had already joined the British army and navy. By the end of March 1915, over two hundred ex-inmates of Clonmel had enlisted for military service.[69] During 1916 a further forty-eight boys volunteered for service and were released accordingly by the lord lieutenant. It was estimated that 270 former inmates were in active service with British forces by March 1916. Recruitment of volunteers from Ireland was particularly significant at this point in the war. After conscription was introduced on the British mainland in 1916, Ireland 'had the only large group of untapped, eligible men in Britain'. The London government came under severe political and public pressure to force the Irish population to 'do their part' in the war effort.[70]

Initial reports suggested that the conduct of the Clonmel borstal soldiers was very good and many displayed exceptional bravery on the battlefield.[71] The number enlisting decreased during 1917, with twenty-one inmates volunteering for service. This brought the estimated total up to 326, according to the GPB's own figures. Fifteen of these soldiers received promotion and four received special mention for gallantry. One former inmate received a Distinguished Conduct Medal.[72] By the end of the war a further fifty-three inmates enlisted for service, bringing the total number to over four hundred.[73] In his visit to Clonmel for the spring assizes in March 1919, Justice Thomas Moloney paid tribute to the 424 Clonmel boys he estimated were engaged in military service during the war. Of these, he wrote, seventy boys 'made the supreme sacrifice'. He revealed that Major Dobbin had already framed the names of the deceased soldiers from the borstal but suggested that a more permanent stone tablet memorial would be a more fitting tribute.[74]

Any number of factors can explain the motivation of borstal inmates to join the British armed forces. Without actual evidence, it might be suggested that many saw military service as a means of leaving the institution for a future that was somewhat more certain than the insecurity of their past lives. Recruitment within certain parts of Ireland was particularly strong during the first two years of the war. While the western seaboard counties produced few volunteers, the southern midlands had particularly high enlistment figures.[75] This suggested that the recruitment campaigns in the area around the town of Clonmel were particularly effective, the borstal institution being an obvious target. Army life was going to be unpredictable, yet they would have their freedom, steady employment and be taken under the charge of one of the regiments. Ironically, for some boys, life in the trenches was going to be more secure than that in the slums of Dublin or Belfast. Fitzpatrick points out that, even in peacetime, recruits from both Ireland and Britain were typically males in their late teens for whom the risks of military life were outweighed by the benefits.

He cites evidence suggesting that, between 1905 and 1913, half of all recruits from Ireland defined themselves as unskilled urban workers, holding positions such as porters, carters, servants or even casual labourers.[76] This corresponds with the profile, outlined earlier, of the juvenile-adult offender in Clonmel borstal. A further reason for the high prisoner uptake of military service was that many of those men and boys came from unstable and undisciplined backgrounds. In the army, they were brought under the control of command structure that forced them to lead regular lives and punished them if they did not.[77]

A number of extracts from accounts of discharged inmates were reproduced in the 1918 report of the GPB. This evidence should be viewed in light of the fact that the Board was anxious to maximise the positive nature of Clonmel borstal and the quotations published in 1918 demonstrate the heroism, bravery and honour of the ex-inmates. There is of course, no reason to think that any young man from the institution demonstrated anything other than positive characteristics and the Board's readiness to exploit this shows the importance of continuing to win public support and patronage. Two of the extracts quote the words of senior commanding officers. The first described the progress of an unnamed former inmate who enlisted directly from the institution. He was now promoted to the rank of sergeant and 'repeatedly distinguished himself both in trench warfare and in the recent open fighting'. A colonel reported that another boy died while trying to save the life of a native soldier, though the location was not specified. An ex-inmate of Clonmel wrote that he had been wounded by a Bulgarian sniper the previous July and was currently undergoing 'necessary repairs'. He extended his greeting to the inmates and staff and expressed his hope that the governor was still providing film and slide shows for the boys. Another inmate wrote to the governor and apologised for not making contact sooner because he was 'very busy going through gas and musketry', passing both with 'flying honours'. The Irishmen of the flying corps, he declared, 'are the bravest of the brave. It fills one's blood with pride when we see our colours on top again.' The same boy singled out the drill and gymnasium practice he received at Clonmel as contributing greatly to his fitness and performance in the army. A number of the inmates expressed a similar opinion – one pointed out that it had saved his instructor a great deal of time and effort. When he was asked if he had ever been trained anywhere else in the past he was forced to tell him the truth. The senior officer paid tribute to Clonmel, stating that he had trained many soldiers from there and none had ever been a problem.[78] At the end of the war, the English Prison Commissioners paid tribute to the military service of former inmates and prisoners from institutions under their control. Whether it was a man recruited directly from penal servitude, a borstal inmate, a petty thief or an habitual drunkard, 'their country's call has touched a fiber in the hearts of many whose lives hitherto have been shown to be unresponsive to all other calls'.[79]

The selection and inclusion of these extracts in an annual report that typically drew a good deal of press attention almost amounted to a propaganda exercise by the GPB. In this context it is difficult to gain a truly accurate reading of the battlefield experiences of the inmates of Clonmel borstal. A number of unpublished documents have survived within the Board's correspondence register and provide more, albeit very limited, detail.

In August 1917 a former inmate, Michael O'Brien, wrote to Clonmel borstal from Cheshire. Following a military incident during which he lost an eye, he was discharged from the army with a pension for life. The government provided for his medical care, which included the fitting of an artificial eye. O'Brien was now working in a munitions factory in England and earning over three pounds per week. His letter reveals a deep affection for the borstal and he enquires after a number of named officers, including the chief warder and Warder Nunan. He also referred to the garden and the field at the institution 'where I spent all my good time'.[80] Governor Dobbin forwarded this letter to the GPB, with a note attached outlining his own recollections of former inmate O'Brien. He was, wrote the governor, 'a typical juvenile class corner boy known as The Slinger'. He was almost certainly on a path to habitual criminality but he, and the public, were saved from this fate because of his time at Clonmel.[81] The register of inmates shows that the boy, a labourer from Longford, was convicted of larceny and sentenced to three years' penal discipline at the institution.[82] His letter provides some insight into the realities of the war and was probably representative of many stories of discharged borstal inmates. His story was not included amongst the many glowing accounts in the 1918 GPB report because it is not a totally happy one, so did not necessarily fit in with the image that the Board wanted to promote. The letter is important in providing a rare glimpse into the subsequent attitude of an inmate to his life at Clonmel.

There is some limited evidence to suggest that the British military authorities were well disposed towards receiving discharged borstal inmates into their ranks. In 1915, Colonel Francis Findlay of the 4th Royal Irish Rifles wrote to Governor Dobbin from his base in County Down. He had recently been due to receive a group of boys discharged from Clonmel but because of a bureaucratic error all but two had been sent to another regiment. He expressed his regret at this situation because he had a very positive first impression of the entire group and was hoping to give them a chance for quick promotion through the ranks. He pledged to pay particular attention to the two boys he had and requested the governor to send him any amount 'of such smart, clean and nice mannered young men'.[83] The records of the GPB showed that an inmate who volunteered for release to join the armed forces was subjected to a procedure as rigid as that for regular discharge. Firstly, it was essential that an inmate had reached the point at which he would have otherwise been eligible for release on licence. The BAI and the visiting justices obtained the consent of his parents or guardians, then interviewed him. At this stage the army's recruiting officer interviewed the inmate on his next visit to the borstal and he was also examined by an army medical officer, before the various reports and recommendations of these parties were forwarded to the GPB for final approval. Once the Board sanctioned the discharge of a boy to the armed forces, he was confirmed for service with the corps of his choice, issued with a uniform and handed to the custody of the recruiting officer, thus ending his detention.[84]

EFFECTIVENESS OF BORSTAL TREATMENT AND AFTERCARE

Such was the ambitious nature of the borstal method that it sought not only to reshape its subjects as law-abiding citizens but endeavoured to change the course of the rest of their lives. The boys faced their greatest challenge when they left the institution and returned to their liberty, which came with the proviso that they would begin a new existence, turning their back on the people and environment they had known before. There is no indication that the intention was to sever all links between the boy and his past completely, merely place him at an inaccessible distance. This feature distinguished the borstal method from other branches of the juvenile penal system. Writing in 1901, E.D. Daly complained that, when a child left the industrial school system at sixteen, the state then had no legal role in his or her life. Children drifted back to the 'evil influences' of parents and inevitably into a life of crime.[85] Using the authority vested in the Association, the state challenged former borstal inmates to become proactive in their own reform.

On an almost annual basis both the GPB and BAI maintained a positive publicity campaign to win public support and higher levels of patronage for the borstal system. Between 1910 and 1921 the reports of both organisations often contained brief accounts on the progress of selected groups of inmates. These accentuate everything positive about the borstal system and highlight its achievements. The reports were quite impressive but failed in many ways to convey anything of the reality of life post-discharge: the GPB/BAI accounts paid little or no attention to the trials and tribulations boys may have faced in society bearing the stigma of the borstal.

In May 1912, the BAI reported that many boys released as far back as five years previously continued to make positive progress: in fact, twelve were already married. One former inmate who had been convicted of a 'serious offence and leading a bad life' was now 'sober and well conducted', earning twenty-four shillings per week. Another boy, convicted of assault, had now obtained a position far from home and had been earning twenty-two shillings per week 'for years past'. A third boy had been taught shoemaking in Clonmel and went on to work with a relative in the same trade. He was now 'in charge of a branch house' and sent a Christmas card to the borstal thanking the governor and officers for the way he was treated.[86] Several further examples were given in the report for the year 1913–14. In 1915 the committee reported on further inmates. John Bell had been convicted of receiving stolen property and was discharged in July 1911. He had since obtained permanent employment, was married and owned his own cottage. T.W. was convicted of larceny and detained in the borstal in 1912. Since his discharge he 'improved in every way and is a good workman at his trade'. In the same year, Jeremiah Dillon was convicted of larceny but since his discharge he remained in employment with the same farmer and had maintained good conduct.[87] To convey to its audience that the training the boys received at Clonmel would be of benefit to employers, the BAI reported in 1916 that John Wilson, convicted of breaking and entering in 1909, was 'now in constant employment as a repairer of boots'.[88] In 1917 the Association reported on two further inmates who were employed in boot-mending and another in tailoring.[89] While it was essential that the BAI promoted the positive effects of their work in this way, the altogether more private records of the GPB reveal the somewhat different experience of at least some inmates, though the extent to which it is representative is difficult to gauge.

A far from smooth transition into society was exemplified by the case of inmate Peter Cawley, who was convicted of manslaughter in 1912 and sentenced to one year of borstal detention. His last residence was listed as Trim Industrial School and his next-of-kin was his mother, whose address was registered as Drogheda union. Cawley was a carpenter and entered Clonmel at the age of sixteen.[90] In 1915, after discharge, he wrote to Governor Dobbin to express his dismay that his previous offence and borstal detention were haunting his now honest existence. He had been brought to court to give evidence in a dispute between his employer and a neighbour. Under oath he was questioned about his past by the neighbour's lawyer, who asked where he had come from, to which he answered, 'a respectable place'. He was then directly confronted in open court about the offence that had sent him to borstal, his involvement in the killing of a schoolmaster. In his letter Cawley expressed his devastation at this exposure, given that he was now leading an honest life and was in court as a witness. He wrote that he was 'trying to earn my living honest and decent and wouldn't you think it was wrong in the eyes of the law to injure my character in such a way'.[91] One of the most important issues facing a discharged inmate sent to work amongst a new community was the protection of his identity as a reformed juvenile-adult offender. In some cases, members of the local farming community were aware that farm labourers had come from the borstal because they had themselves applied for inmates to work for them. Generally the most important aspect of the period after discharge was that a boy should be given a fresh start and an equal opportunity without having to live down the stigma of his past offence.

In the late spring and early summer of 1912 the borstal authorities were faced with a full-scale crisis when Governor Connor received a murder threat against future discharged inmates. The incident began on the evening of 27 March 1912, when the governor received a letter from an address in County Cavan. The letter was badly written and disorganised but the main text reads as follows:

> We protest and strongly advise you to send no more of your Jail Robbers to this county of County Cavan. The next you send is to be murdered by day or night. This county lived without Jail

Robbers a long time and can do yet. You have sent three already we warn you to send no more not matter how many applicants you get we warn you again and again in case you send another there is not one you have already sent but will be murdered and drowned so take warning in time and save murder. We will allow no more Jail Birds to this county or any of the adjoining countys having a lot of bothers in the face of the people keep them there til they are full time served but send no more here, take a warning in time.[92]

The letter was signed by sixteen individuals 'and several other farmers protest against youre Jail Robbers'.[93] Governor Connor became concerned for the safety of four inmates that were currently working in the county and immediately reported the incident to the GPB. The Board ordered him to report swiftly on the placement of the four inmates and provide any other available information about their progress. Three of the boys had been in employment without incident and their conduct was reported as good. A fourth inmate, William Doyle, had been released on licence on 11 September 1911 and placed in employment with Mr D. Sanders, a County Cavan farmer. Nothing occurred until early March 1912, when Doyle left Sanders' employment and went into local lodgings. The farmer reported the boy's departure to the BAI, who began proceedings to have his licence revoked. On the same day, a letter was received by Governor Connor from another farmer in the area, Mr J. O'Connell, seeking to take Doyle into his employment as a labourer. The Association confirmed O'Connell's suitability with local police before approving the request. Doyle's licence was not revoked and he was formally transferred to the employment and care of O'Connell.[94] The BAI only recommended the revocation of a licence in the most extreme circumstances or when there had been a clear breach of the rules.

The GPB reported the murder threat to the RIC in Cavan, who immediately began an investigation of the local farming community. On 9 April the county inspector in Cavan reported back to the Board, stating that the local sergeant could detect no ill feeling towards any of the four boys in the county and the conduct of all was reported as satisfactory. Some of the signatories to the letter were interviewed and claimed that they knew nothing of its existence and had no problem with the boys. It was ascertained that the letter was written by Mr D. Sanders, the farmer from whom Doyle 'was taken away'. The Board replied to the police, pointing out that Doyle was not taken away from Rogers but left his employment 'owing to some disappointment with his master'. A discreet inquiry as to the nature of the boy's unhappiness was requested, along with a specimen of the farmer's handwriting.⁹⁵ Two weeks later the local police again reported to the GPB. It was found that Doyle had left Mr Sanders' farm because of alleged ill-treatment, principally at the hands of Mrs Sanders. The local sergeant found that the handwriting did not match that of Mr Sanders but the letter was almost certainly dictated by him, and probably written by his wife. The other fifteen signatures were believed to have been forgeries, meaning that there was no widespread discontent amongst the farming community of Cavan regarding discharged borstal inmates.⁹⁶ There is no record of how this matter was ultimately resolved, though it was likely to have been in Doyle's favour as the governor and the GPB appeared to rise to his defence at every opportunity. Undoubtedly the boy's initiative in finding alternative employment so quickly after leaving the Sanders' farm commended him to the governor and the BAI. The dispute demonstrates the vulnerability of discharged inmates in the face of potentially unscrupulous employers and adverse circumstances. During the period of their licence they were expected to behave impeccably: any minor transgression could have meant a return to Clonmel.

The GPB and the BAI claimed varying but overall positive levels of success for Clonmel borstal during the period 1906–21. To interpret the statistics, however, it is important to understand their definition of success. The phrase 'doing well' was repeated frequently in these reports and was used to express satisfaction with the progress of the boys. It should be noted, though, that this conclusion was based on their performance in their place of work. There is no clear indication of whether this success reached into other areas of their personal life. The Association's criteria for success were based on the assumption that, if a boy had not re-offended and was working satisfactorily, then he had probably succeeded in becoming a useful member of society. There were no studies to determine, for example, significant rates of suicide, mental illness or alcoholism among discharged inmates, though the authorities were able to find out whether or not a boy came to the attention of the police or the courts after discharge. The statistics do not reveal anything substantial regarding the personal effect of the institution on an inmate's life: it is not known how many former inmates were married or perhaps became homeless. Part of the problem of information gathering was that, beyond the period of a boy's licence, the Association had no legal grounds on which to investigate his circumstances. In most cases, any knowledge acquired depended on an employer or the boy himself furnishing it.

Although an accurate statistical survey of discharged inmates is not possible, an examination of the annual reports of the BAI does provide some account of the success rate, or otherwise, of the system. The Association's assessment appears to be largely based on information received from employers. For the year ending May 1912, forty-six out of fifty-four boys discharged were deemed to be 'doing well'.[97] A year later it was reported that seventy-seven boys had been released on licence and favourable reports had been received from sixty of their employers.[98] In 1914, the BAI provided an overall assessment of the progress of former borstal inmates released since the passing of the Prevention of Crime Act (1908). During that time, 387 boys had been held at Clonmel borstal. Of that number, 229 were subsequently handed over to the care of the Association, which found employment for the 'vast majority'. The report claimed that 73 per cent were known to be 'doing well'; most were working with farmers as untrained labourers.[99] Table 8.1 features a selection of positive comments from employers.

The most comprehensive survey on the success rates of discharged inmates was carried out by Governor Dobbin in 1919 and circulated among the GPB and interested members of the judiciary. This concluded that 467 inmates were detained at Clonmel borstal from the passing of the Prevention of Crime Act in 1908 and March 1919. Of

TABLE 8.1
EMPLOYER COMMENTS ON DISCHARGED INMATES, 1912–13

Name*	Offence	Date of discharge	Comment
T. W.	Larceny	March 1912	'Gives employer every satisfaction'
M. Mc F.	Larceny	May 1912	'Conducting himself admirably'
J. D.	Shopbreaking	September 1912	'A good sober boy'
P. C.	Serious offence	February 1913	'A good honest servant'
A. Mc G.	Housebreaking	March 1913	'No better man ever served another'
J. J.	Housebreaking	April 1913	'Have risen his wages; would trust him with untold gold'
P. P.	Housebreaking	Not given	'Employed now in foundry and earning 35 shillings per week'

Source: Borstal Association of Ireland, *Fourth Annual Report*, 1913–14

* Full names were not provided in the report.

that number, 360, or almost 78 per cent, were known to have conducted themselves satisfactorily after discharge (up to March 1919).
The report deemed that forty-nine, or 10.5 per cent, of the boys had
been unsatisfactory. Over 6 per cent, or thirty inmates, were returned
to the borstal or to prison; fourteen boys were transferred to prison
from Clonmel borstal.[100] These are the most detailed and reliable set
of figures available on discharged inmates during the time period of
this book. They claim an impressive success rate but it bears repeating
that this meant only that these boys did not come to the attention of
the courts again during the period of the survey. They were not
known to have re-offended or to have kept bad company. If a boy
failed to avoid any of these problems the success of his borstal treatment was called into question by the borstal authorities. In the
absence of comprehensive personal accounts from the boys themselves it is impossible to quantify the effects, positive or negative, of
their detention and aftercare in the borstal system in Ireland. Within
the vast GPB correspondence register one single letter survives that
illuminates the impact on at least one former inmate at Clonmel. In
December 1910, Michael Murphy was sentenced to three years in
Clonmel borstal for a number of serious and wilful breaches of the
rules at his last known residence, Philipstown Reformatory. He was
discharged from Clonmel on 29 June 1912. In July 1913 a letter was
received at Clonmel borstal from an address care of the post office in
Townsville, Queensland, Australia. Michael Murphy had written to
Governor Connor to update him on his progress since he was discharged from Clonmel. Murphy wrote that he remained in Ireland for
only a few months before going on to Glasgow, where he earned his
fare to Australia. Since arriving there he had obtained work as a carpenter and was earning thirteen shillings per day. His letter urged the
governor to pass on the same advice to the boys still in the institution
as he had to him, giving them to understand that perseverance with
their trade training will bring enormous benefits when they leave. He
passed on his regards to various named warders and hoped that the
boys would 'gather some sense and learn now while they have the
chance to become decent and respectable to those who are in charge
of them'.[101] Murphy's words were warm in tone and obviously the
sentiments of an inmate with fond recollections of his time in
Clonmel. His letter cannot be taken as representative of the experience of every discharged inmate but there was no escaping the depth
of his gratitude in his final message to Governor Connor; 'I hope you

live to see all the boys grow up good men. God Bless You Sir for your kind advice for it has made a man of me now.'[102]

During the nineteenth century, aftercare bodies had played a limited role in the lives of men and women discharged from Irish prisons. At first, the Clonmel Discharged Prisoners' Aid Society appeared to be no different from previous organisations. The differences became apparent as the CDPAS realised that it was essentially servicing the needs of discharged boys from all parts of the country. Despite the country-wide reach of its activities, the Borstal Association of Ireland was also largely dependent on local patronage. The BAI wielded a power and influence over discharged inmates like no other such organisation, though its work for inmates in the institution and those on licence was often restricted because of the dual problems of under-funding by the GPB and lack of support from the cities for which it was doing the most work.

One of the merits of the borstal system was the extent to which it continued to intervene in the life of its inmates after they left the institution. Owing to the fact that those released on licence were subject to being returned to the borstal at any time if they were deemed to be in breach of their terms, the progress of inmates appears to have been quite positive. A Clonmel borstal survey showed that, up to 1919, as many as 78 per cent of discharge inmates were doing well. It should be noted, though, that the authorities placed a strong emphasis on the successful outcomes of borstal treatment, with little reference to its failures, so it is difficult to come to a firm conclusion on the effect of detention in Clonmel borstal on the wider inmate population. Anecdotal evidence suggests that for some of the boys the experience was positive and certain inmates looked back on their detention with gratitude for the changes it brought to their lives.

NOTES

1. This was how the *Freeman's Journal* described the effect of borstal treatment upon juvenile-adult offenders in a report published on 30 May 1912.
2. Ruggles-Brise, *The English Prison System*, p. 165.
3. Ruggles-Brise, *The English Prison System*, p. 166.
4. NLI, *Report from the Departmental Committee on Prisons*, vi, 1 [C 7702-1], H.L. 1895, 3.
5. Leslie, *Sir Evelyn Ruggles-Brise: A Memoir of the Founder of Borstal*, pp. 141–2.
6. NAI, GPB, CR, Ruggles-Brise memorandum on borstal aftercare, GPB/1824/1911.
7. Hood, *Borstal Re-assessed*, p. 162–3.
8. Hood, *Borstal Re-assessed*, p. 163.
9. NAI, GPB, CR, Ruggles-Brise memorandum on borstal aftercare, GPB/1824/1911.
10. James G. Alcorn, 'Discharged prisoners' aid societies' in *Journal of the Social and Statistical Inquiry Society of Ireland*, 1881, 8, pp. 220–3.

11. Alcorn, 'Discharged prisoners' aid societies', p. 218.
12. NLI, *Second Report of the General Prisons Board*, x [Cl-4432], H.L. 1879–80, xv, 21.
13. NLI, *Third Report of the General Prisons Board*, i [Cl-4430], H.L. 1880–1, iv, 23.
14. Oonagh Walsh, 'Protestant female philanthropy in Dublin in the early twentieth century', in *History Ireland* (Summer, 1997), p. 28.
15. NLI, *Twenty-second Report of the General Prisons Board*, ii [Cd-3340], H.L. 1899–1900, xxx, 131.
16. *The Nationalist*, 19 May 1906.
17. NLI, *Twenty-eighth Report of the General Prisons Board*, ii [Cd-3404], H.L. 1905–06, vi, 136.
18. Osborough, *Borstal in Ireland*, pp. 19–20.
19. *The Nationalist*, Clonmel, 19 May 1906.
20. Michael Ahern, 'The Grubbs of Carrick-on-Suir', in *Tipperary Historical Journal*, 2006, p.103.
21. NAI, GPB, CR, Ruggles-Brise memorandum on borstal aftercare, GPB/1824/1911.
22. Mary O'Dowd, 'Bagwell, Richard', *Oxford Dictionary of National Biography* (http://www.oxforddnb.com/view/printable/45883) (28 November 2006).
23. NAI, GPB, CR, letter to GPB reporting the death of Richard Bagwell, 4 December 1918, GPB/7717/1918.
24. NAI, GPB, CR, Governor Dobbin's report on the borstal's participation in the funeral of Richard Bagwell, 7 December 1918, GPB/1918.
25. NLI, *Twenty-third Report of the General Prisons Board*, vi [Cd-5785], H.L. 1910–11, ii, 15.
26. NLI, *Proceedings of the International Penitentiary Congress*, vi [Cd-5286], H.L., 1909–10, xxxix, 12.
27. Hood, *Borstal Re-assessed*, p. 165.
28. Osborough, *Borstal in Ireland*, p. 17.
29. Osborough, *Borstal in Ireland*, p. 19.
30. Cherry, 'Juvenile crime and its prevention', p. 446.
31. Osborough, *Borstal in Ireland*, p. 21.
32. Cherry, 'Juvenile crime and its prevention', p. 446.
33. *Irish Times*, 29 July 1910.
34. Osborough, *Borstal in Ireland*, p. 21.
35. *The Nationalist*, 26 May 1909.
36. NAI, Clonmel Borstal Memoranda, BAI, *Second Annual Report*, 1911–12, GPB/XB5.
37. NAI, GPB, CR, William Casey's address to the Society of St Vincent de Paul, June 1908, GPB/8040/1908.
38. NLI, *Thirty-third Report of the General Prisons Board*, v [Cd-3440], H.L. 1910–1, xvii, 17.
39. *The Nationalist*, 31 May 1911.
40. NAI, GPB, CR, Casey to GPB, 11 August 1909, GPB/1825/1911.
41. NAI, Clonmel Borstal Memoranda, 1908–32, BAI, *Second Annual Report*, 1911–1912.
42. NLI, *Thirty-fifth Report of the General Prisons Board*, i [Cd-6996], 1912–3, H.L. xxxii, 12.
43. NAI, CSORP, Casey to Augustine Birrell, March 1913, 1A/81/1/1913.
44. NAI, Clonmel Borstal Memoranda, 1908–32, letter from Borstal Association, London, to Governor at Clonmel Borstal Institution, 22 February 1910.
45. NAI, Clonmel Borstal Memoranda, 1908–32, 1909 Regulations with respect to Borstal Institutions for Males in Ireland.
46. NAI, Clonmel Borstal Memoranda, 1908–32, Memorandum from Borstal Association, London, to Governor at Clonmel Borstal Institution: Method used at Borstal, January 1910.
47. NAI, Clonmel Borstal Memoranda, 1908–32, Memorandum from Borstal Association, London, to Governor at Clonmel Borstal Institution: Method used at Borstal, January 1910.
48. NAI, GPB, CR, Governor's discharge report to GPB, 9 July 1913, GPB/5098/1913.
49. NAI, Prison register, Clonmel prison and borstal institution, 1903–23, 1/7/14.
50. This is a fictional name inserted by the author.
51. NAI, GPB, CR, Governor's discharge report to GPB, 9 July 1913, GPB/5098/1913.
52. NAI, Prison register, Clonmel prison and borstal institution, 1903–23, 1/7/14.
53. NAI, GPB, CR, Governor's discharge report to GPB, 9 July 1913, GPB/5099/1913.
54. NAI, Clonmel Borstal Memoranda, BAI, *Second Annual Report*, 1911–12, GPB/XB5.
55. NAI, Clonmel Borstal Memoranda, BAI, *Third Annual Report*, 1912–13, GPB/XB5.
56. NAI, GPB, CR, _____ to Dobbin, 10 January 1919, GPB/2939/1919.

57. NAI, Prison register, Clonmel prison and borstal institution, 1903–1923, 1/7/14.
58. NAI, GPB, CR, _____ to Dobbin, 20 February 1919, GPB/2939/1919.
59. NAI, Prison register, Clonmel prison and borstal institution, 1903–1923, 1/7/14.
60. NAI, GPB, CR, _____ to Dobbin, GPB/2939/1919.
61. NAI, GPB, CR, _____ to Dobbin, 2 March 1919, GPB/2939/1919.
62. NAI, GPB, CR, Dobbin's report to GPB, 5 March 1919, GPB/2939/1919.
63. NAI, GPB, CR, _____ to Dobbin, GPB/2939/1919.
64. NAI, GPB, CR, Dobbin to Ballinamore Sub-district R.I.C, 14 January 1919, GPB/2939/1919.
65. NAI, GPB, CR, Ballinamore Sub-district R.I.C. to Dobbin, 20/01/1919, GPB/2939/1919.
66. Edith Abbott, 'Crime and the war', *Journal of the American Institute of Criminal Law and Criminology*, (May, 1918) 9, 1, p. 34.
67. Carey, *Mountjoy: The Story of a Prison*, p. 180.
68. NLI, *Twenty-seventh Report of the General Prisons Board*, v [Cd-2659], H.L. 1914–5, xxxi-ii, 12.
69. NLI, *Twenty-seventh Report of the General Prisons Board*, v [Cd-2659], H.L. 1914–5, xxxi-ii, 12
70. Alan J. Ward, 'Lloyd George and the 1918 Irish conscription crisis', *Historical Journal*, (March, 1974) 17, 1, p. 109.
71. NLI, *Thirty-eighth Report of the General Prisons Board*, iv [Cd-8450], H.L. 1915–6, xx, 9.
72. NLI, *Thirty-ninth Report of the General Prisons Board*, xxi [Cd-9882], H.L. 1916–7, xii, 5.
73. NLI, *Forty-first Report of the General Prisons Board*, ii [Cmd-687], H.L. 1918–9, xxiii, 9.
74. NAI, GPB, CR, Justice Moloney to GPB, 31 March 1919, GPB/4879/1919.
75. David Fitzpatrick, 'The logic of collective sacrifice: Ireland and the British army, 1914–18', *Historical Journal*, (December, 1995), 38, 4, p. 1025.
76. Fitzpatrick, 'The logic of collective sacrifice', p. 1026.
77. Abbott, 'Crime and the war', p. 34.
78. NLI, *Fortieth Report of the General Prisons Board*, x [Cm-42], H.L. 1917–8, xxvii., 21.
79. Abbott, 'Crime and the war', p. 38.
80. NAI, GPB, CR, _____ to Governor, 26 August 1917, GPB/4879/1919.
81. NAI, GPB, CR, Dobbin to GPB, 29 August 1917, GPB/4879/1919.
82. NAI, Prison register, Clonmel prison and borstal institution, 1903–1923, 1/7/14.
83. NAI, GPB, CR, Findlay to Dobbin, 04 March 1915, GPB/8333/1918.
84. NAI, GPB, CR, Procedure for discharging inmates to the armed forces, 17 May 1918, GPB/3361/1918.
85. Daly, 'The Juvenile Offenders Act 1901', p. 149.
86. NAI, Clonmel Borstal Memoranda, 1908–32, BAI, *Second Annual Report*, 1911–1912.
87. Quoted in *The Nationalist*, 25 August 1915.
88. Quoted in *The Nationalist*, 2 August 1916.
89. GPB, Clonmel Borstal Memoranda, BAI, *Seventh Annual Report*, 1917, GPB/XB5.
90. NAI, Prison register, Clonmel prison and borstal institution, 1903–1923, 1/7/14.
91. NAI, GPB, CR, _____ to Dobbin, 22 January 1915, GPB/8333/1918.
92. NAI, GPB, CR, Murder threat against discharged inmates, 27 March 1912, GPB/3001/1912.
93. NAI, GPB, CR, Murder threat against discharged inmates, 27 March 1912, GPB/3001/1912.
94. NAI, GPB, CR, Connor's report on discharged inmates in Cavan, 29 March 1912, GPB/3001/1912.
95. NAI, GPB, CR, County inspector's office initial report to GPB, 2 April 1912, GPB/3001/1912.
96. NAI, GPB, CR, Second RIC report on treatment of discharged inmate _____, 15 April 1912, GPB/3001/1912.
97. NAI, Clonmel Borstal Memoranda, 1908–32, BAI, *Second Annual Report*, 1911–1912.
98. NAI, Clonmel Borstal Memoranda, 1908–32, BAI, *Third Annual Report*, 1912–1913.
99. NAI, Clonmel Borstal Memoranda, 1908–32, BAI, *Fourth Annual Report*, 1913–1914.
100. NAI, GPB, CR, Statistical table on progress of discharged inmates, GPB/4879/1919.
101. NAI, GPB, CR, _____ to Governor, 17 June 1913, GPB/8683/1921.
102. NAI, GPB, CR, _____ to Governor, 17 June 1913, GPB/8683/1921.

CHAPTER NINE

Clonmel borstal, 1922–40

The second phase of the Irish borstal project began in December 1921 with the signing of the Anglo-Irish Treaty by plenipotentiaries of Dáil Éireann and the British government, and the formal granting of independence. The penal system was just one of many elements of state administration that would be handed over, firstly to a provisional government and then to the permanent Free State government headed by W.T. Cosgrave. While the transfer of administration was carried out with a good deal of efficiency, it did take place in the context of a bitterly fought Civil War, which was to leave a lasting impression on many facets of Irish political, administrative and social life. This chapter will examine the ways in which the borstal system was operated by the Irish government during the eighteen-year period from 1922 to 1940.

THE BURNING OF CLOGHEEN BORSTAL

The Anglo-Irish Treaty was the first formal step in the birth of the Free State and marked the beginning of the transition of Ireland's administrative institutions from British to Irish control. The relatively narrow vote accepting the Treaty in January 1922 highlighted a deep political division that ultimately led the country into a devastating Civil War in the summer of 1922, lasting until the ceasefire in April 1923. Nonetheless, the business of state-building continued apace and a transitional government was established during 1922 as Irish political representatives drafted a Free State constitution. Kevin O'Higgins was appointed minister for home affairs in the interim administration, thus holding responsibility for the country's prisons and borstal institution.

It should be remembered that much of the work in assuming control of the apparatus of government in 1922 was carried out under the shadow of, first, the threat of physical hostilities, including the possibility of renewed British action, and then the actual outbreak of

Civil War between pro and anti-Treaty forces. The unrest had severe consequences for many aspects of government, with a particular burden falling on the prison system. Most of the prisons under the control of the GPB were taken over by the Free State army, leading to greatly reduced capacity for civilian prisoners. The army used the various institutions for the detention of internees, incarcerated for their anti-Treaty military activity, as well as for the accommodation of their guards. In 1923 the GPB reported that this incursion into the day-to-day operation of the penal system caused much overcrowding and this in turn had a detrimental effect on prison discipline.[1] At the political level, it was also impossible for the Home Affairs ministry to implement any long-term strategies for the penal system as it planned, with other departments, for the implementation of a permanent Free State constitution. Under questioning at a Dáil committee dealing with budgetary estimates for the GPB in November 1922, Minister O'Higgins was unequivocal in his opinion on the short-term prospects for the country's prisons. Labour Party deputy Cathal O'Shannon, representing the Louth–Meath constituency, enquired whether the minister had considered a thorough overhaul of the prison system. He described his own experience in prison as similar to being deposited 'into a criminal factory'. He went on to point out that the prisons were very much overcrowded at that particular time and this created sub-standard conditions.[2] It was a fact that, for a time during and particularly following the Civil War, there was an increase in the prison population.[3] Minister O'Higgins responded by declaring that serious reforms of the prison system were unrealistic: 'one does not build or try to build in the path of a forest fire'. The situation could be revised once the unrest subsided.[4] As this and other debates on the condition of prisons under the transitional state continued, the country's only borstal institution experienced what can best be described as a catastrophe.

The Civil War manifested itself in two parts. The first phase consisted of a series of direct confrontations that saw the pro-Treaty side removing the anti-Treaty forces from all of their urban bases by the end of August 1922. Crucial to the success of the provisional government was rapid recruitment to the Free State army, no doubt accounted for by the absence of public support for the anti-Treaty side.[5] After proving ineffective in this phase of the conflict, the anti-Treaty forces resorted to the tactics that had served them so well in the Anglo-Irish war of independence and for the remainder of the year they carried out a campaign of ambush and guerrilla warfare. This activity was particularly focused on their stronghold province of Munster but once again the government forces would prove successful and by the end of December the anti-Treaty forces were all but defeated.[6] It was in the context of this second phase of violent activity that the attack on the borstal, now at Clogheen, took place.

After years of campaigning for an improvement in the condition, or even the location, of the Irish borstal system, the change came about unexpectedly and was perhaps not of the nature that supporters of the institution had hoped for. It is not possible to determine the exact date of the transfer from Clonmel to Clogheen workhouse, which were about twenty miles apart.[7] Osborough states it was during the summer of 1922, while others suggest it was early October. The *Clonmel Chronicle* drew attention to strong rumours of a planned move in late September. In a lengthy editorial protesting against the move, it pointed out that the town could ill afford to lose this community of 150 inmates and staff.[8] It appears that the most likely date for the departure of the inmates was 3 October 1922. The same newspaper reported that the boys were transported, along with their belongings and bedding, by motor to Clogheen workhouse. It went on to discount a rumour that the new borstal had already been burned down.[9] *The Nationalist*, on 11 October, confirmed that 'the Irish Borstal Institute has now been transferred completely from its first home in Ireland, the old County Prison in Clonmel, to Clogheen Workhouse'.[10] One week later, during questioning in Dáil Éireann, Kevin O'Higgins explained that the decision to transfer the borstal to Clogheen was taken in order to make the buildings at Clonmel available to the minister for defence, 'who urgently required them for military purposes'.[11]

In October 1922, military authorities requested the minister for home affairs to hand over possession of the borstal institution, 'owing to the scarcity of suitable buildings to be utilised for the accommodation of troops in the neighbourhood of Clonmel' during the continuing Civil War. After October, the premises were used as a barracks and headquarters of the Waterford command of the national army.[12] When the inmates and staff were evacuated in October 1922, there were over one and a half acres of potatoes, one-quarter acre of parsnips and one-eighth acre of carrots growing in the gardens of the complex.[13]

Clogheen workhouse was fully functioning when it, in turn, was forced to evacuate its inmates in October 1922, to the care of other unions. *The Nationalist* claimed that the move from the 'ordered conditions' of Clonmel to a workhouse environment was difficult for all and the borstal staff found their working conditions to be 'rather irksome'.[14] O'Higgins was more enthusiastic about the suitability of Clogheen. The workhouse was selected following the inspection of a number of potential locations; it had all the necessary requirements for the eighty inmates and staff. The buildings were in 'perfect repair', well lit, equipped with electricity and an independent water supply, and had up-to-date sanitation. There was excess accommodation for inmates and staff and the complex was fitted out with all-important workshops and a gymnasium.[15] Little else is known about the period that the borstal institution spent in Clogheen. Less than one week after the transfer from Clonmel, there was, however, a successful escape attempt. Seventeen inmates escaped on Monday night, 9 October, and by 14 October just two had been apprehended.[16] Since its foundation in 1906, *The Nationalist* had been an ardent supporter of Clonmel borstal and the work of the BAI. The year 1922, though, was something of a watershed in the relationship between the institution and the newspaper. Even though the borstal would eventually return to Clonmel, the newspaper would never again provide such detailed regular coverage of the work of the borstal or the BAI. Nonetheless, *The Nationalist*, like O'Higgins, was enthusiastic about the move to Clogheen, though, unfortunately, in light of the ongoing unrest in the country, these sentiments were to prove short-lived.

Clogheen residents went to bed on the night of Saturday 4 November 1922, safe in the knowledge that they were protected by a 'competent garrison' of the national army. They awoke early on the Sunday morning to find that they had been left defenceless following the 'mysterious evacuation' of national troops from the town. The decision to withdraw from the area was puzzling to the residents because valuable government property was left undefended.[17]

Following this evacuation by the national army, the anti-Treaty forces arrived in the town and established their own base. At 4.00 am on the following Wednesday morning, 8 November, a message for the governor was presented to the external guard of the borstal by a number of armed men, to the effect that the complex should be evacuated within the next twenty minutes. The eighty-one inmates, as well as the staff, were awoken and collected their belongings and equipment. They moved to a nearby fever hospital. The attackers then proceeded to pour petrol over the workhouse buildings and, within a few minutes of being set alight, the porter's lodge, clerk's offices and a boardroom all collapsed. Soon the main building and some out-houses were gutted. All the while it was raining heavily. The anti-Treaty forces left the complex at around 6.00 am.[18] The residents of the town later claimed that any buildings that were saved from this attack survived only because of their own 'courage and civic sense'.[19]

The destruction of the workhouse was inevitably the main subject of discussion by the board of guardians for Clogheen at a meeting on 9 November. The clerk reported that all bedding, furniture and clothing had been destroyed. Seeing that he was able do little to save the burning buildings, he had engaged two men to 'remove two splendid presses' from an outer section of the registry office, along with some books. His report to the board highlighted his own 'personal risk' in the salvage operation. Certain buildings did survive, including the infirmary, apartments previously used by the hospital sister, the fever hospital and the night nurses' quarters. The clerk recommended that all the furniture he had managed to save should be auctioned immediately and the board should employ 'some capable men' to guard the remaining buildings as he feared both would be subjected to a similar attack.[20] The board of guardians and the clerk were more concerned for the financial and material implications for Clogheen union than for the future of the borstal system.

The ramifications of this event were significant not only for those on the scene but for the wider penal system in Ireland. In the space of two hours the physical manifestation of the borstal system in Ireland, carefully crafted over the previous sixteen years, was burned to the ground. The entity now consisted of only the inmates and the staff appointed to look after them; for most of that day the Irish borstal institution had no walls, as the authorities devised a response to that morning's misfortune. The most urgent task for the staff was to re-house the inmates as quickly as possible. Soon after the attackers departed Clogheen, the boys were gathered together and marched to the town of Cahir 'in great fettle, singing songs, about ten o'clock'. Meanwhile, temporary quarters were established, while a medium-term solution was put in place.[21] The disaster that had just befallen the Irish borstal system was the most dramatic event to have occurred in the history of the institution. Up until November, the daily lives of inmates were subject to the strictest control and the boys were rarely allowed to set foot outside the borstal. It is impossible to interpret the inmates' good humour: as triumphalist or merely a reaction to this extraordinary crisis, which had brought some much-needed excitement to their otherwise mundane lives in borstal. The boys remained two or three days in Cahir, during which time there was some discussion of temporary accommodation being sought in Dublin.[22] They were returned once again to the original borstal in Clonmel but soon removed to Kilkenny workhouse, where they were to remain until the withdrawal of the national army from Clonmel in 1924.[23]

Meanwhile, Clogheen residents launched a campaign to have the borstal moved back to their village. A letter to the Department of Home Affairs, dated 15 May 1924, and signed by twenty-three residents of Clogheen (including four Roman Catholic and Protestant clergymen), provides an interesting insight into the local attitude to the borstal. Their approach was two-fold. The first aspect highlighted the physical attributes of the workhouse at Clogheen: although three quarters of the complex had been destroyed by the fire, the walls of the buildings were solid and expenditure of approximately £5,000 would be enough to reconstruct them. Further to this, there was an excellent water supply, electricity cables in place, modern sanitation and spacious grounds surrounded by secure boundaries that would prevent any escapes. The residents were obviously well-versed in the needs of the borstal system as they went on to make reference to the fact that the former workhouse complex was adjoined by approximately one hundred acres of land, which could be purchased or leased for the purposes of training the boys. The final physical selling point was a 'magnificent house and grounds for the Governor'.[24]

The Clogheen residents were not solely concerned with the future condition of the juvenile penal system in Ireland, however. In attempting to have the borstal returned to Clogheen the signatories saw an opportunity for some badly needed financial investment because 'no town of the size has suffered more at the hands of the incendiaries than Clogheen'. Many public buildings, including the borstal, courthouse, police and military barracks were all affected by fire in some way or other, and plans to open a woollen mills in the military barracks had not yet materialised. Unemployment was high in Clogheen in 1924; with a population of about six hundred people there were few economic prospects. It was envisaged that bringing the borstal back to the town could have a dual advantage. Much of the restoration work could be done locally, involving a certain amount of employment. This would in itself be a cost-saving measure for the state, which would not need to bring in outside labour or equipment.[25] The borstal institution never returned to Clogheen. Instead, it went back to its original home in Clonmel on 16 July 1924.[26] Fifty boys were moved from Kilkenny to Clonmel in military lorries, along with the governor, chief clerk and around eighteen warders and their families.[27] This marked an end to a particularly turbulent period in the history of borstal in Ireland and the beginning of another phase in its existence.

One of the most revealing aspects of the attack on Clogheen borstal was the lack of any substantial coverage from the national newspapers. In many respects this was understandable given all the incidents taking place in the country. The *Irish Times* made only passing reference to the fire, while other national titles appear to have ignored it. This was typical of the place that borstal held in the Irish public consciousness. Over the course of its first sixteen years of development one of the loudest complaints from supporters of Clonmel borstal was the singular lack of support it received from around the country. Neither was there any political outcry: the incident was not raised in the Dáil at the time and only received a passing mention a number of years later when the borstal returned from Kilkenny. This could be seen as indicative of the borstal system, despite the success of its regime, failing to ignite the public or political imagination. This has to be weighed against the fact that the attack took place in the context of the bitter Civil War, in which the future direction of the Irish people was at stake. Government infrastructure was attacked on a daily or weekly basis and the national newspapers were filled with accounts of atrocities. The reality was that nobody was killed or injured in the Clogheen workhouse fire and, therefore, the matter may not have merited any large-scale coverage. In returning the borstal system to Clonmel in July 1924, the Irish penal authorities demonstrated the same lack of imagination as their British predecessors. Despite the best efforts of those operating the institution on a daily basis and of the philanthropists involved in the aftercare process, they and most outside observers agreed that this former county gaol was not a suitable location for the reform of juvenile-adult offenders. The GPB had undoubtedly wasted an opportunity to reinvent the Irish borstal system in a new and altogether more reform friendly environment, which should have almost certainly included land for farming.

Since its foundation in 1906, Clonmel borstal, along with the remainder of the penal system, had been under the control of the GPB. This remained the case after the Free State government took power. The Board had been in place since 1877 under the chairmanship of Sir

Walter Crofton and its very existence had both a stabilising and a modernising influence on the network of prisons in Ireland. The retention of this particular agency by the Irish government ensured a certain level of administrative continuity for the penal system, even in the midst of the turmoil of 1922–3. This Victorian-era apparatus of prison management seemed to have served its purpose by the end of the decade, however, and on 18 December 1928 the General Prisons Board was dissolved. Using authority provided by the Minister and Secretaries Act 1924, all of the functions and powers of the Board were transferred to the minister for justice and his department.[28] This marked the conclusion of a very distinctive period in the history of the Irish penal system, with the passing of a body whose most adventurous innovation was the foundation of a borstal institution. The task of managing the punishment and rehabilitation of Ireland's juvenile-adult offender class now fell to the Department of Justice.

ADMISSIONS, 1922–8

In assessing admissions to the Irish borstal institution after Independence it is only possible to examine the years 1922–8 because the register of inmates for the borstal beyond this period is not available. The changes of 1922 in the political and administrative structure in Ireland affected the composition of the borstal inmate community. Between 1906 and 1910 more than 30 per cent of the boys listed their previous residence as Belfast or County Antrim, but after 1922 Clonmel no longer accepted offenders from Northern Ireland.

Another key feature of the post-Independence population of Clonmel was the growth in the number of inmates from Dublin. Between 1922 and 1928 (including the period of its relocation to Kilkenny), there were 163 admissions to the borstal. Of that number, 111 or 68 per cent of boys reported their most recent residence as being in Dublin, compared to 29 per cent in 1910–21.[29] This increase in numbers from the Dublin area could be indicative of a rise in lawlessness characterising the first years of Free State Ireland as the government worked to maintain its authority. There is no evidence, however, to suggest that any of the borstal inmates during the immediate post-1922 period were detained for crimes relating to anti-Free State sentiment.

The highest contributing counties after Dublin were Wexford and Waterford with six inmates each, while Galway and Tipperary both registered five boys. Apart from Dublin, the other major urban centres

TABLE 9.1
GEOGRAPHICAL ORIGINS OF INMATES, 1922–28

County	Number of Inmates
Dublin	111
Waterford	6
Wexford	6
Galway	5
Tipperary	5
Cork	4
Kerry	4
Limerick	4
Mayo	4
Meath	4
Westmeath	3
Wicklow	3

Source: NAI, GPB, Prison register, Clonmel prison and borstal institution, 1903–28.

registered low numbers of inmates in Clonmel for this period. Limerick and Cork contributed just four inmates each, as did Kerry, Mayo and Meath. Three boys came from Westmeath and three from Wicklow.[30] Table 9.1 fails to reveal an urban-rural divide in the sphere of Irish juvenile criminality. So, while County Kerry produced the same number of boys as the cities of Cork and Limerick, Dublin accounted for more than twice the rest of the country combined.

Continuity was demonstrated in the profile of reported occupations of inmates. Labouring was once again the numerically highest occupation, with fifty-nine or 36.2 per cent of the inmates, compared with 50.2 per cent prior to 1922. The second predominant occupation was messenger or message boy. Among the rest were van boy, grocer's assistant and porter. Occupation was not listed by 16 per cent of inmate.[31] Once again these trends indicate that those sentenced to periods of detention in borstal, and thereby consigned to the juvenile-adult offender class, came from the unskilled labouring classes. In this respect, little had changed between 1910 and 1928.

The distribution of offences was also greatly unchanged from the pre-1922 position. Larceny again proved to be the most common crime for which a sentence of borstal was handed down, with eighty-five boys convicted for this offence. Thirty-three inmates were detained for housebreaking and twenty-nine for shopbreaking. Breaking and entering, and receiving, were the fourth and fifth most common offences, with twenty and ten inmates respectively.[32] These five most common criminal acts mirrored those for the earlier period, with a slight alteration in their order. These statistics, and the previous findings on geographical origins, reflect the fact that the majority of criminal acts by juvenile-adult male offenders continued to be urban-based and opportunistic in nature. Large cities and towns, particularly Dublin, provided the most tempting environment for larceny, housebreaking and shopbreaking.[33]

Though the most common offences were of a non-violent nature, there were a number of inmates in this period sent to borstal for physical actions on others. Nineteen-year-old Michael Sweeny from Sligo resided with his mother Anne prior to his detention in Kilkenny borstal in July 1924, when a two-year sentence was imposed at the central criminal court in Dublin for manslaughter.[34] This was by far the most serious crime for which any offender was sent to borstal in Ireland between 1922 and 1928 – it was not, however, the longest sentence. A useful comparison is the case of sixteen-year-old John O'Brien from County Clare. His offence was described as 'discharging a shotgun at residence with intent to prevent persons from doing what they had a legal right to do'. This offender lived with his father and was employed in farming. Despite the fact that his offence, like many others in borstal, did not cause physical harm to others, he received the longer sentence of three years.[35] Only one offence of a sexual nature appeared during this period: eighteen-year-old David Tobin from Dublin was sentenced to three years' borstal detention for the 'indecent assault on three boys aged under thirteen years'.[36]

The common borstal offence of larceny was, of course, not exclusively confined to Dublin or other cities. Sixteen-year-old Jame Grace, a newsboy, from Monaghan was sentenced to three years in borstal in 1928. Among his crimes were the larceny of a tabernacle lock from St Macarten's Cathedral in Monaghan and damage to an outer tabernacle door. He also pleaded not guilty to a charge of breaking into another premises with intent to commit a felony. The judge in the case noted that the boy remained in bed until 10.00 am each Sunday morning and apportioned some blame to his parents as 'that was not the way for a Catholic boy to be brought up'.[37]

The year 1928 saw another physical act committed against a Roman Catholic church, for which the guilty party found himself in Clonmel. As we have seen throughout this book, a recurring theme surrounding the borstal sentencing and detention process was that of removing the individual from his criminal environment. This arose in the sentencing of seventeen-year-old Michael Whyte from Clifden in

Galway. At a sitting of Galway circuit court on 12 March the offender pleaded guilty to entering a church at Ballyconneely and stealing money from an offertory box. The boy already held a conviction for breaking and entering: the judge declared that 'the sooner he was taken away from the people surrounding him the better'. The judge did not accept the boy's contention that he committed the crime alone and, in passing sentence, he promised him that his experience in Clonmel would make 'him forget that he had been twice convicted'.[38] Michael Whyte reported his occupation as being a labourer and resided with his family. He was sentenced to two years' detention in Clonmel borstal.[39]

As in the pre-Independence period, not all of the borstal offenders worked in isolation. Gerald Davis was part of a small but active gang of bicycle thieves operating in Dublin and brought before the recorder of Dublin at the court in Green Street in January 1924. Along with two other boys, he pleaded guilty to stealing bicycles and passing them on to an older man for sale. Evidence was given by several men who had left their bicycles outside various offices around Dublin and came out of work to find they were gone. Garda investigations led to a shop in Francis Street where the proprietor revealed he had purchased the 'machines' from three boys; the man was found guilty by a jury and held over for sentencing. The recorder underlined that this type of criminal activity was a scourge, declaring that there would be 'none of this nefarious robbery of bicycles in the city if it were not for the receiving merchants like the accused'. Two of the boys were sent to an industrial school until they reached the age of sixteen.[40] Davis, who was already sixteen years old and whose employment was listed as 'nil', was sentenced to three years' borstal detention, having pleaded guilty to twelve counts of larceny.[41] This case highlights the phenomenon of gangs of youths operating with relative ease in co-operation with an older and more experienced leader, in the city with which they were so familiar.

Despite the fact that Ireland was embroiled in a Civil War during 1922–3, it appears that Clonmel borstal was not utilised for the punishment of political offences: the institution was not founded for such purposes, of course. Neither is there anything to suggest that the borstal was used to detain anti-British or, later, anti-Treaty fighters. The borstal was a reformative institution and continued to be seen as such by the penal and judicial authorities during the emergency conditions that prevailed in Ireland between 1919–23.

DAY-TO-DAY LIFE IN BORSTAL, 1922–40

In the absence of full archival material for the entire post-1921 period, it is not possible to construct the daily routine of the inmates in detail. It is possible, however, to reconstruct their general routine. Upon reception by the institution, each boy continued to be interviewed by the governor, who learned something of his character and his potential for trades training. The Roman Catholic and Protestant chaplains played the same role as they did prior to Independence: ministering to their respective congregations and giving occasional lectures on various topics. The Sisters of Charity visited the Catholic inmates every Sunday but the nature of their work remains unclear.[42] Additionally, during the late 1930s a Roman Catholic priest visited the institution three or four times per week. On Sundays, priests delivered Mass to the Catholic inmates, administered the sacrament of confession and made contact with the individual boys. The departing Roman Catholic chaplain noted in late 1940 that individual spiritual instruction was necessary, as a number of boys arrived each year 'in complete, or almost complete ignorance of the catechism'. In addition to this, when the annual retreat organised by the Redemptorist order took place in the town of Clonmel, these priests usually made themselves available to the borstal. It was also noted that the Blessed Sacrament was 'constantly reserved in the chapel of the institution'.[43] The medical officer still played a vital role and physical exercise remained central to each day in Clonmel. Boys were weighed and measured on a regular basis to track their progress. Any inmate not developing physically as well as expected would be sent to the medical officer for examination. Well-behaved inmates were allowed to receive visitors and letters each month and at certain times of the year, such as Christmas and Easter, they were permitted parcels from relatives containing luxuries such as fruit and cake.[44]

Minister for justice James Fitzgerald-Kenney explained in 1927 that 'as far as our means permit, we train the inmates for some calling which will enable them to pursue an honest life on their discharge'. The reality, however, was that there were no 'regular trading workshops' to train the boys in anything beyond the long-practised trades of shoemaking, tailoring and some carpentry.[45] In the same year, the GPB highlighted the poor educational attainment levels of inmates committed to the borstal. Of the sixty-seven inmates in custody in December 1926, thirteen were deemed totally illiterate. Of the remaining fifty-four, just seven were able to read and write 'fairly well', while thirty-eight had no knowledge of arithmetic. The GPB's vice-chairman, Inspector MacDermot argued that this situation caused great difficulties for the Board, and indeed the BAI, as both bodies sought to find employment for discharged inmates. He argued for the appointment of an officer whose sole purpose would be to oversee the education of the inmates. This would have the dual purpose of addressing the educational standard of the boys, as well as freeing up the governor's time for the running of the institution.[46] It is not clear whether this request was granted by the government at the time.

Some attempt was made by the borstal management to help the boys escape the monotony of their daily routine. On Thursday night, 31 October 1938 a variety evening was held at the institution. This event took the form of a concert in which the audience was presented with music, dance and comedy acts, along with conjuring tricks, and a one-act play was staged by the Clonmel Operatic and Dramatic Society. The concert performers 'were loudly applauded' and 'much merriment' was had by the audience. The evening was concluded with the singing of the National Anthem.[47] A newspaper report related how there was repeated applause and loud cheering, forms of human expression not necessarily associated with a penal institution. The variety concert appears to have been a success and was undoubtedly an attempt to inject something of a non-penal atmosphere into the institution and, therefore, move it closer to its original intention. No other published account has been found of other similar concerts having taken place between 1922 and 1940 but it will be shown later that this was not an isolated event.

It appears that the institution itself played a limited role in the life of the town of Clonmel. One resident in the late-1930s, Mary, made her confirmation at the Roman Catholic church of SS Peter and Paul alongside around six inmates from the borstal. Seated together at the top right-hand side of the church and dressed identically in a 'sort of grey serge', the boys were accompanied by at least two warders and they were described as having been 'a little group apart'. They were confirmed as the last of the boys, directly preceding the girls. The inmates stood out because of their 'apartness' and the fact that they were clearly in custody, although the warders were not in uniform.[48] This is in keeping with the more relaxed policy that emerged in both Irish and British borstal policy in the 1930s and 1940s. If inmates, for any reason, went outside the institution they were typically accompanied by non-uniformed officers, though their clothes might have set them apart. Another resident of Clonmel remembers very little interaction between the borstal and the townspeople. He emphasises 'a sense of apartness', as the borstal existed as something of a closed community within the town and when one passed its gates there was an awareness of the presence of an authority within that should not be disturbed. For him, as a young man, the borstal was perceived as a type of prison for 'all sorts of people, you presumed they were terrible types, savages. You didn't go near the place, you treaded very carefully.'[49]

Indeed, by 1940 the barrister Edward Fahy was highly critical of the state of the institution, not only condemning the lack of open space for sport or training, but also underlining the dire condition of the cells. Fahy felt that the Irish authorities had not embraced or come to terms with the original notion of borstal not being a prison. The complex retained all of the features of the Victorian gaol, including the high walls, stern-looking front gate and, quite significantly, the institution continued to use the original prison cells.[50] One of the most disturbing comments made by Fahy was a comparison he made between Clonmel borstal and Portlaoighise convict prison. The cells in the borstal were 'gloomy, about twelve feet long and four-and-a-half feet wide', and were very poor when compared with the 'bright roomy cells' at Portlaoighise.[51] It is not clear exactly why Clonmel borstal still remained when better conditions had developed in English borstals.

THE BORSTAL ASSOCIATION OF IRELAND, 1922–40

One of the most significant changes in the Irish borstal system following the Anglo-Irish Treaty and Civil War was the almost complete disappearance of the BAI from the public discourse. Although it traditionally styled itself as a non-denominational organisation and, indeed, this was borne out by membership from both religious traditions, its leadership would have been strongly identified with the Protestant community. Its founder, Richard Bagwell, was, after all, a staunch Unionist and, although he died in 1918, the Association would have been publicly identified with the strong Protestant philanthropic tradition that existed in Clonmel at the time. No public meetings of the BAI were reported after 1921: such gatherings might have been a target for political violence. This does not mean, however, that the Association went out of business.

It transpired that from August 1923 onwards the government grant to the BAI of two pounds per discharged inmate was discontinued. In the subsequent period the Association was left with a financial shortfall of over two hundred pounds and by late 1927, according to Governor Barrows, the aftercare body was in crisis as it struggled to carry out its basic functions. Barrows wrote to the GPB in 1927 that the BAI provided more than just an aftercare service to the juvenile-adult offenders in Clonmel. The institution now possessed a cinematograph projector and, if the necessary finance was made available to the BAI, it could hire films that 'would be carefully chosen and would contain a large proportion of instructional matter'. This would provide welcome relief for the boys, whose activities were limited to playing indoor games such as draughts or football on a relatively small patch of ground outdoors. As well as this, discharged inmates would benefit from the provision of tools to help them get straight to work in their given trade.[52] The Association had continued its work during the 1920s, although it cannot possibly have operated at the pre-Independence level, given that it was wholly dependent on charitable subscriptions from August 1923 onwards. In January 1928 the Department of Finance consented to Governor Barrows' request and sanctioned a payment of fifty pounds to the GPB/BAI for the year 1928–9. This was on the basis that approximately twenty-five boys were discharged form Clonmel borstal each year, therefore providing a grant of two pounds each, to be spent however the BAI saw fit.[53] By the mid-1930s the Department of Justice referred to the BAI as 'a voluntary body of gentlemen' who kept [an inmate] under 'friendly supervision' for a period of three years after his discharge from the borstal.[54] Despite reduced reference to the BAI, a significant advance had been achieved in the length of supervisory power over discharged boys.

THE ABSENCE OF A FEMALE BORSTAL

During the entire lifetime of Clonmel borstal there was never any equivalent provision for juvenile-adult females. Prior to 1921 the reason offered by the GPB was the very low number of female offenders in this class. In 1924, the prominent Jesuit clergyman, Rev. Richard Devane, as part of a wider discussion on provision for young and abandoned mothers who turned to prostitution, pointed out that females between sixteen and twenty-one were persistently detained in regular prisons, where they associated with unsavoury characters. He called for the foundation of a female borstal, which would be influenced by the Roman Catholic Church.[55] Devane's proposal would have presented a range of difficulties, however, as the borstal treatment method was so firmly controlled by the apparatus of the state. The existing system for males had no in-built provision for the kind of influence suggested by Devane and any such moves would almost certainly have resulted in a radical revision of the ways in which borstal treatment was applied. Kilcommins et al. point out that a further call for a female borstal was made in 1924 by district judge G.P. Cussen. While the recommendation did receive a somewhat promising response from government, no action was forthcoming.[56] In 1925 the Free State minister for justice, Kevin O'Higgins, was questioned in the Dáil about any potential plans for providing borstal-type provision for females offenders. He responded that when juvenile-adult age females were committed to prison they were treated 'on borstal lines' but that, in any event, the numbers would be too low to justify such an institution. He briefly outlined what it meant for females to be treated 'on borstal lines'. Girls between sixteen and twenty-one years of age were segregated from the main prison population, taught light trades and given some primary education.[57] This suggests nothing more than a watered-down version of borstal. In 1927 Sir Thomas Moloney echoed O'Higgins' earlier contention that the number of female juvenile-adult offenders remained too low to justify the opening of a separate borstal. In fact, he questioned the overall usefulness of borstal treatment for girls, arguing that his experience with the English system showed that some females required an altogether more individualised approach as well as 'more varied forms of appeal'.[58] In retrospect it is easy to see why those calls for a female institution, while acknowledged, were not acted upon at the time. The male borstal which had been in existence since 1906 had come close to extinction a few months earlier. The notion of establishing a second such institution was most probably far down the list of political priorities in the unstable political and security environment that prevailed in early 1920s Ireland.

Calls for some form of appropriate custodial provision for female juvenile-adult offenders continued, however, and supporters continued to underline the futility of prison as an option.[59] Interestingly, many of the reasons put forward for prison as a less-desired option mirrored those advanced decades earlier in the case of male offenders. In a set of notes provided to the Roman Catholic archbishop of Dublin, John Charles McQuaid, in 1941, three Dublin-based probation officers outlined the need for a remand home specifically for girls. For 'the more respectable type of first offenders', the risks associated with a sentence of imprisonment were many. Associating with hardened criminals, even for a few days, often had the effect of changing the attitude of the most well-intentioned of young first offender. Any length of time spent in prison could lead to the removal of any feelings of 'terror' for first offenders. The probation officers went so far as to argue that many convicted females opted for a short prison sentence rather than a lengthy term of probation as this course expedited their freedom from the shackles of supervision.[60] The notion of prison 'hardening' and removal of first offenders' fear of imprisonment was a well-rehearsed argument in the history of borstal, both in Ireland and England. While the probation officers made no mention of a potential female borstal, they did not highlight the thinking among those working in the penal system that, even two decades on from Independence, there remained a pressing need for some course of action in this area. With the government once again struggling to maintain the existing male borstal, as the next chapter will show, any possibility of a response to the problem of the female juvenile-adult offender was almost non-existent.

While it was inevitable that a shift in administrative control at government level was always likely to cause some upheaval, the confusion that reigned over the Irish borstal system for the first two years of the Free State could scarcely have been predicted. The survival of the borstal following the attack at Clogheen is a testament not to the provisional government (which was busy trying to defeat the anti-Treaty forces in the Civil War) but to the will of those on the ground on the day. Once the boys and the officers guarding them had evacuated the ruins of Clogheen workhouse, the Irish borstal was reduced to an idea and it no longer had walls or cells. The reconstruction of the borstal system during the 1920s and its survival into the 1930s can both be largely credited to staff and volunteers of the BAI and their ability to maintain the institution during a time when it remained severely under-funded. This second phase of borstal in Ireland is largely marked by the absence of any significant development or initiative that advanced its ability to fulfil its oft-stated vision of rehabilitating or reforming juvenile-adult male offenders rather than punishing them. The lack of a female borstal was further evidence of a lack of progressive thinking in the treatment of the juvenile-adult offender. In the absence of any great political enthusiasm it was hardly surprising that, following the beginning of World War Two the borstal complex was once again the target for occupation and the system was moved again, this time to Cork city. This marked the beginning of the third and final phase of the Clonmel borstal story and will be the focus of the next chapter.

NOTES

1. NLI, Forty-fifth Report of the General Prisons Board, 1922–1923, p. iv.
2. Dáil Éireann, Dáil in Committee – General Prisons Board, 28 November 1922.
3. Carey, Mountjoy: The Story of a Prison, p. 205.
4. Dáil Éireann, Dáil in Committee – General Prisons Board, 28 November 1922.
5. Lyons, Ireland since the Famine, pp. 462–3.
6. Connolly, The Oxford Companion to Irish History, p. 265.
7. Official records do not cover the specific discussion and events of the evacuation of Clonmel borstal to Clogheen.
8. Clonmel Chronicle, 27 September 1922.
9. Clonmel Chronicle, 4 October 1922.
10. The Nationalist, 11 October 1922.
11. Dáil debates, 18 October 1922.
12. The Nationalist, 19 July 1924.
13. NAI, Maher to Department of Home Affairs, 15 December 1923, H201/3.
14. The Nationalist, 11 October 1922.
15. Dáil debates, 18 October 1922.
16. Clonmel Chronicle, 14 October 1922.
17. NAI, Clogheen residents to Minister for Home Affairs, 15 May 1924, H201/3.
18. The Nationalist, 11 November 1922.
19. NAI, Clogheen residents to Minister for Home Affairs, 15 May 1924, H201/3.
20. Tipperary Studies, 'Minutes of proceedings of the Board of Guardians, Clogheen Union', 9 November 1922.
21. The Nationalist, 11 November 1922.
22. Clonmel Chronicle, 11 November 1922.
23. Osborough, Borstal in Ireland, p. 60.
24. NAI, Clogheen residents to Minister for Home Affairs, 15 May 1924, H201/3.
25. NAI, Clogheen residents to Minister for Home Affairs, 15 May 1924, H201/3.
26. The Nationalist, 19 July 1924. This was the process of reducing the Free State army to a size required for peacetime.
27. Clonmel Chronicle, 26 July 1924.
28. NLI, Saorstat Éireann, Annual Report on Prisons for the Year 1928, H.4, p. 3.
29. NAI, Prison register, Clonmel prison and borstal institution, 1903–1928, GPB1/7/14.
30. NAI, Prison register, Clonmel prison and borstal institution, 1903–1928, GPB1/7/14.
31. NAI, Prison register, Clonmel prison and borstal institution, 1903–1928, GPB1/7/14.
32. NAI, Prison register, Clonmel prison and borstal institution, 1903–1928, GPB1/7/14.
33. NAI, Prison register, Clonmel prison and borstal institution, 1903–1928, GPB1/7/14.
34. NAI, Prison register, Clonmel prison and borstal institution, 1903–1928, GPB1/7/14.
35. NAI, Prison register, Clonmel prison and borstal institution, 1903–1928, GPB1/7/14.
36. NAI, Prison register, Clonmel prison and borstal institution, 1903–1928, GPB1/7/14.
37. Irish Independent, 28 July 1928.
38. Connacht Tribune, 17 March 1928.
39. NAI, Prison register, Clonmel prison and borstal institution, 1903–1928, GPB1/7/14.
40. Freeman's Journal, 22 January 1924.

41. NAI, Prison register, Clonmel prison and borstal institution, 1903–1928, GPB1/7/14.
42. NLI, Saorstat Éireann, *Annual Report on Prisons*, 1934, p. 14.
43. *The Nationalist*, 30 October 1940.
44. NLI, Saorstat Éireann, *Annual Report on Prisons*, 1934, p. 14.
45. Quoted in *The Nationalist*, 26 November 1927.
46. NAI, *MacDermot to Department of Justice*, H268/6, 21 December 1927.
47. *The Nationalist*, 2 November 1938.
48. Interview with Mary, 20 November 2008.
49. Interview with Michael, 20 November 2008.
50. Fahy, 'The boy criminal', p. 147.
51. Fahy, 'The boy criminal', p. 148.
52. NAI, Barrows to GPB, H268/7, 03 December 1927.
53. NAI, Department of Finance to GPB, H268/7, 17 January 1928.
54. NLI, Saorstat Éireann, Annual Report on Prisons, 1934, p. 14.
55. James M. Smith, *Ireland's Magdalen Laundries and the Nation's Architecture of Containment* (Manchester: Manchester University Press, 2007), pp. 50–1.
56. Shane Kilcommins, Ian O'Donnell, Eoin O'Sullivan, Barry Vaughan, *Crime, Punishment and the Search for Order in Ireland* (Dublin: Institute of Public Administration, 2004), pp. 44–5.
57. Dáil debates, 30 April 1925.
58. Sir Thomas Moloney, 'The treatment of young offenders', *Journal of the Social and Statistical Inquiry Society of Ireland*, (June 1927), p. 451. Sir Thomas Moloney (1865–1949) was born in Dublin and educated at Trinity College. In 1906 he was appointed crown counsel for Carlow and in 1813 he became attorney-general for Ireland. Moloney showed a particular interest in the borstal systems of both Ireland and Britain, having visited the institutions in both jurisdictions on several occasions.
59. Smith provides a particularly useful analysis of this debate.
60. Letter and notes to Archbishop John Charles McQuaid, 22 December 1941.

CHAPTER TEN

Decline of borstal in Clonmel, 1940–56

The beginning of the third phase of borstal in Ireland was largely dictated by external events. The onset of World War Two in 1939 necessitated the restructuring of many aspects of government administration as the country struggled to cope with the security threats and economic hardships brought about by a conflict in which it was neutral. The removal of the borstal from Clonmel for the duration of the war was not surprising. Such institutions were also targeted by the authorities in Britain as they were suitable sites for the relocation of soldiers, prisoners or even supplies in a wartime environment. This chapter will examine the fate of the Irish borstal system from its removal to Cork during the emergency and its subsequent return to Clonmel in 1946. It will also evaluate the treatment of inmates in the 1940s, when the Irish borstal institution came to be defined by its almost complete lack of progress in the rehabilitation of the juvenile-adult offender. Finally, it discusses one of the most significant controversies to befall the Irish penal system during the first half of the century. The public statements of Boys' Town founder Monsignor Edward Flanagan on the state of Ireland's prisons and borstal institution hit a raw nerve with both government and opposition political parties. Ironically, it is likely that the controversy did have some positive side effects for the inmates of Clonmel borstal when the system was reinstated in the town in 1946, thereby delaying its closure.

THE BRITISH BORSTAL SYSTEM ON THE EVE OF WORLD WAR TWO

For every reverse of fortune suffered by the Irish borstal system during the 1920s, it seemed that the opposite was happening to the expanding network of institutions in Britain. The Ruggles-Brise era came to an end in 1921 with the appointment of Sir Maurice Waller as chairman of the Prison Commissioners for England and Wales. By this time, there were three borstal institutions in England: the original in Kent, another in

Feltham and a third in Portland in Dorset, opened in 1921. Alexander Patterson was appointed in 1922 as a Prison Commissioner with special responsibility for borstals.[1] During the next two and a half decades under Patterson, the British borstal system underwent a series of transformations, becoming the subject of constant scrutiny and evaluation. While the Irish borstal was struggling to find a home during the turbulence of 1922–4, Patterson was examining ways of consolidating and expanding the system. Widely experienced in the ways of delinquent young people, having lived among them for the previous twenty years in the slums of south-east London, Patterson shared 'with them the ups and downs of war in trench and shell hole'.[2] McConville characterised Patterson's task as an ambitious one in which he needed to refashion the borstal system for a new generation whose social ideas had been dented by the effects of World War One.[3] This was achieved in a number of ways.

Among the first of the sweeping changes implemented by Patterson was a set of ideas based on the public school system that had existed in England since the previous century. While most of the core principles of borstal such as discipline and hard work remained intact, the institution would now be subdivided into a 'house' system. This entailed re-assigning the cell blocks as 'houses', each with their own individual name and housemaster. A system of prefects and monitors was also initiated as a means of placing some measure of responsibility onto the shoulders of more trustworthy inmates.[4] Sporting and other competitive and social activities were encouraged between the houses as a means of fostering teamwork and instilling a sense of loyalty and belonging among the inmates.[5] This appears to have been part of a concerted effort to move the borstal away from the prison and closer to the spirit of an educational environment. It also most likely contributed to the institution sometimes being referred to as a 'borstal school' in newspapers and elsewhere. Patterson devised this particular strategy out of a need for 'something deeper' than the tried and tested methods that were employed in borstals. The house system came about because the boys required time for positive influences to take hold and self-confidence to build. The role of the housemasters was, therefore, seen as one of the most important factors in this process of individualisation.[6]

The second major initiative of the post-World War One British borstal system came about not necessarily because of a growing inmate population but because the penal authorities felt the need to develop a new type of institution altogether. In an event that has now passed into British penal legend, in 1930 a group of inmates and staff marched cross-country from Feltham borstal to a country estate, Lowdham Grange.[7] Under the leadership of Governor William Llewellin, the party began work on what was to become Britain's first open borstal institution.[8] Roger Hood describes the development as 'a revolutionary move in English penological history'. The open borstal was meant only for those boys who had performed well in the early stages of their detention in the closed institutions. The arrival of the open borstal meant that classification had become somewhat more refined than the three-grade system that had marked the pre-1921 institution.[9] One underlying principle set Lowdham Grange, and the other three open borstals that were in place by the outbreak of the World War Two, apart from the closed institutions. The security and rigid custodial nature of the traditional borstal was replaced by notions of 'trust, cooperation, mutual confidence, all based on a firm discipline and the exercise of self-control'.[10] The new regime came to an abrupt halt, though. By 1.00 pm in the afternoon of 3 September 1939, the operation of Lowdham Grange as a borstal institution was brought to a premature, although not permanent, end. An early morning telegram from the Home Office in London ordered that the institution was to be used to house adult convicts.[11] Despite the interruption of war, however, Britain's borstal system had been set on a new course as Ruggles-Brise's ideas were modified or replaced to cope with new generations of offenders and those charged with their detention. Even though the evolving British system was undoubtedly marked by many imperfections beyond the scope of this study, it was clear that by 1939 its Irish counterpart, in contrast, had fallen behind both in terms of resources and an ability to apply modern ideas to its development.

One of the most noted inmates of any British borstal institution was the Dublin writer Brendan Behan, though his profile was not typical of the Irish borstal inmate. In the pre-1921 period there is no record of any boy having been detained for political agitation of any nature. The available records for the post-1921 period suggest that this remains the case. Borstal was not established for the detention of political prisoners, accused bombers or those fighting for the freedom of a nation. The juvenile-adult was a very specific class of offender, a late nineteenth-century creation identified as a cause of many social ills, but not of the aforementioned and altogether more idealistic crimes. While the British authorities may have adopted their own strategies in this regard, it appears that the Irish Department of Justice chose to retain the borstal for its original purpose. As Brendan Behan was serving his sentence in England, the Irish system was once again undergoing a transformation.

BORSTAL IN CORK

On 1 September 1939 the German invasion of Poland threw the world into a devastating six-year world war on a scale that dwarfed that of 1914–18. Ireland's neutral stance was announced the following day, when the taoiseach, Eamon de Valera, outlined the policy in Dáil Éireann. Two days later the house passed a First Amendment of the Constitution Bill and an Emergency Powers Bill.[12] Between them, these provisions prevented constitutional challenge to any act of government that was declared to be in the interest of public safety during a time of war or internal revolution; in the case of war it was not necessary for Ireland to be a participant.[13] It is out of these developments that the period between 1939 and 1945 came to be known in Ireland as 'The Emergency' rather than the Second World War.

In the following years, many publicly owned buildings, including prisons, were taken over by the government in response to perceived internal and external security threats arising from the war. Sixteen years after its return to Clonmel, the Irish borstal institution was once again on the move. In late 1940 the complex was taken over by the army 'in connection with the scheme of national defence'. On this occasion the system was relocated to Cork prison.[14] Minister for Justice Gerry Boland announced the move to Cork, as well as attempts to locate a more appropriate, lasting home for the institution. The government, he claimed, was faced with the problem of the high cost of funding such a venture.[15] The minister did not use the emergency circumstances as an excuse for the government's inability to ensure proper funding for the borstal; the reality was that successive governments since 1922 failed to plan or fund the borstal for the long term. The move to Cork suggested that the much-needed overhaul of the system would be deferred again.

The problems with the institution in Cork were very much in line with the extensive criticisms that had been levelled at that in Clonmel since 1906. One of the most vocal parliamentary advocates of properly reforming the borstal system was the Fine Gael deputy James Dillon.

During the 1930s and 1940s, he raised the inadequacy of the conditions of training and reformation, both in Clonmel and now in Cork. In November 1940, following the transfer, Dillon described the new home of borstal as possessing an 'even less attractive interior than that from which they [the boys] were removed'. He termed the housing of the borstal inmates in a hard-labour jail as a 'public scandal'.[16] The following year, Boland rejected Dillon's call for a commission to investigate and make recommendations on the Irish borstal system and appeared to suggest that the problems encountered by the institution were not so complex as to warrant such a move. His contention was that suitable premises and a tract of land sufficient for agricultural training would resolve the matter.[17]

One of the most significant and detailed accounts of Cork borstal comes in the form of a lecture delivered by the barrister Edward Fahy and published in *Hermethena* in 1941. Fahy reveals that the internal classification system within which inmates had existed since the inception of borstal in Clonmel in 1906 remained in operation when the institution moved to Cork. All boys were placed within the penal, ordinary or special grades and the daily regime contained many of the same elements as Clonmel, with some slight variations in the times. Training, education, gardening and sokol drill comprised the main day-to-day activities, with time also set aside for meals and prayer. Sokol drill was a form of gymnastics that began in Czechoslovakia in the 1860s. Special grade inmates were allowed to play football in a small yard at the back of the complex.[18] Fahy highlighted the serious official neglect of the Irish borstal, so that by the early 1940s no material or theoretical differences from the pre-1921 institution had emerged. Over this time, neither the Cumman na nGaedheal nor Fianna Fail governments had developed the borstal idea using up-to-date penal theory. As a consequence, Ireland's juvenile-adult offenders were punished and reformed in a sort of institutional time-warp in a borstal that had fallen completely out of step with its former parent system in Britain.

Whether it was in response to Fahy's criticisms or to pressure from James Dillon in the Dáil, in 1942 the minister for justice revealed a number of improvements to the borstal in Cork. The use of a playing field had been obtained from University College, Cork, and bicycles were also acquired, with cycling trips organised for the inmates. Boland claimed that this helped to eliminate one of the most serious defects of the Cork borstal: the absence of outdoor activities. An

indoor recreation hall had recently been completed and included a
stage, a piano, a radiogram and tables at which the inmates could play
chess and draughts.[19] This latter development could not necessarily be
deemed progressive, however, as inmates at Clonmel had been
involved in those particular indoor activities since 1906. In 1943
Boland repeated his defensive line that conditions had improved at
Cork borstal, now adding that the new recreation hall was used for
lectures and cinematic presentations. 'Conditions', he argued, 'are
very much better than they have ever been since the Borstal system
was started.'[20] Boland was showing his unfamiliarity with borstal, as
lectures had always been an integral part of the borstal process and,
indeed, films were shown as soon as the technology became available
during the World War One years.

Two years later the Department of Justice pointed out that the
majority of the boys entered the institution with poor levels of literacy
and a low standard of religious knowledge. Even though the same level
of schooling as before was provided to the inmates, there appears to
have been an increased clerical presence in the institution during its
time in Cork. Religious instruction was provided by the Sisters of
Charity under the supervision of the chaplain and there was a weekly
visit from a member of the Presentation Christian Brothers, who gave a
lecture to the inmates.[21] While the official records did attest to a female
religious presence in Clonmel borstal, there was no mention of visits by
the Christian Brothers. By 1944, the boys also had access to the Cork
city public swimming baths courtesy of the city manager, a gesture 'very
much appreciated by the inmates'.[22] In general terms it would appear
that the boys detained in Cork borstal had advantages over those in
Clonmel purely because of the physical location of the institution. For
the entire duration of the life of Clonmel borstal there was certainly no
access to facilities such as playing fields or public baths. If public
accounts of the two institutions are to be accepted, however, this is
where the positive aspects of the Cork facility seem to end.

Under questioning from Dillon in the Dáil in late 1944, Boland
stated that sites had been identified near Dublin that might be able to
provide a permanent home for that borstal but none turned out to be
acceptable.[23] Two locations had been under active consideration. The
first was a forty-six acre site at Ballyfermot Upper, owned by a Mr
Hogan, but it was somewhat problematic: it was crossed by two over-
head electricity cables and, under regulations at that time, it was not
permitted to build within twenty-five yards of these lines. A further

complication came in the form of a tentative plan by Dublin Corporation to construct a road that would divide the site into two unequal parts. The Board of Works concluded that it would be unwise to enter negotiations on this particular site. The second location was close to Mr Hogan's and was first purchased by Dublin Corporation with a view to constructing a tuberculosis hospital but the idea had been dropped. The Department of Justice and the Board of Works approached the Department of Local Government and Public Health with a view to entering negotiations but they were unsuccessful as the Department of Health wanted to build an auxiliary mental hospital on the site.[24] A new borstal was, however, part of the government's planning for post-war capital spending: the only planned capital investment for prisons was the construction of a new borstal with an estimated cost of £50,000. The 'long-standing need for such a building' was accepted and the planning report described the existing provisions as 'totally unsuitable for the imparting of reformative treatment'.[25]

Dillon's criticisms of the institution in Cork came to a head in 1945 when he accepted an offer from the minister for justice to explore the facility for himself, with complete access to all parts of the borstal. Later Dillon described the institution as 'deplorable' but quickly made it clear that it was not unsanitary. He described it as 'nothing but a jail in the middle of the city of Cork' and pointed out there was 'not a hen-run on which you can exercise the boys'.[26] Yet, one of the selling points of Cork borstal, as outlined earlier, was the provision of a playing field by the university. Dillon minimised the significance of this particular feature, however, by stating that the boys were allowed out to play the 'occasional' game of football. What was much more serious than any of the other deficiencies was the fact that the complex was 'so unsuitable for a borstal' that it was becoming difficult to maintain discipline. The deputy argued that the inadequacy of the buildings meant that the authorities were making concessions to the inmates on humanitarian grounds and this was having a detrimental effect on discipline.[27]

As late as March 1946, Minister Boland agreed in the Dáil that neither was the facility at Clonmel suitable as a borstal institution.[28] Before the end of the year, however, the minister was forced to defend an apparent change of heart by the government as it was revealed that the military occupation of the former Clonmel borstal complex was now at an end, allowing for the return of the inmates and staff from Cork. Again in response to Dillon, Boland reversed his position of previous years and stated there would be a return to

Clonmel, which was superior to Cork in its accommodation, the acre of ground for outdoor activities, the large rooms for workshop and classes, as well as indoor recreation.[29] Whatever the situation with the attempts to build or acquire a completely new borstal during the emergency period, that project never came to pass. On 21 January 1947, the inmates and staff returned to South Tipperary for the third and final chapter in the life of Clonmel borstal. By this time, however, the Irish juvenile penal system was somewhat ambushed by a controversy that originated from a wholly unexpected source.

THE MONSIGNOR FLANAGAN CONTROVERSY

Born in Ballymoe, County Roscommon, in 1886, Edward Flanagan is most commonly remembered as the founder of the Boys' Town home for destitute boys at Omaha, Nebraska, in December 1917. This organisation began life in a simple house in Omaha but quickly grew to become an organised 'town' in the literal sense of the word. Much responsibility for its day-to-day operation was placed in the hands of the boys who lived and worked there. The overall administrative structure included a mayor, six boy commissioners and a municipal court. There was also a Boys' Town high school and instruction in trades training. The movement was operated solely on a charitable basis.[30] Flanagan developed his idea for the home out of a mix of his own experience and his 'Christian faith'. The emphasis of the treatment of those who lived in Boys' Town was not one of punishment but of 'love, care and encouragement'.[31] In 1938 the idea further gripped the imagination of the American and international public with the release by Metro Goldwyn Mayer of a motion picture, 'Boys' Town', based on the life and work of Monsignor Flanagan, who was played by Spencer Tracy. The film earned Flanagan worldwide respect for his efforts. One such admirer was Patrick Wynne, who worked at the Franciscan Abbey, Clonmel. Having seen the film, Wynne had written to Flanagan to congratulate him on his work and in early 1940 was 'delighted' to receive a personal letter of response. Flanagan thanked Wynne for his support for 'the work I am trying to do for poor homeless boys of all colours, nationalities and creeds'. He described the film as 'a beautiful and spiritual presentation' and anticipated a greater financial windfall for Boys' Town in the planned follow-up.[32] In 1947 Monsignor Flanagan was asked to tour Asia to ascertain the needs of children orphaned by World War Two; his

report was received in person by President Harry Truman at the
White House in July of the same year. He died in May 1948 in Berlin
while on a tour to raise funds and awareness of his work. Such was
the esteem and respect that Flanagan had earned, Truman placed a
wreath on his grave at Boys' Town two weeks after his death.

Though he may have grown in respect and stature in the United
States, Monsignor Flanagan managed to gravely offend the Irish political establishment during the two years leading up to his death. His
public statements on the country's juvenile penal system, including
industrial schools, reformatories and borstals, caused extreme discomfort to the all-powerful Irish Catholic church hierarchy that ran
many of these institutions, as well as a state that was not ready to take
responsibility for them. His words were eerily prophetic but would
not be fully vindicated for almost another half century.

'From what I have seen since coming to this country, your institutions are not all noble, particularly your borstal, which are a disgrace.'[33]
Monsignor Flanagan spoke these words during a lecture delivered at
the Savoy cinema in Cork city on 7 July, 1946, in the course of his tour
of Ireland. He was well received by capacity audiences and, in places
such as Limerick and Waterford, Catholic bishops attended the events.[34]
Central to the allegations made by Flanagan during this period was
his contention that physical punishment and brutality were common
practice in the prisons and borstal institutions in Ireland. The claims
provoked a fierce reaction from both politicians and public alike. The
first parliamentary response of Minister for Justice Boland on 23 July
attempted to undermine Flanagan by pointing out that he had not actually visited any prison or borstal institution during his visit, and was,
therefore, not in a position to comment.[35] In October James Dillon
asked whether the minister was seriously considering returning the
inmates to 'a dirty, damp antediluvian prison'. Dillon continued, 'it is a
small wonder that Monsignor Flanagan should say what he did about
this country'.[36]

The controversy was also played out on the pages of the *Irish
Times*, with mixed reactions to Flanagan's views. One high-profile
correspondent, Maud Gonne MacBride, praised Flanagan's courage
for speaking out, 'painful as it is to read'. Her letter intimated that the
public did not know much about the conditions within the country's
borstal, reformatories or industrial schools at that time. She then went
on to challenge one of the core principles upon which borstal was
originally founded. 'The mere fact,' she argued, 'of keeping young

offenders apart from older ones won't do much good if any of these establishments have adopted the standards of our prisons and employ the same punishments.' Among those punishments used at borstal was the most 'dangerous' of all in her opinion: solitary confinement.[37] Not all correspondents were sympathetic to this viewpoint, however, with one letter-writer, 'Northman' from Dimamanagh, County Tyrone, calling for the return of 'the old-fashioned stocks and ducking-stool' as a means of subjecting the offender to public 'ridicule'.[38] Another, whose name was withheld by the editor, presented a series of arguments that highlighted the failings of officialdom and its depiction of the prison system. Firstly, the writer pointed out that the question of whether or not Monsignor Flanagan had actually visited any Irish penal institutions was not necessarily relevant. Had he attended a prison, his visit, according to the correspondent, would have followed a set pattern. The tour would commence with a visit to the governor's house, where he would have been entertained. Flanagan would then have inspected the sundial on the governor's lawn and 'beautifully kept' flower-beds. He would have been shown a number of carefully chosen cells and would have 'noted the spotless cleanliness of the long main hall, the shining brasswork and the carefully blacked stairs'. The guest would possibly also have visited the farm, where he would see a number of prisoners 'working industriously, and apparently quite happily under the watchful eye of a warder, who would spring to attention'.[39] This letter serves to call into question many of the so-called 'independent' inspections to which the various penal institutions had been subjected over the course of many decades. It would, perhaps, be somewhat stronger had the identity of the author been revealed. It is obvious that the individual had considerable insight into the day-to-day operations of a prison in Ireland during this period. The letter went on to highlight what Monsignor Flanagan would not have been shown. The convicts who tended to the flower-beds were typically short-term prisoners who were sentenced to between six months and two years; these individuals were only given this job under exceptional circumstances and the average convict in a prison only caught sight of the flower-beds twice during his sentence – the day he arrived and the day he left. Secondly, the cells that a visitor would inspect were 'show cells' only made available to impress outsiders. The 'spotless hall' and 'shining brasswork' was only possible because of the 'back-breaking' efforts of those convicts selected for this labour from 7.00 am until 8.30 pm. As for the prisoners working 'happily on the farm, their existence would become "unendurable" if they did not follow the set pattern in the presence of visitors. A prisoner could possibly end up in a punishment cell for fourteen days existing on a diet of bread, potatoes and water.' 'I know,' said the writer, giving the strongest hint of his former position within the system, 'I was there.'[40] While this letter could rightly be challenged as being the biased and resentful opinion of a former prisoner with an obvious axe to grind against the system, it is powerful because of the level of detail and the careful construction of its arguments against government criticisms of Flanagan. It gives voice to contemporary suspicion, and indeed a wariness among historians of the validity of independent inspections of penal institutions. An editorial note printed immediately below the letter pointed out that the author had been advised to make the allegations known to the appropriate authorities. In December 1946, Monsignor Edward Flanagan responded to some of the criticisms that had been levelled at him since his visit to Ireland. He again stressed an awareness of 'brutalities' that existed in the Irish prison and borstal systems, and that these had been denied but not disproved. Flanagan pointed out that 'if such a denial came from an impartial group of investigators who had made a thorough study of the entire situation, such proof would be convincing'. He went on to call for the establishment of such a group and the uncensored publication of its findings. Flanagan made an impassioned defence of his pride in his heritage, rejecting out of hand any suggestion that he was anti-Irish. He argued that his criticisms of the Irish borstal system were similar to those he had made against American prisons and reformatories, where he had identified similar brutalities and injustices.[41] In defending himself against this particular allegation, Flanagan was attempting to disarm one of the most serious and damaging claims that could have been made against his reputation.

The controversy surrounding Monsignor Flanagan's visit to Ireland rumbled on and surfaced once again in the Dáil in late March 1947. In a robust defence of the Irish borstal and reformatory systems, James Dillon described Flanagan's allegations as 'falsehoods and slanders'. Dillon reminded the house that there was no more severe critic of Boland and the Department of Justice's administration of the borstal system than himself. He had no choice, however, but to publicly criticise a cleric whose words led American cartoonists to depict an Irish penal system in which 'muscular warders are flogging half-naked fourteen year old boys with a cat-of-nine-tails'. Dillon urged the minister for justice not to fall into the trap of feeling obliged to defend every aspect of the borstal system against Monsignor Flanagan's 'ill-informed nonsense'.[42] Dillon's comment was representative of the political system closing ranks against any criticism of the highly sensitive area of juvenile penal discipline. While the political and religious establishment in Ireland was extremely unwelcoming of any criticism of the borstal, their comments were often accompanied by a strong defence of religious orders such as the Christian Brothers and therein, potentially, lay the real source of this indignation. Monsignor Edward Flanagan's death in 1948 ensured a permanent end to the controversy between himself and the Irish political establishment but there is no doubt that the debate he initiated did reap some unexpected dividends for Clonmel borstal.

THE RENEWAL OF CLONMEL BORSTAL?

When juvenile-adults were once again returned to Clonmel in January 1947 they encountered an institution that was undergoing something of a physical transformation. The most significant alteration was in its name – it was now to be known as 'St Patrick's Borstal Institution, Clonmel'. The Department of Justice reported that the facility was in a poor state of repair by the end of the six-year army occupation, a factor that necessitated a 'complete renovation'. Part of this process included an attempt to shake off some of the physical characteristics of a prison and introduce a sense of openness to the complex. This entailed the demolition of certain old buildings and walls as well as the removal of bars from all the windows. The institutional garden was also over-hauled, having been used as a dump during the military occupation. There was also a plan to renovate all of the remaining cubicles used for sleeping the inmates and to install 'shower baths'. Although the refurbishment was not complete upon the return of the inmates, it was anticipated that there would eventually be sleeping quarters for eighty to ninety boys.[43] It is unlikely that these specific changes amounted simply to a knee-jerk reaction to the ongoing public controversy about the state of prisons and borstals in Ireland. For the most part they were the type of modifications that would have been necessary for returning the institution to an acceptable physical state for its original function. Real physical change was to come the following year.

It is now clear that, by 1948, any plans by government for a completely new borstal institution were scrapped. The public and private reasons for the decision were somewhat different, however At a government meeting held in May it was decided that, as 'an economy measure', plans for a new borstal building would be dropped.[44] The following year, internal correspondence from the Department of Justice reaffirmed this decision. In a private letter to the Department of the Taoiseach it was pointed out that, 'I am to state that considerable improvements and renovations have since been carried out at the existing Institution (St Patrick's, Clonmel). In the circumstances the proposal to erect a new Borstal has been dropped.'[45]

1948 was something of a landmark year for the borstal in Clonmel for two different reasons. Firstly, it appears that the Department of Justice implemented the mid-twentieth century equivalent of a public relations drive to improve the image of the institution. In early May *The Nationalist* published a lengthy article headlined 'the borstal has a new look'.[46] The article reproduced a report, *Notes by the Visiting Committee*, published by the Department of Justice. This commented on reception, health, food, education and training, religion, discipline and punishment, staff, discharge and aftercare. There can be no question that it was compiled and published in response to the Monsignor Flanagan controversy. This is confirmed by the third sentence of the introduction, which states that 'the need for some such publication may be illustrated by reference to two very misleading newspaper articles on this subject published, one in the United States of America and the other in Dublin'.[47] The piece goes on to describe an allegation of flogging at an Irish penal institution for males between the age of sixteen and twenty-one – presumably the borstal – and to refute this claim in the strongest terms. The Visiting Committee suggested that flogging was not at that time, or previously, a punishment that was used in the Irish borstal. Neither had it been permitted for use in the wider prison system for over two decades.[48] Flanagan's allegation of flogging was one of the most contentious aspects of the controversy and it is, therefore, appropriate that this is the first issue addressed by the Visiting Committee.

Accepting that the Visiting Committee report failed to identify any serious weakness in the institution, it did demonstrate that some significant structural changes had moved Clonmel borstal some distance from the Victorian prison structure that had so long been a target of vilification and criticism. Among the additions that would directly impact on the lives of the boys were the construction of a ball-alley and a playing field (the latter located just outside the outer wall of the complex). In the area of training one of the most important additions was a cabinet-making workshop. Officers of the institution remained in traditional prison uniform but this had been toned down to such an extent that it was now approaching civilian style.[49] This particular development had taken place a quarter of a century earlier in the British system with the arrival of open borstals.[50] The reality was that Britain's borstal had long ago surpassed the structures and facilities that were achieved in Clonmel by 1948.

The second important development in St Patrick's Borstal Institution occurred later in 1948 and so was not included in this report. In early October the 'stern looking, steel-plated' front gate of the institution was replaced. The new structure was a decorative bar gate over which the words 'St Patrick's Institution' were placed, allowing outsiders to glimpse through the archway and catch sight of lawns and flower-beds.[51] The governor of St Patrick's borstal, John A. Furlong, stated his desire to turn the institution into a 'rehabilitative centre'. He commented that his overall philosophy was to bring Clonmel borstal closer to the spirit of 'Boys' Town' 'by bringing them [the boys] something of the atmosphere of home and all that the term implies'.[52] It is interesting that the governor would be keen to publicly embrace the Boys' Town idea, given the poor relationship between the Department of Justice and the deceased Monsignor Flanagan. Furlong outlined the new openness of the borstal and its commitment to 'enlightened treatment', describing how one of the boys who was recently discharged 'wept unashamedly' when it came time to leave.[53]

These positive developments came forty years too late. Enlightened, humanised treatment and a sense of openness and rehabilitation were all part of the original borstal philosophy set out by its founder, Evelyn Ruggles-Brise, but had been lost in Clonmel. Furlong was staunchly anti-capital punishment, having witnessed a number of executions himself. His opposition centred on the possibility that a condemned person may actually be innocent. Secondly, he emphasised the effects the process had on those charged with carrying out and witnessing the execution. In a lecture delivered in 1953 to women in Clonmel as part of a University College Cork lecture series, he recounted one execution he witnessed in Mountjoy. In keeping with common practice, the chaplain had given the condemned man a crucifix to hold. After the execution had taken place and the body was removed from the gallows, it was discovered that the long part of the crucifix had gone all the way through the hand of the now-deceased prisoner. The profound effect of this incident seemed to contribute to Furlong's opposition to executions. The last governor of Clonmel,

Furlong was described by local resident 'Mary' as 'a big man ... he was charming and was a very good communicator'. Above all he projected an impression of being something of a social revolutionary, someone who was very 'humane'.[54] If this 'public' Furlong was as enlightened in his attitudes during his borstal governorship then it appears that the Department of Justice had indeed found the correct official to steer the course of the post-war, post-Flanagan institution.

Features of the Irish borstal that did seem to move somewhat closer to the British institutions during the final phase of Clonmel were physical exercise and sport. While British borstal boys had been advantaged since the early part of the century by access to fully equipped gymnasia and playing fields, the Irish system was only now realising its potential in this regard. A number of key developments took place during the late 1940s to open a new horizon of sporting activity for the boys in Clonmel. The playing field mentioned earlier allowed inmates to engage in football and other such field sports. One of the most important introductions to the borstal sporting schedule was the formation of a boxing club. In 1947 the Department of Justice announced the establishment of 'St Patrick's Boxing Club', with three tournaments held between the institution and outside clubs that year.[55] The club expanded the following year when it was affiliated to the Irish Amateur Boxing Association. Inmates took part in a number of tournaments inside the institution and two external contests, one in Clonmel and another in County Tipperary.[56] In addition, a former Irish amateur lightweight champion, J. Healy, was appointed trainer of the club.[57] On a visit to the borstal on 1 October 1948, minister for justice Sean McEoin lauded the achievements of the institution since its return to Clonmel and spelled out to the inmates the benefits of the boxing club. Having witnessed the boys in competition in the boxing ring that night, he was pleased to note that they proved they could obey the rules, punch straight and follow the instructions of the referee. He encouraged the wider inmate population in the audience to apply these rules to their own lives once they left the institution.[58] The boxing initiative had clearly taken hold in the borstal and was reported in *The Nationalist* and the Department of Justice annual prison reports over the next few years. In 1949 the club participated in tournaments in Clonmel, Waterford and Kilsheelan.[59] It was obvious that, by the late 1940s, the Irish authorities had finally discovered a useful sporting pursuit for juvenile-adult offenders that both caught the imagination of the boys themselves and was not cost-prohibitive for the Department of Justice.

It appears that the practice of presenting variety shows of the kind outlined in the previous chapter continued during the late 1940s. 'Mary' was affiliated to a local amateur drama group and assisted with the props of the show in the borstal institution at Christmas 1949 or 1950. About twelve local people performed *The Monkey's Paw* by W.W. Jacobs. 'Mary' remembers a claustrophobic feeling as she passed through the front gates of the borstal, describing the sense of being in what she describes as 'a place apart'. The group approached the stage not from the back or the side but were forced to walk through the audience of borstal inmates: as a result they were greeted by 'a gale of shouts and cheers'. This was the prevailing mood of the evening as the play was accompanied by 'a big jeer from the start to the finish'. She describes a distinct sense of 'threat' from the boys themselves because of the nature of the jeering and, while she realised that there was not any real physical danger, there was a strong feel of menace. While the boys themselves did have an enjoyable evening, a point that is repeated frequently by 'Mary', the members of the drama group were left with the feeling that 'this was no way to spend a Christmastime'. Physically the borstal complex was described as 'a grim place' on the inside, in keeping with the 'dark and fore-boding' external appearance it had always projected.[60] 'Mary's' account certainly contradicts some of the public pronouncements on the borstal, particularly those published in the 1948 Visiting Committee report. Neither that report nor the annual Department of Justice publications ever described the institution as 'grim'; in reality, all of the officially generated accounts of the borstal since its foundation seemed unrealistically positive in their descriptions of the structure and atmosphere in the complex. While this oral account is the testimony of just one individual, its credibility is in its independence: the witness had no connections either with the bureaucracy of the borstal or with those detained within its 'foreboding' walls.

THE END OF BORSTAL IN CLONMEL

Despite the attempted rejuvenation of the borstal in the years imme-diately following the return from Cork, there was one dark spectre looming over the whole system, from which the authorities could not hide. In its 1947 annual report the Department of Justice announced that a new scheme had been introduced whereby convicted juvenile-adult age boys serving sentences in adult prisons could be transferred to Clonmel. This was necessitated by the low number of inmates sent to the institution by the courts. With a daily average of just twenty-six inmates who had been sentenced to borstal, sixty-six boys in the same age category who had been sentenced to upwards of three months in regular prison were transferred from other prisons to Clonmel. The department justified the programme on the grounds that it served two purposes: firstly it enabled the institution to operate to its fullest potential once it had a sufficient number of inmates and, secondly, it removed the 'short-termers', as they became known, to more suitable surroundings than an adult prison.[61] This was in fact something of an act of desperation on the part of the Department of Justice, which was struggling to find a way to keep the borstal operational. Table 10.1 indicates that the numbers fluctuated over the following years

TABLE 10.1
LONG AND SHORT-TERM INMATES, 1947–56

	Juvenile-adults	Short-termers
1947	20	66
1948	11	85
1949	39	57
1950	15	46
1951	24	30
1952	9	50
1953	26	43
1954	17	29
1955	14	23
1956	16	23

Source: NLI, Department of Justice, *Annual Report on Prisons*, 1947–56.

and it became increasingly difficult to justify the continued operation of the institution.

From the early 1950s onwards the post-war renewal of Clonmel borstal was discontinued. There were no new initiatives, no significant infrastructural changes and a decrease in public statements of support for the institution from government and other quarters. The Department of Justice in its 1955 report on prisons gave the clearest indication that borstal in Clonmel had indeed entered its final years. With just fourteen borstal sentences and twenty-three short-term inmates admitted during that year, the report pointed out that such low numbers made it increasingly difficult to sustain the training classes that had once been so central to the borstal day.[62] This was one of the first public admissions of failure by one of the agencies charged with administering the borstal system since its foundation. While many reports had pointed out weaknesses and areas for improvement, there was a foreboding tone here that signalled a bleak future for the system in Clonmel. By the end of the twelve-month period covered in the 1955 report it became necessary to end a number of the educational classes provided by the borstal 'school'. The low numbers of inmates attending these lessons did not justify the investment in labour necessary for the continued maintenance of this aspect of the institution.[63] The decline in the borstal population appears to be in line with a reduction in the number of prisoners and indeed institutions in the wider penal system in Ireland. Between the dissolution of the GPB in 1928 and the mid-1950s the number of prisons was reduced from eight to four and the daily average number of inmates had fallen to 400.[64]

The question of the future of the borstal entered the public arena in the summer of 1956. Answering questions from the South Tipperary T.D. Michael J. Davern, the minister for justice, James Everett, confirmed in the Dáil that his department was studying the question of removing the borstal from Clonmel. Two factors placed a question mark over its continued existence in the town. Firstly, the low numbers did not justify the expense of running the institution and, secondly, it had become 'practically impossible' to provide the necessary training for inmates.[65] A week later, the minister was told that visitors to inmates at Clonmel were suffering considerable financial and other hardship as a result of its geographical location. Everett stated that the government was aware of this fact and would be taking it into account when considering Clonmel's future.[66] In fact, this would turn out to be one of the key publicly stated factors influencing the decision on the fate of the borstal. In August, the *Irish Times* reported that a section of Mountjoy prison in Dublin was a likely location for a new borstal institution. The women's section of the complex, with accommodation for about one hundred inmates, had been identified by the Department of Justice as a suitable location.[67]

In early October, Minister Everett visited Clonmel borstal as part of what one of his officials termed 'a routine inspection of Irish jails'. The party also stopped at the Bulmer's cider plant in the town. When questioned by a *Nationalist* reporter, the same official confirmed that a decision on the future of the borstal had still not been made.[68] While the Department of Justice did not say so publicly, it was likely that the real purpose of this visit was to sign off on the removal of the borstal from Clonmel. On 24 October it was reported in the *Irish Times* that a decision had finally been reached. In a move that mirrored the way in which the institution had originally been set up in Clonmel, the Minister for Justice announced that the disused women's prison at Mountjoy would be set apart for use by juvenile-adult male offenders sentenced to detention in a borstal. Work was already underway to completely segregate the new borstal from its parent institution.[69] It was pointed out that the new location would make it easier for the families of inmates from Dublin to visit the institution, one of the long-standing complaints against Clonmel.[70] Other problems were identified by the Department of Justice; it reported that, with training discontinued, it had become necessary to employ inmates to keep the institution running. On 1 December 1956, over a half century after its foundation in Clonmel, the Irish borstal institution vacated the former county gaol complex for the final time.[71] In April 1957 the Minister for Justice, Oscar Traynor, outlined the official thinking behind the decision. In the five years prior to its removal the average number of inmates sentenced to borstal detention had not exceeded sixteen; on one particular year it was as few as nine. This made the education and industrial training of the boys almost impossible. The absence of both of these important features of borstal treatment meant that their rehabilitation would essentially be compromised. It was, therefore, agreed that the borstal system could no longer be administered in Clonmel.[72] The borstal was reopened as St Patrick's Borstal Institution, North Circular Road, Dublin, where it remains, in the twenty-first century, as a controversial and much-criticised place of detention for juvenile male offenders.

Compared to the developments that had already taken place in Britain, the Irish borstal system during the 1940s and 1950s could best be described as lamentable. The Fianna Fail and later the first Inter-Party governments failed to seize the initiative and develop and modernise the rehabilitative methods of the borstal. While the British government engaged with new penal thinking to improve and diversify its borstal system, successive Irish administrations failed to bring Clonmel up to the standards that Britain had already achieved by 1921. Once World War Two commenced, the government was able to hide behind the constraints of the Emergency when explaining its lack of progress. Any changes that were to come to Clonmel borstal were not to the nature of treatment, not to the theoretical approach to rehabilitating offenders and certainly not to the restructuring of the system. Instead, the institution was subjected to certain, limited physical improvements brought about by the Monsignor Flanagan controversy. These were essentially token gestures by a Department of Justice aware that the unwelcome spotlight shone on the borstal by Flanagan meant that it became necessary to quickly shake off its appearance as a Victorian penal institution. The changes were merely cosmetic, however, and the absence of any official imagination sealed the fate of Clonmel borstal. With inmate numbers having fallen to an all-time low, the institution became unsustainable and, despite some moderate successes, Clonmel's fifty-year borstal project ended in failure in December 1956.

NOTES

1. Hood, *Borstal Re-assessed*, p. 103.
2. Molly Mellanby, R.L. Bradley, 'The English borstal system after the war', *Probation*, 1948, p. 19.
3. Sean McConville, 'The Victorian prison', p. 142.
4. Hood, *Borstal Re-assessed*, p. 108–9.
5. McConville, 'The Victorian prison', p. 142.
6. Mellanby, Bradley, 'The English borstal system after the war', p. 19.
7. McConville, 'The Victorian prison', p. 143.
8. Mellanby, Bradley, 'The English borstal system after the war', p. 20.
9. Hood, *Borstal Re-assessed*, p. 116.
10. C.T. Cape, 'The Lowdham Grange borstal institution', *Probation*, 1941, p. 34.
11. Cape, 'The Lowdham Grange borstal institution', p. 34.
12. Dermot Keogh, *Twentieth-Century Ireland: Revolution and State-building* (Dublin: Gill and Macmillan, 2005), p. 111.
13. Connolly, *The Oxford Companion to Irish History*, p. 169.
14. NLI, *Annual Report on Prisons 1947*, J4, p. 12, 1947.
15. Dáil debates, 16 October 1940.
16. Dáil debates, 6 November 1940.
17. Dáil debates, 17 September 1941.
18. Edward Fahy, 'Borstal in Ireland', *Hermethena*, June, 1941, p. 80–1.
19. Dáil debates, 15 October 1942.
20. Dáil debates, 4 February 1942.
21. NLI, *Annual Report on Prisons 1944*, p. 9, 1944.
22. NLI, *Annual Report on Prisons 1944*, p. 9, 1944.
23. Dáil debates, 30 November 1944.
24. NAI, Department of Justice memorandum, S13074B.
25. NAI, Extract from report on post-war planning, 30 December 1944, S13074B.
26. Dáil debates, 12 April 1945.
27. Dáil debates, 12 April 1945.
28. Dáil debates, 27 March 1946.
29. Dáil debates, 14 November 1946.
30. *The Nationalist*, 21 February 1940.
31. Daire Keogh, '"There's no such thing as a bad boy": Fr Flanagan's visit to Ireland, 1946', *History Ireland*, (Spring 2004), 12, 1.
32. Reproduced in *The Nationalist*, 21 February 1940.
33. *Irish Times*, 8 July 1946.
34. Mary Raftery, Eoin O'Sullivan, *Suffer the Little Children: The Inside Story of Ireland's Industrial Schools* (Dublin: New Island, 1999), p. 189–90.
35. Dáil debates, 23 July 1946.

36. Dáil debates, 28 October 1946.
37. *Irish Times*, 12 October 1946.
38. *Irish Times*, 5 October 1946.
39. *Irish Times*, 28 September 1946.
40. *Irish Times*, 28 September 1946.
41. *Irish Times*, 28 December 1946.
42. Dáil debates, 27 March 1947.
43. NLI, Department of Justice, *Annual Report on Prisons*, J4, 1947, p. 12.
44. NAI, Department of the Taoiseach memorandum, S13074B, 14 May 1948.
45. NAI, Department of Justice to Department of the Taoiseach, S13074B, November 1949.
46. *The Nationalist*, 8 May 1948.
47. The Borstal Institution at Clonmel, Notes by the visiting committee, 1948, p. 3.
48. The Borstal Institution at Clonmel, Notes by the visiting committee, 1948, p. 3.
49. The Borstal Institution at Clonmel, Notes by the visiting committee, 1948, p. 3.
50. McConville, 'The Victorian prison', p.142.
51. *The Nationalist*, 2 October 1948.
52. *The Nationalist*, 2 October 1948.
53. *The Nationalist*, 2 October 1948.
54. Interview with 'Mary', 20 November 2008.
55. NLI, Department of Justice, *Annual Report on Prisons*, 1947, p. 14.
56. NLI, Department of Justice, *Annual Report on Prisons*, 1948, p. 14.
57. The Borstal Institution at Clonmel, Notes by the visiting committee, 1948, p. 14.
58. Quoted in *The Nationalist*, 2 October 1948.
59. NLI, Department of Justice, *Annual Report on Prisons*, 1949, p. 20.
60. Interview with 'Mary', 20 November 2008.
61. NLI, Department of Justice, *Annual Report on Prisons*, 1946, p. 13.
62. NLI, Department of Justice, *Annual Report on Prisons*, 1955, p. 18.
63. NLI, Department of Justice, *Annual Report on Prisons*, 1955, p. 18.
64. Eoin O'Sullivan, Ian O'Donnell, 'Imprisonment and the crime rate in Ireland', *Economic and Social Review*, Spring 2003, 34, 1, p. 34.
65. Dáil debates, 12 June 1956.
66. Dáil debates, 19 June 1956.
67. *Irish Times*, 28 August 1956.
68. *The Nationalist*, 2 October 1956.
69. *Irish Times*, 24 October 1956.
70. *Irish Independent*, 24 October 1956.
71. NLI, Department of Justice, *Annual Report on Prisons*, p. 13.
72. Dáil debates, 26 April 1957.

CHAPTER ELEVEN

Conclusion

Historically, the term 'juvenile offender' referred to any person under the age of sixteen. The juvenile-adult offender somehow got lost in the midst of historical investigations of criminal and delinquent children, prostitutes, and transported convicts of the nineteenth century. This book identifies the juvenile-adult male offender in Irish society and places him within the historiography of the early twentieth-century penal system. The establishment of borstal institutions in Kent, Feltham and Clonmel was one of the outcomes of the development of political and social attitudes towards imprisonment that had been ongoing for over a century. By the end of the nineteenth century the focus of incarceration had shifted from one concerned with punishment to one that was also intent on achieving rehabilitation. Reformation was seen as desirable not only for the good of the prisoner but also for society. An explosion of juvenile crime during the early Victorian era in England brought the issue into sharp focus as penal administrators and social thinkers struggled to find possible solutions. It is unlikely that the borstal system that emerged in England and Ireland in the early 1900s would have been publicly acceptable even fifty years earlier. Social thinking, however, had evolved to such an extent that innovators such as Evelyn Ruggles-Brise in England, and Zebulon R. Brockway in the United States, were able to justify the expenditure of public money on ambitious new reform programmes for classes of criminals generally demonised by society. The borstal institution was symbolic of a new, more compassionate approach. It was part of an enlightenment of the penal system that attempted a move away from the darkness and despair of the past, towards a more open and hopeful future that sought to tap into the potential of the offender through individualisation rather than demonisation.

The opening years of the twentieth century saw a repetition in Ireland of the conditions of criminality that were identified in England during the previous two decades. With recidivism rates in excess of 75 per cent, Ireland's prisons also contained high numbers of males that fell into the juvenile-adult offender category: sixteen to twenty-one years old. By the time it arrived in Ireland in 1906, its English founders had already put the borstal system to the test. A number of controversies surrounded the implementation of the borstal system in Ireland. The first of these was on the issue of sentencing. The persistence of low sentences handed down to juvenile-adult offenders both in Britain and Ireland was seen by those administering the borstal system as harmful. The short sentence did not allow sufficient time for the reform process to take hold nor did it provide enough time for an inmate to learn a trade. A lengthy and sustained public debate included highly vocal contributions from both the GPB and the BAI, both of whom were critical of the judiciary. The debate failed to bring about a change of attitude by the courts and this eventually, in 1914, forced the political establishment to change the law, to a two-year minimum borstal sentence. The majority of inmates came from the country's two main cities, Dublin and Belfast. Locating the institution in Clonmel may have been a conscious decision to place it as far away as possible from an unsuitable environment. The profile of the borstal inmate typically dictated that he was previously employed in an unskilled manual occupation.

At the core of the borstal philosophy was the reformation of its inmates through the use of education and training. From the first suggestion of the penal reformatory by the Gladstone Committee, all of those charged with operating the system agreed that the key to reforming a juvenile-adult offender was to equip him with the education and skill to enable him to survive in the competitive labour market. Despite the apparent enthusiasm of those who operated Ireland's first borstal, including the GPB and the BAI, it is obvious from contemporary accounts that the complex was unsuited to its purpose. The original county gaol in Clonmel was constructed in the 1830s, with an altogether different class of offender in mind. Edward Fahy, writing in *The Bell*, depicted a place that was cramped and uncomfortable, both inside and out.[1] This was in conflict with the original intention of the borstal, which was to provide its young inhabitants with a place where they would flourish, physically and intellectually. In fact one of the severe disadvantages of the borstal at Clonmel was its lack of adequate agricultural training facilities. At a time when the Irish workforce remained heavily dependent on farming employment, the BAI repeatedly highlighted the absence of such provisions as one of the strongest impediments to its work in rehabilitating inmates. This problem persisted for the entire lifetime of the institution. It was compulsory that all the inmates at Clonmel achieved a certain standard of education and the institution employed a number of measures to facilitate this. A schoolmaster warder taught the inmates a number of academic subjects, ensuring that they first learned basic numeracy and literacy. The GPB provided the institution with a well-equipped schoolroom and the education of the boys was supplemented by scientific and geography lectures provided by the BAI. This rounded education could be seen as compensation for the institution's shortcomings in the area of training and certainly left the inmates at an advantage over their contemporaries. The education of juvenile-adults was also enhanced by the contribution of the chaplain, who provided lectures, as well as spiritual and moral guidance. Unlike industrial and reformatory schools, the borstal was a non-denominational institution and was not controlled by the churches. However, the clergy did play an important and powerful role in its operation. They placed particular emphasis on the role of religion in the moral improvement of inmates and, as a mark of their stature, the chaplains were always asked to submit a report in advance of an inmate being discharged on licence.

It is clear that there were huge inequalities between the borstal institutions of Ireland and those in England. Comparatives surveys on labour and inmate dietary show that the inmates at Clonmel were severely disadvantaged compared with their contemporaries in Kent and Feltham. While the government, through the lord lieutenant and the chief secretary, can be blamed for the lack of investment in land for farm training, the GPB was clearly responsible for many of the day-to-day shortcomings of the institution at Clonmel. Many of the educational, recreational and other advantages that were enjoyed by the inmates were provided by the BAI and, without the extraordinary efforts of that body and its honorary secretary, William Casey, the GPB would probably have failed in their borstal experiment in Ireland.

Maintaining control over the inmates during their detention in the borstal posed a particular challenge. The discipline of the boys was largely governed by the same procedures to which adult prisoners were subjected in local and convict prisons. The visiting justice adjudicated over matters of indiscipline and usually administered a punishment of confinement or the withholding of certain dietary provisions. One of the key failings of this system was that there was little accountability or independence attached to the process of 'trying' the inmates. There is no evidence to suggest any impropriety on the part of the visiting justices or institutional staff in these procedures but the system was open to many questions. The inmates of Clonmel borstal appeared to be vulnerable to corruption or collusion on the part of the authorities, and victimisation, and possibly abuse, may indeed have been a feature of their lives. Without first-hand accounts from the boys, or indeed the institutional staff, it is not possible to make a definitive conclusion in this regard. It should be stated that no serious or independently recorded accusation of abuse or threatening behaviour against institutional staff has been located to date. As expected from such institutional records, there is no reference to physical or sexual abuse, nor is there any mention of sexual relationships between the inmates or with other officers. All of the inmates existed within a unique system of grades. The penal, ordinary and special grades proved to be a success in that they challenged each boy to conduct himself in a manner that not only prevented his demotion to the grade below but increased his chances of promotion to the next level. For many inmates this required an almost heroic effort – many of these boys had never known order or discipline in their lives and their adherence to the rules of the borstal institution brought numerous tangible and life-improving benefits. It was hoped by those who conceived this system that the efforts that the boys would make in this regard would bring about a sort of revolution in their character whereby they would realise the advantages of persistent good behaviour and put this to good use upon their release.

If the evidence of the both the GPB and the BAI and their criteria for success is accepted, it appears that the system was indeed largely successful between 1906 and 1921. Progress was recorded for almost three quarters of discharged inmates and it is clear that this combination of intensive penal discipline and vigilant aftercare intervention had the desired outcome. Indeed, the BAI was crucial to the success of the overall idea, insofar as these inmates did not re-offend. What is not known is the long-term effect of borstal treatment upon these juvenile-adult offenders. It is impossible to speculate how difficult it was for previously obstreperous young men to make a re-adjustment to free society following an average of eighteen months of intensive reformatory treatment. When the period of a discharged inmate's licence or supervision had expired, he was very much alone in the world. His readjustment was supervised for six months but the BAI did not possess the resources to provide ongoing support for every boy. This study has shown some evidence of the hostility experienced by discharged inmates but it was not in the interest of either the GPB or the BAI to make the details of such problems widely known. Nor is it possible to know the degree to which former inmates of Clonmel borstal suffered from any form of psychological or addiction problems such as depression or alcoholism. At a very basic level, it is not even clear to what extent the inmates were successful in finding and keeping employment. Any evidence put forward from official sources appears to be short to medium-term data.

The borstal system in Ireland fared no better under the Free State and successor governments than it had under British administration. When the institution finally returned to Clonmel in 1924 it was accompanied by the familiar problems of lack of land and adequate training facilities – in short, it remained severely under-funded. Nor was the borstal 'idea' evolved. While other institutions of the state, most notably the police, underwent considerable reform following the commencement of the Free State there is no evidence of any ideological development of or new attitude towards the borstal. Calls for a female borstal were unrealistic at a time when the male institution was barely surviving. The fact that external events, such as the Emergency, caused the removal of the borstal to another location was not an exclusively Irish phenomenon. Similar measures were taken in Britain during the Second World War but the skeletal nature of the Irish institution meant that the effects were felt more severely. While it cannot be stated with complete certainty that the public comments of Monsignor Edward Flanagan on the Irish penal system brought about a number of physical changes to Clonmel borstal from the late 1940s, it is likely that the controversy did provoke the Department of Justice into addressing the subject.

If all of these factors are considered, it is therefore not possible to come to a definitive conclusion regarding the success or otherwise of borstal treatment in Clonmel during this period. The institution, as founded in Ireland, had an ambitious and idealistic set of targets. Like the system already underway in England, Clonmel borstal sought to curb the growth of habitual criminality by attacking it at the source. At best the institution could be deemed only a partial success during its lifetime, as it was not equipped with all of the tools necessary to bring about the required reforms in its inmates. Large-scale government under-funding, a widespread lack of judicial co-operation and

an absence of country-wide philanthropic support for the BAI all contributed to a system that never operated to its fullest potential. To say
that remnants of the borstal system still endure in the twenty-first century does not mean that its principles were the only possible solutions
to the problem of juvenile-adult offending. Rather, it is a statement
that, in many ways, the penal system has apparently failed to find a
better alternative to the ideas of Ruggles-Brise, Brockway, Crofton
and Jebb. What can be concluded from this study, however, is that the
period between 1921 and 1956 marked the long decline of the Irish
borstal system. The majority of the significant developments, whether
infrastructural or otherwise, took place prior to 1921 and, although
this period was flawed because of under-investment, the institution
under Irish administration experienced no radical overhaul of the
kind experienced in Britain.

Previous attempts to change the juvenile penal system had been criticised by a number of reformers because they played no legal role in the
life of a child who was discharged into the same unsavoury environment that had previously contributed to their downfall. The guidance
that was provided to a young man after he left the borstal institution
was equal to, if not more important than, the discipline to which he
had become accustomed during his detention. This was the case
because, outside the borstal, he did not have the safety net of the grade
system or even the institutional staff to ensure that he kept himself out
of trouble. There is no doubt that the efforts of the BAI in improving
the lives of inmates during and after their detention was a key factor
in the establishment and gradual expansion of Clonmel borstal. The
evidence presented in this book clearly proves that the Association and
the institution took up a great deal of its officers' (particularly Casey's)
time, and this work was voluntary. It is fair to conclude that the BAI
was absolutely essential to Clonmel. It fulfilled a role far beyond its
officially designated function and often made up for the shortcomings
caused by a lack of GPB funding in the institution.

It is hoped that this book has shed some light on the process through
which the borstal institution was introduced to Ireland and its initial
progress thereafter. There are clearly some unanswered questions and
a number of specific areas that are worthy of further examination.
The exact reasons for the location in 1906 of this new penal reformatory at Clonmel remain unclear. Based on the reports of the BAI it
would appear that the system did indeed have the desired effects on

its subjects, in that a great majority did not re-offend. These figures are not independent, however, and represent only the alleged successes of the borstal system. The survival of first-hand accounts from discharged inmates would be useful in determining the extent of the effectiveness or otherwise of the system. It is hoped that this book will allow former inmates of the institution to come forward and tell their own stories of life in the Irish borstal, filling in the gaps, perhaps even correcting the official record. Finally, the lives of these juvenile-adult offenders prior to their detention in the borstal institution is worthy of serious and in-depth examination. The complex, daring and disorganised life of the young criminal on the streets of Ireland during the early twentieth century has not yet been fully investigated. Nor has the phenomenon of criminal mentoring – through which young, impressionable males were apprenticed and organised by older, experienced criminals, who educated them in a school of criminality that started with petty theft and continued on to more serious and often violent crime.

NOTE

1. Fahy, 'The boy criminal', *The Bell*, 1940, 1, 2, p. 46–7.

Bibliography

PRIMARY SOURCES

National Archives of Ireland

Clonmel Borstal Memoranda, GPB/XB5
General Prisons Board Correspondence
Prison register, Clonmel prison and borstal institution, 1903–23, GPB/1/7/14

National Library of Ireland

General Prisons Board for Ireland, *Annual Reports*, 1877–1928
Department of Justice, *Annual Reports on Prisons*, 1929–56

Newspapers and Periodicals

Belfast Newsletter
Clare Champion
Clonmel Chronicle
Connacht Tribune
Cork Examiner
Dublin Evening Mail
Freeman's Journal
Hue and Cry: The Police Gazette
Irish Times
Nationalist and Leinster Times
The Nationalist
The Treasury

Internet

Oxford Dictionary of National Biography
(http://oxforddnb.com/view/printable/65325) (28 November 2006).

- Goldman, Lawrence, 'Crofton, Sir Walter Frederick'

- O'Dowd, Mary, 'Bagwell, Richard'
- Priestley, Philip, 'Brise, Sir Evelyn John Ruggles'

SECONDARY SOURCES

Abbott, E., 'Crime and the war', in *Journal of the American Institute of Criminal Law and Criminology*, (May, 1918) 9, 1, pp. 32–45.

Ahern, M., 'The Grubbs of Carrick-on-Suir', in *Tipperary Historical Journal*, 2006, pp. 98–106.

Alcorn, J.G., 'Discharged prisoners' aid societies' in *Journal of the Statistical and Social Inquiry Society of Ireland*, 8 (1881), pp. 217–223.

Bailey, V., 'Churchill as Home Secretary: prison reform', in *History Today*, (March, 1985) 35, 3, pp. 10–13.

Barnes, J., *Irish Industrial Schools: 1868–1908* (Dublin: Irish Academic Press, 1989).

Black, J., 'The Victorian origins of a "Group 4" prison service', in *History Today*, (October, 1993), 43, 10, pp. 10–13.

Bourke, J., 'Effeminacy, ethnicity and the end of trauma: the sufferings of "shell-shocked" men in Great Britain and Ireland, 1914–39', in *Journal of Contemporary History*, (January, 2000) 35, 1, pp. 57–69.

Bourke, J., 'Masculinity, men's bodies and the Great War', in *History Today*, (February, 1996) 46, 2, pp. 8–11.

Bourke, J., *Working-Class Cultures in Britain: 1890–1960* (London: Routledge, 1994).

Boyce, D.G., 'British opinion, Ireland, and the War, 1916–1918', in *Historical Journal*, (September, 1974) 17, 3, pp. 575–93.

Boyce, D.G., *Nineteenth-century Ireland: The Search for Stability* (Dublin: Gill and Macmillan, 1990).

Bradley, A., Valiulis, M. (eds), *Gender and Sexuality in Modern Ireland* (Massachusetts: University of Massachusetts Press, 1997).

Brewster, S., Crossman, V., Beckett, F., Alderson, D. (eds), *Ireland in Proximity: History, Gender, Space* (London: Routledge, 1999).

Burke, W.P., *The History of Clonmel* (Waterford: Clonmel Library Committee, 1983).

Carey, T., *Mountjoy: The Story of a Prison* (Dublin: The Collins Press, 2000).

Carroll-Burke, P., *Colonial Discipline: The Making of the Irish Convict System* (Dublin: Four Courts Press, 2000).

Cherry, R.R., 'Juvenile crime and its prevention', in *Journal of the Statistical and Social Inquiry Society of Ireland*, 12 (1911), pp. 435–50.

Comerford, R.V., 'Ireland 1850–70: post-famine and mid-Victorian', in Vaughan, W.E. (ed.), *A New History of Ireland: Ireland under the Union, 1801–70* (10 vols, Oxford: Oxford University Press, 1989), v, pp. 360–99.

Connolly, S.J., 'Aftermath and adjustment', in Vaughan, W.E. (ed.), *A New History of Ireland: Ireland under the Union, 1801–70* (10 vols, Oxford: Oxford University Press, 1989), v, pp. 1–32.

Connolly, S.J., *The Oxford Companion to Irish History* (Oxford: Oxford University Press, 1998).

Coolahan, J., *Irish Education: Its History and Structure* (Dublin: Institute of Public Administration, 1981).

Crossman, V., *Politics, Law and Order in Nineteenth Century Ireland* (Dublin: Gill and Macmillan, 1996).

Cullen, L.M., *An Economic History of Ireland since 1660* (London: Batsford, 1987).

Daly, E.D., 'The Juvenile Offenders Act 1901', in *New Ireland Review*, (November, 1901), 16, pp. 147–52.

Daly, M.E., *Social and Economic History of Ireland since 1880* (Dublin: Educational Company, 1981).

Daly, M.E., 'The county in Irish history', in Daly, M.E. (ed.), *County and Town: One Hundred Years of Local Government in Ireland* (Dublin: Institute of Public Administration, 2001), pp. 1–11.

Davitt, M., *Leaves from a Prison Diary* (Shannon: Irish University Press, 1972).

Dobash, R.E., Dobash, R.P., Noaks, L., 'Thinking about gender and crime', in Dobash, R.E., Dobash, R.P., Noaks, L. (eds), *Gender and Crime* (Cardiff: University of Wales Press, 1995), pp. 1–19.

Dooley, E., 'Sir Walter Crofton and the Irish or intermediate system of prison discipline', in O'Donnell, I. and McAuley, F. (eds), *Criminal Justice History* (Dublin: Four Courts Press, 2003), pp. 197–220.

Dressler, D., *Practice and Theory of Probation and Parole* (New York: Columbia University Press, 1959).

Dudley Edwards, R., *An Atlas of Irish History* (London: Routledge, 2005).

Duffy, S., *Atlas of Irish History* (Dublin: Gill and Macmillan, 1997).

Emsley, C., *Crime and Society in England: 1750–1900* (Oxford: Oxford University Press, 2005).

Fahy, E., 'The boy criminal', *The Bell*, 1, 2 (1940), pp. 41–51.

Fahy, E., 'The prisons', *The Bell*, 1, 2 (1940), pp. 40–6.

Fahy, E.,'Borstal in Ireland', *Hermethena*, (June, 1941), pp. 80–1.

Ferriter, D., *The Transformation of Ireland, 1900–2000* (London: Profile Books, 2004).

Finnegan, F., *Do Penance or Perish: Magdalen Asylums in Ireland* (Oxford: Oxford University Press, 2001).

Fitzpatrick, D., 'The logic of collective sacrifice: Ireland and the British army, 1914–1918', in *Historical Journal*, (December, 1995) 38, 4, pp. 1017–30.

Girvin, B., *The Emergency: Neutral Ireland, 1939–45* (London: Macmillan, 2006).

Godfrey, B.S., Lawrence, P., *Crime and Justice: 1750–1950* (Devon: Cullompton, 2005).

Guinnane, T.W., 'Age at leaving home in rural Ireland, 1901–1911', *Journal of Economic History*, (September, 1992) 52, 3, pp. 651–74.

Guinnane, T., *The Vanishing Irish: Households, Migration and the Rural Economy in Ireland, 1850–1914* (Princeton: Princeton University Press, 1997).

Harding, C., 'The inevitable end of a discredited system? The origins of the Gladstone committee report on prisons, 1895', in *Historical Journal*, (September, 1988), 31, 3, pp. 591–608.

Hayner, N.S., 'English schools for young offenders', in *Journal of Criminal Law and Criminology*, (January–February, 1937) 27, 5, pp. 696–705.

Heaney, H., 'Ireland's penitentiary, 1820–31: an experiment that failed', in O'Donnell, I., McAuley, F. (eds), *Criminal Justice History* (Dublin: Four Courts Press, 2003), pp. 120–49.

Henry, B., *Dublin Hanged: Crime, Law Enforcement and Punishment in Late Eighteenth-century Dublin* (Dublin: Irish Academic Press, 1994).

Hood, R., *Borstal Re-assessed* (London: Heinemann, 1965).

Hyde, H.M., *Oscar Wilde: A Biography* (London: Farrar, Straus and Giroux, 1976).

Keogh, D., O'Shea, F., Quinlan, C. (eds), *The Lost Decade: Ireland in the 1950s* (Cork: Mercier Press, 2004).

Keogh, D., '"There's no such thing as a bad boy": Fr Flanagan's visit to Ireland, 1946', *History Ireland*, (Spring 2004) 12, 1.

Keogh, D., *Twentieth-century Ireland: Revolution and State-building* (Dublin: Gill and Macmillan, 2005).

Kilcommins, S., O'Donnell, I., O'Sullivan, E., Vaughan, B., *Crime, Punishment and the Search for Order in Ireland* (Dublin: Institute of Public Administration, 2004).

Lee, J.J., *Ireland 1912–1985: Politics and Society* (Cambridge: Cambridge University Press, 1989).

Lentaigne, J., 'The treatment and punishment of young offenders', in *Journal of the Statistical and Social Inquiry Society of Ireland*, 13 (1881), pp. xxvii–xxxvii.

Leslie, S., *Sir Evelyn Ruggles-Brise: A Memoir of the Founder of Borstal* (London: John Murray, 1938).

Lyons, F.S.L., *Ireland since the Famine* (London: Fontana Press, 1985).

McCarthy, J.P., 'In hope and fear: the Victorian prison in perspective', in Augusteijn, J., Lyons, M. (eds), *Irish History: A Research Yearbook* (Dublin: Four Courts Press, 2002), pp. 119–30.

McConville, S., 'The Victorian prison: England 1865–1965', in Morris, N., Rothman, D. (eds), *The Oxford History of the Prison: The Practice of Punishment in Western Society* (Oxford: Oxford University Press, 1998), pp. 117–50.

MacDonnell, H., 'Prisons and prisoners: suggestions as to treatment and classification of criminals', in *Journal of the Statistical and Social Inquiry Society of Ireland*, 10 (1889), pp. 441–2.

MacDonnell, H., 'Review of some of the subjects in the Report of the Royal Commission on Prisons in Ireland', in *Journal of the Statistical and Social Inquiry Society of Ireland*, 13 (1885), pp. 617–23.

McDowell, R.B., 'Administration and the public services, 1800–70', in Vaughan, W.E. (ed.), *A New History of Ireland: Ireland under the Union, 1801–70* (10 vols, Oxford: Oxford University Press, 1989), v, pp. 530–70.

McGowen, R., 'The well-ordered prison: England, 1780–1865', in Morris, N., Rothman, D. (eds), *The Oxford History of the Prison: The Practice of Punishment in Western Society* (Oxford: Oxford University Press, 1998), pp. 71–98.

Moloney, T., 'The prevention and punishment of crime', in *Journal of the Statistical and Social Inquiry Society of Ireland*, 14 (1921), pp. 117–25.

Moseley, S.A., *The Truth about Borstal* (London: Cecil Palmer, 1926).

Mulhall, D., *A New Day Dawning: Ireland at the Turn of the Century* (Cork: Collins Press, 1999).

Murphy, D., *The Two Tipperarys* (Nenagh: Relay Books, 1994).
O'Callaghan, M., *British High Politics and a Nationalist Ireland: Criminality, Land and the Law under Forster and Balfour* (Cork: Cork University Press, 1994).
O'Donnell, S., *Clonmel: 1840–1900 – Anatomy of an Irish Town* (Dublin: Geography Publications, 2000).
Ó Gráda, C., *Ireland: A New Economic History, 1780–1939* (Oxford: Oxford University Press, 1994).
Osborough, N., *Borstal in Ireland: Custodial Provision for the Young Adult Offender, 1906–1974* (Dublin: Institute of Public Administration, 1975).
O'Sullivan, D., *The Irish Constabularies, 1822–1922: A Century of Policing in Ireland* (Dingle: Brandon, 1999).
Pinchbeck, I., Hewitt, M., *Children in English Society*, Vol. 2: *From the Eighteenth Century to the Children Act 1948* (London: Routledge, 1973).
Putney, G., Putney, S., 'Origins of the reformatory', in *Journal of Criminal Law, Criminology, and Police Science*, (December 1962) 53, 4, pp. 437–45.
Radzinowicz, L., Hood, R., *A History of English Criminal Law and its Administration from 1750* (London: Clarendon, 1986).
Raftery, M., O'Sullivan, E., *Suffer the Little Children: The Inside Story of Ireland's Industrial Schools* (Dublin: New Island, 1999).
Robins, J., *The Lost Children: A Study of Charity Children in Ireland, 1700–1900* (Dublin: Institute of Public Administration, 1980).
Rotman, E., 'The failure of reform', in Morris, N. Rothman, D. (eds), *The Oxford History of the Prison: The Practice of Punishment in Western Society* (Oxford: Oxford University Press, 1998), pp. 151–77.
Ruggles-Brise, E., *The English Prison System* (London: Macmillan, 1921).
Ruggles-Brise, E., *Prison Reform at Home and Abroad: A Short History of the International Movement since the London Congress, 1872* (London, 1925).
Russell, C.E.B., *Young Gaol-birds* (London: Macmillan, 1910).
Schlossman, S., 'Delinquent children: the juvenile reform school', in Morris, N., Rothman, D. (eds), *The Oxford History of the Prison: The Practice of Punishment in Western Society* (Oxford: Oxford University Press, 1998), pp. 325–49
Shore, H., 'The idea of juvenile crime', in *History Today, 50*, 6 (2000), pp. 21–9.

Smith, B.A., 'The Irish prison system, 1885–1914: land war to world war', in *Irish Jurist*, 16 (1981), pp. 316–49.

Smith, J.M., *Ireland's Magdalen Laundries and the Nation's Architecture of Containment* (Manchester: Manchester University Press, 2007).

Stratta, E., *The Education of Borstal Boys: A Study of their Educational Experiences prior to, and during, Borstal Training* (London: Routledge, 1970).

Taylor, D., *Crime, Policing and Punishment in England, 1750–1914* (London: Macmillan, 1998).

Tobias, J., *Crime and Industrial Society in the Nineteenth Century* (London: Batsford, 1967).

Vaughan, W.E., Fitzpatrick, A.J., (eds), *Irish Historical Statistics: Population 1821–1971* (Dublin: Royal Irish Academy, 1978).

Von Holtzendorff, F., *The Irish Convict System: Most Especially Intermediate Prisons* (Dublin: W.B. Kelly, 1860).

Walklate, S., *Gender and Crime: An Introduction* (London: Prentice Hall, 1995).

Walsh, O., 'Protestant female philanthropy in Dublin in the early twentieth century', in *History Ireland*, (Summer, 1997), pp. 27–31.

Ward, A.J., 'Lloyd George and the 1918 Irish conscription crisis', in *Historical Journal*, (March, 1974), 17, 1, pp. 107–29.

Whelan, D., *Peter Tyrrell: Founded on Fear* (Dublin: Irish Academic Press, 2006).

Wiener, M.J., *Men of Blood: Violence, Manliness and Criminal Justice in Victorian England* (Cambridge: Cambridge University Press, 2004).

Wolff, M., Prison: *The Penal Institutions of Britain – Prisons, Borstals, Detention Centres, Attendance Centres, Approved Schools and Remand Homes* (London: Eyre and Spottiswoode, 1967).

Index